New Solutions for
House Museums

New Solutions for House Museums

Ensuring the Long-Term Preservation of America's Historic Houses

Donna Ann Harris

ALTAMIRA
PRESS

A Division of
ROWMAN & LITTLEFIELD PUBLISHERS, INC.
Lanham • New York • Toronto • Plymouth, UK

ALTAMIRA PRESS

A division of Rowman & Littlefield Publishers, Inc.
A wholly owned subsidary of The Rowman & Littlefield Publishing Group, Inc.
4501 Forbes Boulevard, Suite 200
Lanham, MD 20706
www.altamirapress.com

Estover Road
Plymouth PL6 7PY
United Kingdom

British Library Cataloguing in Publication Information Available

Library of Congress Cataloging-in-Publication Data

Harris, Donna Ann.
   New solutions for house museums : ensuring the long-term preservation of
America's historic houses / Donna Ann Harris.
      p. cm.—(American Association for State and Local History book series)
   Includes bibliographical references.
   ISBN-13: 978-0-7591-1086-1 (cloth : alk. paper)
   ISBN-10: 0-7591-1086-7 (cloth : alk. paper)
   ISBN-13: 978-0-7591-1087-8 (pbk. : alk. paper)
   ISBN-10: 0-7591-1087-5 (pbk. : alk. paper)
   1. Historic house museums—United States—Management. 2. Historic house
museums—United States—Finance. 3. Historic buildings—Conservation and
restoration—United States. 4. Dwellings—Conservation and restoration—United States.
5. Historic preservation—United States—Case studies. 6. Historic house museums—
Canada—Management. 7. Historic house museums—Canada—Finance. 8. Historic
buildings—Conservation and restoration—Canada. 9. Dwellings—Conservation and
restoration—Canada. 10. Historic preservation—Canada—Case studies. I. Title.

   E159.H265 2007
   363.6'9—dc22   2006102096

Printed in the United States of America

∞™ The paper used in this publication meets the minimum requirements of
American National Standard for Information Sciences—Permanence of Paper for
Printed Library Materials, ANSI/NISO Z39.48–1992.

Table of Contents

List of Figures

All figures and photographs courtesy of Donna Ann Harris.

Acknowledgments

I extend my heartfelt thanks to a number of people who helped shape the contents of this book.

Appreciation goes first to the James Marston Fitch Charitable Foundation in New York City. Their award of a Mid Career Fellowship in 2003 enabled me to undertake travel and research to prepare five case studies of house museums that have made a successful transition to a new use or new owner and develop the bulk of the first seven chapters. Missy Dierickx and Bill Higgins provided trenchant insight throughout this process. The Fitch Foundation grant allowed me to work full time on this project during the first year of establishing my consulting practice, Heritage Consulting Inc. I am forever grateful.

Case study interviewees shared a great deal of information with me. I thank the following people for being so generous with their time and for their enthusiasm about this project.

- Casa Amesti, formerly owned by the National Trust for Historic Preservation—Thompson M. Mayes, Deputy General Counsel, National Trust and Sidney Morris, board member of the Casa Amesti Foundation.
- Nantucket Historical Association—Kirstin Gamble, Dr. Frank Milligan, Niles D. Parker, all formerly associated with the organization, and Ben Simons, assistant curator.
- Robert E. Lee Boyhood Home—Thompson M. Mayes, Deputy General Counsel of the National Trust.

- Heritage Branch, British Columbia Ministry of Community, Aboriginal and Women's Services—John Adams, principal of Discover the Past, Inc., Victoria, and former chief historian with the Heritage Branch; Rhonda Hunter, former director of the Heritage Branch; Jan Ross, site manager of the Emily Carr House, Victoria; Gail Simpson, site manager of the Point Ellice House, Victoria; and Patrick Frey, director of the Heritage Branch.
- Elfreth's Alley Association—Beth Richards and Robert Vosburgh Jr., former executive directors of Elfreth's Alley Association, Philadelphia.
- Hazelwood—Barbara Funk, director of arts and cultural programs, Prince George's County Parks and Recreation Division of the Maryland-National Capital Parks and Planning Commission; Yasmin Anderson-Smith, formerly with the Division; and Pamela Cooper, resident curator of Hazelwood.
- Historic Adams House—Mary Kopco, Executive Director of the Adams House and Museum, Inc.
- Heurich House—Mark G. Griffin, Chairman of the Heurich House Foundation Inc.
- Margaret Mitchell House and Museum—Jim Bruns, President of the Atlanta History Center.

Jennifer Esler, former executive director of Cliveden of the National Trust, was the first person to write about struggling house museums in her 1996 article for the National Trust's *Forum Journal*. This book greatly expands on her initial premise. Gerald George has also chronicled the precarious state of house museums in several books and articles.

Barbara Silberman, Senior Program Advisor with Heritage Philadelphia Program (www.heritagephila.org) started me on this project, and has been a strong supporter throughout the birth of this book. I have been working as the lead consultant since 2005 on the Living Legacy Project, a project she directs that is sponsored by the Heritage Philadelphia Program, funded by The Pew Charitable Trusts, administered by the University of the Arts, with additional support from the William Penn Foundation. The Living Legacy Project is providing one-on-one technical assistance to seven historic house museums in the Philadelphia area as they consider a transition to new owners and uses.

My research and case studies for the James Marston Fitch Charitable Foundation have guided our work with these sites and been tested on these institutions. Material developed for the Fitch Foundation project is being used as the Living Legacy decision-making process outlined in chapter 6. The house museums participating in the Living Legacy Project also were exposed to the eight solutions and case studies outlined in Part II. Our work with these institutions has convinced me that the methodology proposed here can make a real difference when historic house museums sincerely wish to change the way they do business.

Mary Ellen Hern, founding director of the Historic House Trust in New York City, read and edited early drafts of the case studies and this book, and her wisdom and encouragement has been exceedingly welcome.

The following people also read drafts of the book for content and their comments have helped to clarify my arguments. Bill Higgins, principal of Higgins Quasebarth Historic Preservation, NYC; Barb Silberman, Director of the Heritage Philadelphia Program; and Rob Saarnio, associate director of Shangra-La, the Doris Duke Institute of Islamic Art in Honolulu. Terry Dickenson also made helpful suggestions. Jim O'Connell provided excellent internet research on house museum mergers that were useful for some of the case studies.

My editor at AltaMira Press, Serena Krombach, has been very supportive and enthusiastic throughout this venture, for which I am grateful.

Finally, I owe a special debt to my husband, Ian Siler, who read early and later drafts of each case study and the entire book. He has traveled with me to see some of these case study sites and has been extraordinarily enthusiastic and encouraging over the past two years. This book is dedicated to him.

Part I

ASSESSMENT AND DECISION MAKING

CHAPTER 1

Current Trends in Historic House Museums

This book is designed for board and staff members of nonprofit-owned historic house museums that are struggling with insufficient funds or people power to sustain their site to the level that their historic building needs and deserves.

Some board members or staff will pick up this book and be horrified that it advocates mergers, reprogramming, sales, leases, new uses or new owners for historic sites. Others will be relieved that a book has been developed to assist them in their hour of need. My intent is to provide you, the board member, staff member, or volunteer at a struggling house museum, with new options and solutions. Not every historic house museum, whether founded 100 years ago or last month, can be sustained long-term.

Perhaps you as a volunteer board member or staff of a house museum have a nagging feeling that your site has become an ever-increasing burden to your small nonprofit organization. Maybe someone on your board has even said, "we need to do something!" at a recent board meeting.

You are not alone.

In the last two years, I have spoken with more than fifty house museum administrators and all understand your plight. Lack of money and investment in their buildings forces house museum boards to make untenable choices—to offer engaging tours or undertake basic maintenance; to restore the chimney or buy acid-free tissue for the costume collection. All of these alternatives are daunting. There is never enough money. Often stinging choices need to be made.

In their *History News* article "Does America Need Another House Museum?" Carol Stapp and Ken Turino make the statement, "The strongest evidence for questioning the value of museumification of a historic property springs from the paradox that the noble objective of interpretation for the public good may in fact be ill served when a building becomes a museum."[1]

Many of today's historic-house stewards still use the same methodology described by Stapp and Turino—museumification—to preserve their historic house. Many other methods have been developed in the intervening 150 years, and this book will describe several alternatives that other house museums are successfully using across the country.

AN UNCOMFORTABLE FIT

The initial motivation of preservationists who saved the building was to retain the structure as part of the historic fabric of the community. In most cases, the initial group who saved the site chose a museum use by instinct or by default with little understanding of the harsh realities of the costs, skills, and experience needed to actually run a museum. If board leadership knew now what they should have known at the beginning, I suspect that we would have less than half of the house museums across America that we do today.

While it is a noble objective to save a building for the public good, museum use is not necessarily the best conclusion for every hard-won preservation battle. In most cases, the best option is finding a sympathetic owner who loves the house and retains its original use as a home.

House museums can be excellent community and tourism resources if the local community has the leadership and the financial wherewithal to provide for an organization that must be heavily subsidized. Houses that are intact, with furnishings that have a clear provenance to the house, may have a better chance to become legitimate tourism resources. Based on their slim attendance figures, most historic house museums are locally significant, with real meaning only to community members.

Without substantial and continuing financial support, it may be impossible to sustain a historic house museum despite its importance to the community.[2] It is time that struggling historic sites consider new options, perhaps even returning the site to private ownership with legal assurances that the site be protected forever.

This book outlines eight different techniques being used by other nonprofit and government owners of historic houses to sustain their sites for generations to come. The solutions are wide-ranging. Some solutions maintain a house museum use under a different management operation. Other solutions detail compatible adaptive uses for the house to ensure that there are funds for proper maintenance. The most commonly used solution is to return the house to private ownership with easements (also known as conservative restrictions) to protect the building forever. An extensive chapter discusses reuse solutions and includes brief case studies of organizations that have made the transition from nonprofit-owned and operated house museum to something new.

YOUR STEWARDSHIP ROLE

None of these solutions cataloged here are an easy or "quick fix" for a longstanding problem of chronically inadequate investment in the historic property.

Many historic house stewards will make the unconscious or even conscious choice not to address the lingering deterioration of the house, since it is much easier to just do nothing. It is human nature to avoid change. Many boards will hope that the deterioration or restoration needs will go away or be resolved by some unnamed future board of directors. But the future is unknown. There are no assurances that the house will have caring board members after you and other board members decide to retire.

How can you make certain that the site does not end up abandoned and deteriorating after all of the years of your hard work? Will these future boards have enough money to maintain the property? As stewards of your historic property today, you are obligated to plan for its future. No one cares as much as you do, right now, about your site. Ensuring your legacy as a preservation trailblazer requires that you plan for your beloved building right now. Do not leave such an important matter to unknown board members in the future. Take action today.

Your board will need to carefully weigh your alternatives and then take forceful action. You will need an attorney to advise you throughout this process.

I hope that some of these solutions pioneered by other house museum stewards will help you, the historic house museum board member, staff, or volunteer, as you consider other responsible alternatives to historic house museum use. Reading this book can be the first step in your journey.

WHAT THIS BOOK WILL NOT COVER

This book will focus on historic buildings and their stewards. Readers interested in collection deaccessioning and accreditation standards should consult the American Association of Museums (AAM). These important elements of museum management are the subject of many books and articles.

The American Association of Museums website (www.aam-us.org) has an extensive publication series. The AAM also manages a historic house museum professional interest committee. A number of the regional museum organizations have historic house museum resources. Contact the Mid-Atlantic Association of Museums (MAAM) (www .cmiregistration.com/user/splash_org_231.htm) historic site administrator committee, and the New England Museum Association (www .nemanet.org) for further information.

CURRENT TRENDS IN HOUSE MUSEUMS

Richard Moe, president of the National Trust for Historic Preservation (NTHP), began his recent article "Are There Too Many House Museums?" by describing house museums this way. "For many people, the terms 'historic preservation' and 'house museum' are virtually synonymous. While this perception unquestionably represents a narrow and inaccurate view of what preservation today is all about, there can be no question that house museums constitute the bedrock of the American preservation movement."[3] This book will explore other options than creating or continuing struggling historic house museums.

EARLY EXAMPLES

The first historic sites saved by volunteers, rather than by government, commemorate famous men or events in our nation's early history. The tale of Ann Pamela Cunningham and her intrepid band of ladies is often told. They saved Mt. Vernon in 1858 to commemorate George Washington's home and burial place and open it for visitation by patriotic pilgrims. The Mt. Vernon model, where a national nonprofit women's organization solicited funds for a singularly important historic site, was tried for several other important houses, especially the Hermitage in Nashville, Tennessee and at Valley Forge, outside Philadelphia. These preservation efforts did not seem to stir people's heartstrings as much as the Mt. Vernon Ladies Association's work for George Washington's home.[4]

Revolutionary War sites were set aside throughout the East during the nineteenth and early twentieth centuries due in part to the centennial celebration in Philadelphia in 1876. National patriotic organizations such as the Daughters of the American Revolution and the Colonial Dames, through their state chapters, became significant leaders in preservation efforts at the local level all across the country.

In the early years of the twentieth century, historic house museums joined the commemorative shrines dedicated to war and politics. These new house museums were often chosen as exceptional, atypical, or even characteristic examples of a particular style of American architecture. These sites, often stuffed with the finest furnishings, were typically built by the very wealthy or designed by prominent architects.

Starting in the 1960s, still more historic house sites were added to the mix as state and local centennials and other anniversaries were held, and each town wanted to preserve the oldest or the best house to tell their community's story. Around the nation's bicentennial in 1976, there was an explosion of interest in historic preservation, most directed toward homes, fueled in part by the "astonishing fervor to set aside local homes and turn them into museums" for tourists.[5]

However, many of these sites never received adequate funding or support from the community. Today, 150 years after Mt. Vernon was opened to the public, its model of saving historic properties and converting them into historic house museums still remains the most common preservation paradigm.

No doubt your community has one, perhaps several, nonprofit-owned house museums in addition to other house museums that are owned by government entities—cities, counties, states, or the National Park Service. House museums are everywhere.

HOW MANY ARE THERE?

Almost twenty years ago, the National Trust for Historic Preservation conducted a state-by-state survey and identified at least 5,000 house museums, concentrated largely on the East Coast and in the Midwest.[6] According to the American Association for State and Local History's (AASLH) most recent *Directory of Historic House Museums in the United States,* published in 1999, there are now more than 8,000 house museums in the country.[7]

Even this number may be too low, since the Heritage Philadelphia Program noted that less than one-third of the 275 historic sites in the Delaware Valley are included in this tally.[8] There have been no attempts since 1999 to identify all of the house museums in the country, perhaps because the list inevitably would be outdated the year it was printed.

The pace of creation of house museums seems to have quickened since the 1960s. The 1988 National Trust survey of historic houses noted that 59 percent began operation earlier than 1960.[9] The Trust survey noted that 70 percent are in rural locations or places with populations of less than 50,000 people.[10] The most sobering statistic from that study is that "historic properties have been turned into museums on the average of one every three and a half days."[11] Today, organizations' interest in creating house museums continues unabated. The National Trust and similar regional organizations receive several calls each week from volunteers who want to start new house museums.[12]

WHAT'S THE ATTRACTION?

Historic house museums appeal to both preservationists and the public alike, because of their familiar scale and mien. In a world of spinning complexity, house museums can be relied upon because they do not change. They are "rich and diverse learning environments," and real and tangible reminders of the past.[13] They are part of our collective memory of a place.

But the house itself is a dead artifact without active interpretation to bring it to life for visitors. For many of us, historic houses are the first place where the past came alive. We recall the delight on our children's faces when they made the first connection between abstract or dusty facts in textbooks to the physical and authentic artifact in front of them. Gerald George describes house museums as powerful because they "encourage empathy by explaining lives and emotions in other eras."[14] The best sites have excellent interpretation and tell stories that affect people viscerally. What constitutes a successful museum property, according to George, is "what people take away from their visit. . .a deep experience and insight into issues that people are interested in, that changes attitudes and behaviors."[15]

The intense desire to honor and romanticize local forefathers by transforming their homes into historic sites is widespread. According to Moe, the houses that have been turned into museums are mostly those of "dead rich white guys."[16] Most often they are the oldest house in town or a stunning example of an interesting architectural style. Few house museums tell stories about the typical homeowner or work-a-day people. There are only a handful of places that tell stories about women or ethnic groups, and few blacks or Hispanics are memorialized.[17]

In some communities, there are so many house museums that they have become redundant, with multiple house museums telling the same story. Inevitably, some tell their stories better than others.[18] In the Philadelphia region, which has more than 275 house museums in five counties, more than 100 are eighteenth-century examples of domestic architecture, and their interpretations are generic. Most discuss issues related to merchant princes and enormous wealth; few mention women, and none mention slaves, though clearly slaves are integral to eighteenth-century histories of accumulating great wealth. Of these 275 sites, less than ten interpret any other kind of history. A few tell stories about artists and writers; just three are twentieth-century structures; and only five represent important individuals or aspects of African-American history.[19]

There is no way to prevent yet another historic house museum from joining the hundreds of other eighteenth-century house museums in Philadelphia, or anywhere else. All of these sites are owned by different and independent nonprofit organizations, each with its own mission and vision for its future. There is no overarching entity that decides which sites should be preserved, saved, or developed as house museums. The result is that more are added each year by well-meaning preservationists and local historians. Yet those that already exist struggle for their very survival.

HOW DID THESE SITES COME ABOUT?

One of the greatest strengths of the historic preservation movement is that it is a grassroots effort. Anyone with a passion for a historic house can gather together like-minded people and set off on the difficult journey to save it from destruction.

Many historic house museums start out as traditional preservation projects. A house is threatened and a spirited band of volunteers, in the past mostly women, lead the charge to save the structure. The fight to save the building from certain destruction or an insensitive owner galvanizes citizens to spend time, money, and emotional energy for their cause. Sometimes years go by between the threat and the outcome. But once the site is secure, the inevitable question arises: What should we do with the building?

Charles Hosmer, the first historian of the American historic preservation movement, wrote in his 1965 book *Presence of the Past: A History of the Preservation Movement in the United States before Williamsburg* that it was rare for a local preservation organization in the early years of the movement to take a longer view of its stewardship responsibilities.

> whenever a historic building was to be saved. . .funds would have to be raised for the purchase of each property. . . .Payment of the purchase price only changed the ownership; it did not insure that the stability of the structure for years to come. Few preservationists could see beyond the glorious days when the old house was purchased, nor could they trouble themselves with the sordid, day to day maintenance problems.[20]

Most advocates stumble into a house museum use because they become emotionally invested in the site and do not trust any private owner to value what they have saved. Activists want to avoid repeating the threat cycle again at all costs. It is unfortunate that nonprofit ownership becomes the *de facto* choice in these circumstances. Perhaps these local historians believe that the motives of a nonprofit organization are purer than the private sector.[21]

Few groups take the time to assess all possible uses other than a "one-size-fits-all" private house museum. This is partly the fault of the preservation and local history movements as a whole. Until now, no one has attempted to make other solutions generally known through publication and the discussion of alternatives. In the end, the best use may be the original use: as a private home, restored, preserved, and loved by its owners.

STRUGGLING FOR SURVIVAL

For those historic houses that are already museums, the statistics are sobering.[22] The 1988 National Trust survey of historic houses found that 54 percent of house museums received no more than 5,000 visitors a year; 65 percent had no full-time staff; and 80 percent had annual budgets of less than $50,000.[23]

A survey conducted by the Philadelphia-based Heritage Investment Program in 2000 produced similar data in the Philadelphia region. Of that region's more than 275 house museums, 40 percent do not have professional staff. More than half have budgets under $100,000. Less than 10 percent have a sufficient endowment of at least $250,000 to sustain a site into the next generation.[24]

Most stewards of the public's history believe the problem is fundamentally financial, thinking that a large enough endowment will solve all the site's problems.[25] A twin concern is the capacity of the organization itself. Inexperienced boards are unable to carry forward their preservation and interpretation mission. Tired boards and volunteers burn out. Institutions with strong organizational capacity can weather the loss of 5 or 10 percent of their income in a year, because they can boost income from other earned revenue sources and make cuts that do not fundamentally threaten the organization's fragile well-being. Organizations with weak capacity do not have the people power or the financial underpinning—whether it's a reserve or an endowment—that can cushion them from unforeseen reverses.

Overall, house museums are struggling with a variety of issues. Here are some typical concerns.

AGING BOARDS

The people who saved and now manage historic house museums are aging. These dedicated volunteers, mainly women, are now in their 70s and 80s, and few boards are able to attract younger people to serve as these committed people die or move away.

Baby Boomers, defined by the U.S. Census Bureau as adults born between 1946 and 1964, comprise 76 million Americans, which is about one quarter (26.75 percent) of the entire population of the United States in 2005. Statisticians divide this group in two parts. Younger Boomers, born between 1956 and 1964, still have children at home, are actively in the workforce, and have mortgage payments. Older Boomers, those born between 1946 and 1955, are the ones reaching retirement age in the next ten years.[26]

Most of the members that make up the current boards of house museums belong to the so-called Greatest Generation, born from 1911–1924 and with personal histories directly impacted by the Second World War. These are the parents of the Baby Boomers. This generation is in the midst of an enormous transfer of wealth as the Greatest Generations dies and leaves its estates to family and philanthropic organizations during the next five to fifteen years.

Whether the Baby Boomer generation will step up and take the place of their parents on house museum boards remains to be seen. This generation is not being routinely cultivated by many house museum organizations, and that is a shame. The Older Boomers are just now starting to retire, while the Younger Boomers are in their peak earning years.[27] Both of these groups may have other priorities for their leisure time. Even younger people, those that belong to Generation X (those born between 1961 and 1981), or their youngest brothers and sisters, the Generation Y (born between 1977 and 2003), are not being asked to serve on boards or committees.

The sheer number of Baby Boomers makes this a ripe group to solicit for board seats and as volunteers. But following them, there is a relative paucity of Generation X and Y members.

Another culprit may be the bylaws of the organization itself. Boards that are self-perpetuating do not rotate board members yearly and do not allow new board members with ideas, money, or connections to be recruited to serve.

The continuing vitality of house museums is directly related to board succession planning. House museums with already depleted board ranks may have few people to groom to succeed current leadership to carry the organization forward into a new generation. In addition, strategic planning may be viewed as a frill when there are many other pressing issues at hand. If the organization does not have paid staff and the house is being run entirely by volunteers, the board may not be able to sustain the momentum of even the most successful operation over time. And finally, the entire nature of volunteerism has changed. The traditional volunteers of the past—women—now work outside the home, leaving little time for community activities. Families with working parents have little time available for volunteer activities that don't involve their children.

FEW ENDOWMENTS AND LITTLE PLANNED GIVING

It is true that house museum organizations struggle because they are not able to raise enough money to cover operations and maintenance, let alone restoration costs. The building's failing condition becomes a drain on the organization's finances and the public mission of interpretation is forced to compete with maintenance and repairs for limited dollars. These organizations are perhaps not sustainable long-term because the twin missions of the organization—restoration and interpretation—cannot be fully supported. Many boards must behave like Solomon, choosing which bill to pay or which mission to promote, because the organization's budget may be just too small.[28]

It is troubling that many house museum organizations lack the sophistication necessary to sustain a simple membership drive or to solicit individuals for larger gifts. While the days of bake sales to pay the electric bill may be in the past, raising money through a capital campaign or endowment drive may still be a far-off dream if the organization does not yet have the capacity to take on this work. The transfer of wealth between the "Greatest Generation" and the Baby Boomers is currently underway, yet many house museums are not tapping into this opportunity effectively. Most groups simply do not ask (or know how to ask) their members for planned gifts.

It is estimated by Paul Schervish, Director of Social Welfare Research Institute at Boston College and a National Research Fellow at the Center on Philanthropy at Indiana University, that the transfer of wealth between generations will reach $41 trillion dollars.[29] Baby Boomers may inherit $7.2 trillion, but the majority of this wealth will go to their children and grandchildren. As the Baby Boomers age and die, their role as benefactors will come to the fore. Those in the planned giving field acknowledge that universities, hospitals, foundations, and large nonprofits are already active in planned giving, but small and mid-size organizations have not begun to cultivate or solicit these gifts. Three reasons are given: "we are already too busy, we need more training, and we don't have the resources." To not solicit these gifts is "leaving money on the table," according to Randy Schackmann.[30]

In his article "Is Your Nonprofit Walking Away from Money?" on the On Philanthropy website (www.onphilanthrophy.com), Mr. Schackmann notes, "If you are not helping your supporters to give through their estates and with planned gifts, someone else will. And you may lose out on their gift completely."[31] He suggests getting basic information from a trusted advisor or attorney to structure your program, even a small one to solicit gifts from estates, from those that have a long history with the organization. These people, past board members, leaders, or donors, are the easiest ones to approach about possible gifts because they already have good and longstanding relationships with the mission of the organization. One on one meetings are needed with the potential donor to explain why the organization is seeking gifts as part of their estate planning.[32]

Nor is an endowment automatically a saving grace. Sites that are lucky enough to have an endowment, even a small one, may find that it does not generate enough income to make a real difference. Increasing restoration costs may make invading the principal of an endowment of any amount seem very tempting. For sites fortunate enough to have staff, the employees are often encouraged to chase increasingly scarce government and foundation dollars, even though these two sectors produce only one-third of all philanthropic dollars.[33]

SPIRALING DEFERRED MAINTENANCE OBLIGATIONS

As anyone who owns an antique home knows, they require constant attention. Small maintenance needs can turn into larger and more costly repairs if neglected even for a season. Restoration costs can be overwhelming. For historic sites that seek to present their site to the public as a pristine artifact that requires exacting restoration, they must first undergo the necessary and expensive studies that precede the work—then pay for the restoration itself.

VISITOR SERVICES

House museums compete for visitor time and dollars across the whole range of leisure time activities.[34] For the all-volunteer house museum, simply being open regular hours is a challenge. Staffing the site when visitors want to come—in the summer and on weekends—is the same time when volunteers want to be with their own families. When visitors do appear at the door, they want engaging and meaningful tours that relate to their lifestyle—all ages, all races, all political persuasions.

If the organization is not successful in their volunteer recruitment and staffing efforts, the site then becomes "open by appointment only." These hours are of little use to a family seeking an educational outing for their children, particularly if they plan their travels at the last minute from a website. Sites that are open irregular hours are almost bound to face the self-fulfilling prophecy—no one visits, because no one knows when they are really open. And finally, it is no secret that some boards really do not want visitors at all, because the house has become a finely furnished, members-only clubhouse.

WHAT IS BEING DONE?

In the last ten years, the chorus of preservation professionals who are dismayed by these issues has become larger and louder. In 1999, with support from the National Trust, the American Association for State and Local History (AASLH) formed its historic house committee to address this agenda of concerns. Moe's 2002 *Forum Journal* article baldly stated the central question: "Are there too many house museums?"[35] That year, the committee gathered two dozen leading professionals from nonprofit house museums at a conference to consider a challenge issued by James M. Vaughan, the National Trust's Vice President for Stewardship of Historic Sites:

> In the increasing competition for visitors, members and financial support, many, if not most, historic sites are struggling for survival, and the quality of preservation and maintenance of many such sites has declined precipitously. In addition, the quality and appeal of traditional house museum interpretation does not successfully compete with other contemporary sources of educational leisure time activities. Is it time for new models, new standards and new approaches?[36]

The AASLH historic house committee has responded to Vaughan's query with a strong affirmative and is now working on a multifaceted approach to these issues.

Since the conference, additional articles have appeared in the professional history publications, including the Summer 2004 *History News* article entitled "Does America Need Another House Museum?"[37] Several educational sessions at national history, preservation, and museum conferences have also addressed this issue during the last two years.

AASLH historic house committee members are developing a series of publications about this issue. The first title, Gerald George's *Starting Right: A Basic Guide to Museum Planning,* describes the criteria for deciding when to start a house museum. Subsequent volumes will treat issues of preservation, interpretation, and other aspects of historic house operations. The committee believes it must formulate criteria for assessing when house museums are no longer sustainable. It is crucial to support the individuals who care for historic sites and offer them positive choices as they develop new alternatives to the traditional house museum paradigm.[38]

Another project is surveying what makes a historic house museum successful. Although many historic site professionals have great anecdotal answers to all of these questions, no one has any real data. Within the next several years, quantifiable measures will become available to historic sites that are interested in measuring their success.[39]

Through a Mid Career Fellowship from the James Marston Fitch Charitable Foundation, I spoke with more than fifty historic site leaders and service providers and then developed twelve case studies of historic house museums that have made the transition from a house museum use to something new. This book is designed to be another part of the planned publication series and to offer alternatives to house museums that are struggling for survival.

NOTES

1. Carol B. Stapp and Kenneth C. Turino, "Does America Need Another House Museum?" *History News* 59, no. 3 (2004): 7.

2. Few historic sites, even the largest ones are able to survive based on admissions and other earned income (shop sales, food). Recent declines in attendance are discussed in the article by Carolyn Brackett. Carolyn Brackett "Why Is Historic Site Visitation Down?" *Forum Journal* 19. no. 2 (2005): 14.

3. Richard Moe, "Are There Too Many House Museums?" *Forum Journal* 16, no. 3 (2002): 1.

4. Charles Hosmer, *Presence of the Past: A History of the Preservation Movement in the United States before Williamsburg.* New York: G. P. Putnam's Sons, 1965, 60–61.

5. Gerald George, "Historic House Museum Malaise: A Conference Considers What's Wrong," *History News* 57, no. 4 (2002): 2.

6. George, "Museum Malaise," 3.

7. Patricia Chambers Walker and Thomas Graham, compilers, *Directory of Historic House Museums in the United States.* Lakewood, CA: AltaMira Press, 1999, 2.

8. Barbara Silberman, interview with author, 23 May 2003, and Barbara Silberman, e-mail correspondence with author, 26 July 2005. Less than 33 percent of the 275 house museums in the Philadelphia region appear in the 1999 AASLH Directory of House Museums.

9. Gerald George, "Historic Property Museums: What Are They Preserving?" *Forum Journal* 3, no. 4 (1989): 4.

10. George, "Property Museums", 5.

11. George, "Property Museums," 6.

12. James M. Vaughan, interview with author, typescript of telephone conversation, Washington, D.C., 26 June 2003.

13. George, "Museum Malaise," 4.

14. George, "Museum Malaise," 4.

15. George, "Museum Malaise," 4.

16. Moe, 2.

17. Donna Ann Harris and Barbara W. Silberman, "Exploring Alternate Stewardship Arrangements for Historic Houses, joint grant proposal to the William Penn Foundation and The Pew Charitable Trusts," November 2004, 7.

18. Harris and Silberman, "Grant," 12.

19. Harris and Silberman, "Grant," 10.

20. Hosmer, *Presence of the Past*, 288.

21. Moe, 4.

22. Jennifer Esler, "Historic House Museums: Struggling for Survival," *Forum Journal* 10, no. 4 (1996). Available at forum.nationaltrust.org/default.asp.

23. George, "Property Museums," 5.

24. Harris and Silberman, "Grant," 3. Donna Ann Harris, "Field Research for Heritage Philadelphia Program, Internal Revenue Service Form 990 Reports for 27 Historic Sites." Heritage Philadelphia Program, December 2005.

25. Thomas Wolf, *Managing a Non-profit Organization in the Twenty-first Century*. New York: Simon and Schuster Inc., 1999. Wolf describes how large endowments in and of themselves do not create sustainable organizations. He highlights the Symphony Orchestra Stabilization Program, funded in the 1960s, a massive infusion to endowments of some of the nation's premier orchestras. This program has not produced its desired outcomes some thirty years later. "Orchestra endowments had grown as predicted but only by an inflation-adjusted 37 percent—not enough to cover the tenfold increase in the annual financial shortfall. By century's [20th] end the industry and its funders are still scratching their heads trying to figure out what they could do to solve the structural problems that this 'stabilization' program had helped create." Clearly a one time infusion of lots of cash "is not a permanent guarantee that endowments will assure long-term sustainability." Wolf says "discipline is required." 318–19.

26. Met Life, Mature Market Institute Demographic Profile, American Baby Boomers. Available at www.metlife.com/Applications/Corporate/WPS/CDA/PageGenerator/0,4132,P8895,00.html (accessed 31 October 2006).

27. Susan Carey Demsey. "Still Bullish on Boomers," available at www .onphilanthropy.com/site/News2.html (accessed 25 September 2006).

28. Wolf, 323. Wolf gives a case study of an all-volunteer land conservation organization called Happyspring Inc. that was too small to be viable. "It could not assure that essential jobs would get done or if done would get done well. The organization was not on the radar screen of local citizens who might support it. Institutional donors would not support it because of its small size and limited impact. . . .Without support and visibility it was difficult to recruit the trustees who could change the situation." 323.

29. Randy Schackmann, "Is Your Nonprofit Walking Away from Money?" Available at www.onphilanthropy.com/site/News2?.html (accessed 25 September 2006).

30. Randy Schackmann.

31. Randy Schackmann.

32. Giving USA Foundation's annual report on philanthropy for 2005 says that individual giving is still the largest pool of charitable support to nonprofit causes in America. Foundations and corporations are generous, but individuals still provide the bulk of support. View their report at www.aafrc.org/gusa .htm.

33. Giving USA Foundation.

34. Brackett, 14.

35. Moe, 1.

36. George, "Museum Malaise," 4.

37. Stapp and Turino, 4.

38. Harris and Silberman, "Grant," 5.

39. Barbara Silberman, e-mail correspondence with author, Philadelphia, PA, 26 July 2005.

CHAPTER 2

Is This Your House Museum?

The following five scenarios depict fictional historic house museum organizations that are facing tough challenges. While your house museum organization may not be confronting these dire circumstances today, these situations may prompt you to evaluate your current situation, and to think about your ability to sustain your site into the next generation.

DEFERRED MAINTENANCE—ORANGE HOUSE

Our house museum organization is now more than 100 years old, having saved the 1780 Orange House from destruction in 1899. Over the years we have had many successes, including acquiring many original Orange family pieces of furniture from family members to furnish the parlor and one bedroom. These rooms were restored in the early 1960s, and our curator has determined that we should undertake paint analysis to determine the original colors of the walls and woodwork.

Our property maintenance committee has done a great job with general repairs to the house and several outbuildings, but our roof needs repair. We were able to put on an asphalt roof in the 1960s but have never been able to raise the money to restore it properly with cedar shakes. Now the roof is past its useful life and another capital campaign to raise $40,000 for a new asphalt roof seems beyond our grasp.

We have a small endowment of $120,000 from an Orange family bequest, but our visitation has been declining, and shop sales are slowly eroding. Several board members are very concerned about the pointing on the building as well, and we have an estimate from a restoration contractor for $60,000 to repoint the house. While the declining attendance and shop sales can be countered with additional rentals of our grounds for weddings, our board does not have the capacity to mount a capital campaign for $40,000—much less $100,000—to fully repair our building.

We are beginning to feel like the repair and restoration needs of our building are crushing us, and we see no end in sight. We feel we have to do something, but what?

AN AGING BOARD OF DIRECTORS—BROWN HOUSE

Our house museum organization, made up of preservation activists in our neighborhood, was successful in the late 1960s in saving more than forty houses from certain destruction when the state planned a new road that would have demolished two square blocks of our neighborhood. Throughout this eight-year fight, we kept focusing our efforts to save the Brown House, the oldest one in town, which happened to be on one of the two blocks. When we were finally successful in getting the highway rerouted, we listed our neighborhood on the National Register of Historic Places. The owner of the Brown House donated the house to us in 1975, right before the nation's bicentennial celebration.

Some of the organization's original founders are still on our board, and they are now in their seventies and eighties. The average age of our board is more than sixty-five years old, and we now have four vacancies out of twelve seats.

Most of the people moving into our neighborhood have young families and both parents work because the housing in our historic district has become extremely expensive. We have made some approaches to these neighbors to serve on our board, but all claim they are already overcommitted. Several of our board members have questioned the continued viability of our organization because we cannot attract new board members.

What will happen to the house when our eight board members "retire" or move on?

NO ENDOWMENT OR ORGANIZATIONAL RESERVES—
VIOLET MANSION

Ever since our house museum organization acquired the Violet Mansion from the family, we have been under pressure to restore the building. The Violet family had maintained the house for generations when they donated it to us in 1950. However, it did not come with any endowment.

In the meantime, we were able to get some government grants in the 1970s and 1980s to partially restore the building. We have had staff since the beginning because we promised the Violet family that we would run educational programs for children. We have a good relationship with the local school system and provide more than 120 class visits a year to public, private, and parochial schools.

Our problems began last year, when the government funding agency that provided 80 percent of our educational program budget had its budget cut by one-third. Our grant this year was down by 35 percent and we had to let our part-time educator go and reduce our educational programming by one-third. We have no other funds to rely on, no endowment to support our operations, or "rainy day" fund.

Our board members are talking about giving back the grant money and letting the rest of the educational staff go because we cannot sustain our educational programming anymore, much less maintain the house. Some board members even think we should give the house back to the Violet family.

DWINDLING ATTENDANCE, INCREASED COMPETITION—
BLACK'S CASTLE

Our staff members noticed it first. Attendance at Black's Castle has fallen 3–5 percent each year for the last five years, and we see no improvement this year. This means that, from our peak attendance year in 2001, our visitation has now dropped by almost 25 percent in just five years. We believe the neighboring historic sites are seeing similar drops, but do not have strong enough relationships with them to ask. Shop sales have been erratic during the last five years, but when all is said and done, this revenue center has fallen off by 10 percent in the same period. We noticed the declining attendance in subtle ways. First, school bookings came in more slowly than usual. In our peak month of May, we had room in the parking lot for the first time ever. Second, we noticed that fewer families came, despite the fact that we changed our admission structure to make admission free for all children under twelve. Finally, couples and small groups from nearby states became our mainstay, rather than local visitors. Most came in the afternoon, after visiting another historic site in the area. We have made up for some, but not all, of this lost visitation revenue from food sales at the tea shop on-site, our online gift catalog, and catering after hours. We are committed to increasing our attendance figures as we derive more than 70 percent of our revenue from visitor tickets and visitor spending on-site. We do not know what to do to bring back local visitors, and cannot afford to spend the vast sums needed to market our site to out-of-state visitors through the local convention and visitor's bureau. We feel alone and adrift, like we are on a leaking vessel heading into the Bermuda triangle.

RELEVANCE TO THE LOCAL COMMUNITY—WHITE ROW

Our board has been worried about the neighborhood around our historic house museum for more than thirty years. We have seen the area change during that time, but still have kept our doors open two days a week for tourists and school visits. We tell the story of the fighting White family from the War of 1812, and the patriarch Major White, who died in the house in 1850.

Today the White Row is deep in the midst of our city's ever-expanding Chinatown. Our docents and visitors say they have a hard time finding a place to park since we have no parking lot ourselves. We struggle with trash around our building and have had to add an alarm system after several break-ins. We have tried to reach out to our neighbors a few times but they are not interested in the story of Major White. Several board members have even suggested offering English as a second language classes in our basement classroom, but that idea never seems to go anywhere.

Our board is trying to uphold the story of Major White, but no one seems interested anymore.

SUMMARY AND PREVIEW

This chapter presented fictional scenarios that many historic house museums are currently facing. If any of these fictional stories resonate with you, then the following chapters might be useful. They will help you, your staff, and your board think about whether your house museum organization can confront its challenges or is ready to discuss new alternatives.

This book has a chapter describing solutions that house museum organizations have successfully tried to meet the overarching objective of ensuring that the historic building is preserved for generations to come. Other chapters describe a model decision-making process. The book also provides suggestions on how the board should commemorate the organization's stewardship of its historic site if the building is transitioned to a new owner or use so that the history and legacy of your work can be passed on to future generations.

In Part II, extensive case studies of historic house museums that have made a successful transition to a new owner or user will provide inspiration and reassure you that that your problems are not unique. The case studies will show you that there are good solutions pioneered by other nonprofit organizations just like yours.

The next chapter deals with legal and ethical issues for house museum boards. It discusses the legal responsibilities of nonprofit organizations in general, and the special responsibilities for house museum stewards. It discusses the specific challenges of the fictional house museums profiled above and provides some solutions for them. Finally, the chapter discusses attitudes toward investment in real estate.

CHAPTER 3

Legal and Ethical Issues

Board members of historic house museums have a fiduciary responsibility to preserve and educate the public about the property. Museum objects and assets such as endowments are held in the public trust.[1] Board members or trustees should take this responsibility seriously because their museum, housed in a costly piece of real estate, demands their full attention. Board members must be good stewards of the assets that the organization's constituents have entrusted to them. The literature on the roles and responsibilities of nonprofit boards is vast, but the most common duties can be reduced to four concepts.[2]

1. Board members set the strategic direction of the organization according to the organization's mission. All of the organization's actions should adhere to the basic reason the organization was put into place. Education and preservation of the building and collections should be the house museum's organizations key functions, according to its mission statement.

2. Board members ensure that the organization has the financial resources to undertake the work necessary to accomplish its mission. Boards need to raise funds for both operating costs and for capital repairs and restoration to the building to ensure its proper maintenance over time. Diligent board members should ensure that the building is at a minimum weather tight and in good repair, and restoration work is planned.

3. Board members oversee the financial accountability for the organization, and verify that its money is wisely and effectively

used. A house museum's largest asset is probably the historic building itself. The board should ensure that adequate funds are available for annual maintenance and that they are not wasting this asset by putting off repairs.

4. Board members develop the leadership necessary for the organization now and into the future. Succession planning is not simply who will be the next president. Rather, it informs a whole host of forward-looking activities, including how the organization is making incremental progress toward its overall goal of preservation of the historic structure. The board should always be looking for new talent at every level of the organization and promoting new volunteers, board members, and staffers whenever possible. Talented committee members should become committee chairs, and committee chairs should become board members and officers.

ATTORNEY GENERAL'S OFFICE

The entity that polices nonprofit charitable organizations is the attorney general in your state. The state attorney general enforces the charitable trusts or gifts to charity on behalf of the people of that state. His or her office oversees the management of charities by requiring them to register annually and by responding to charity-related complaints from the public.[3]

Concerns about mismanagement of charities in recent years have heightened scrutiny, especially regarding executive compensation, fundraising activities, accountability of nonprofits, deaccessioning, and financial instability.[4] Boards that allow themselves to float toward insolvency without taking aggressive action can open themselves up to liability for failure to act.[5]

"When a History Museum Closes," a recent ethics position paper prepared by the American Association for State and Local History's standing committee on standards and ethics, discussed the steps board and staff members must take when a history museum closes due to bankruptcy. This paper does not include historic house museums within the definition of a history museum, because house museums pose special concerns, which will be the subject of subsequent ethics papers in the coming years.[6]

The attorney general plays an important role as the public guardian of assets held for the people of the state by nonprofit organizations. Anyone can initiate complaints about neglect or harm to museum assets to the state's attorney general. For nonprofit boards facing difficult decisions, instruct your organization's attorney to discuss the organization's situation with the state attorney general at the earliest possible stage, regardless of which of the eight options to be discussed later you choose.

PRACTICAL MATTERS: RESPONSIBILITIES AND SOLUTIONS

House museum boards face many thorny issues in their everyday effort to maintain and restore their historic site. Organizations like the ones profiled in the previous chapter "Is this your house museum?" have real problems to address. The following paragraphs provide practical advice for these fictional historic houses and some commonsense solutions to the problems posed.

Orange House Board Responsibilities

Board members of the fictional Orange House must address their most basic responsibility to the house, to ensure its preservation while maintaining an active educational program. However, because the board has not been able to raise sufficient funds to invest in their building on a regular basis, the accumulated deferred maintenance is now very costly, even threatening the survival of the organization itself.

Furnaces, paint, roofs, and water heaters, for example, eventually reach the end of their useful lives and must be replaced. Failure to act promptly to replace these items only causes more damage and more expensive repairs. Board members unable to plan in advance for such predictable expenditures by raising money and putting it aside as a reserve for replacement costs, only saddle future board members with ever-larger capital expenditures that should have been amortized or paid for over a longer period of time. In this case, the board of Orange House must make Solomon-like decisions, because they have not been able to gather the necessary financial resources to support the mission of the organization, which is the preservation of the historic house.

Orange House Solutions

For the Orange House board to solve their deferred maintenance problem they will need to fundamentally change their efforts to raise funds. The organization must build its capacity to raise more money.[7] Broadening their donor base and seeking larger gifts and donations for specific restoration projects are likely the best prospects for raising the money they need to repair the roof immediately. They should also seek grants from governmental entities, private foundations, and direct appropriations from city, county, and state government.

Existing board members may have to recruit new board members who understand that their fundamental role is as fundraisers. The board may have to adopt the old adage "give, get, or get off" for their board members despite the upheaval that attitude may cause. The board must decide whether the staff needs to be augmented with consultants who can write grants for a fee, if staff grant writing has been unsuccessful in garnering larger gifts for restoration purposes. The board may also need to decide whether the current staff has the skills necessary to undertake all the jobs necessary to service the Orange House and its current pressing preservation needs. The board should make a several-year good-faith effort to raise the necessary funds, including staff realignments (if necessary), and adding new fundraising board members. If these efforts are unsuccessful and the Orange House board is still not able to address the deferred maintenance problems, they should consider exploring other options detailed in the rest of this book.

Brown House Board Responsibilities

The board of Brown House is made up of preservation activists who have a forty-year history with the organization, but their recent inability to gather new board members to serve is a concern. While they have recruited new potential board members from the neighborhood, they all have declined, leaving the Brown house board diminished, perhaps unable to muster a quorum to transact business. Leadership is a critical element of any organization's success. Boards that are unable or unwilling to successfully recruit new board members are placing the house at risk, too. A depleted board, whether through resignations, death, or inactivity, leaves the organization's largest asset, its real estate, vulnerable. In this case, the natural attrition of the board could eventually lead to the abandonment of the property because there are too few board members to act in its best interests.

Brown House Solutions

For the Brown House board to solve their board vacancy problems, they will have to make a concerted effort to recruit new, younger area residents to the organization and make these new board members feel welcome. Board members are volunteers who have a fiduciary responsibility to the house, but they are first and foremost volunteers who are donating their time to a cause that they must feel is worthy and where their contribution will be appreciated and respected.

This transition of the organization from one generation to another can be made less traumatic, if the original board members help identify new members and mentor them for one or two years so the new recruits are able take over their respective roles as overseers of their precious historic property. If, after making a concerted effort to solicit new board members and immersing them into the organization's history and culture, the Brown House board has still not addressed their fundamental board attrition issues, then they should consider some of the alternatives explored in the coming chapters.

Violet Mansion Board Responsibilities

The Violet Mansion has an excellent educational program that positively impacts local children, but changes in funding have created a deficit, and part-time educators have been laid off. For the board to withstand the current crisis, they must decide how valuable the educational program is to the organization's mission. Nonprofits, because of their reliance on grants, donations, and service contracts, are often loathe to diversify their income sources because of the staff time needed to execute a successful new funding venture. The board must raise the necessary funds to support the already-depleted educational staff. Additional layoffs and attrition threaten the public programming at the site. Here, if no progress is made, the board has failed to meet its basic responsibility to set the strategic direction as outlined in the mission of the organization, and provide adequate financial resources.

Violet Mansion Solutions

For the board of the Violet Mansion to solve their immediate funding short fall and save their valued educational program, they must diversify their funding base, and raise sufficient funds above the annual operating budget to create a reserve. Ideally, the reserve should be large enough so that the organization could continue to operate with current staff for several months, while new fundraising appeals are implemented. The board must regain control of their strategic fundraising responsibilities and guide the staff to diversify the organization's income sources. The staff, however, must have the capacity to take on these new duties on top of their already existing projects.

Often this fundamental change in fundraising strategy may result in board member resignations, because these individuals cannot or will not take on the now-necessary fundraising efforts. The board should not consider the bleak alternative of turning back the house to the original donors, the Violets, until they have made a sustained effort to solve this crisis and build a reserve or endowment. If, after a good effort to sustain their high-quality educational program with new funding, the board is unable to find new sources of support, then they might consider some of the alternatives described in the rest of this book.

Black's Castle Board Responsibilities

Despite the real efforts being made by Black's Castle board and staff to market and interpret their site, they are frustrated that their visitation is dwindling. The decline in visitation to house museums is almost systemic throughout the house museum community nationwide. Carolyn Brackett, who wrote about this issue in the Spring 2005 *Forum Journal,* attributes the decline in historic house museum visitation to many factors, including national events, plethora of choices, changing travel patterns, and the need to engage diverse visitors.[8]

Here, the staff of Black's Castle has been proactive and changed their admissions policies, hoping that free admission for children would spark additional attendance. It is unclear whether these changes were based on market research or rather educated guesses. It is also unclear if the staff or board members understand their competition, whether it is the historic site down the road, the nearby water park or the outlet mall ten miles away. All of these activities compete with historic sites for the precious leisure time that Americans have available.

The board must reinforce its responsibility to set the strategic direction of the organization and provide leadership to the staff to better understand its new visitors and audience and respond appropriately to these challenging new market realities. The board must also carefully monitor the financial performance of the organization through the financial statements and other indicators like admissions, website hits, and news stories, for example.

Black's Castle Solutions

The Black's Castle staff has collected statistics that indicate that their audience is changing, which provides a good start to begin to explain the revenue downfall. However, the organization needs more detailed information about their current visitors. These data can be garnered through a formal survey process by brief questionnaires, surveys on their website, or through telephone interviews. Once the organization understands what these new visitors want, they must refashion their programming to meet their needs. Market research will allow staff to be more strategic with the limited funds available for marketing and advertising. Another strategy would be to develop joint marketing campaigns or partnerships with neighboring sites or attractions. At a minimum, they should share visitor statistics formally or informally so that the decline in attendance at Black's Castle can be judged against others.

Certain board members and staff may not be able to adjust to these new realities. If so, the board should be clear about the new strategic direction and encourage all to join together to solve the problem. The board may also need to rethink all of its revenue streams, and invest in other visitor services such as a shop or food service to expand these revenue sources. The board should also review its overall budget and carefully monitor the monthly financial statements to ensure that the board is effectively and wisely managing the resources entrusted to the organization. If, after changing programming to better suit the new audiences, adjusting the marketing program, developing partnerships, and monitoring the financial performance of the organization, the board still sees a downward trend in their financial outlook, then they may wish to consider several of the options noted in this book.

White Row Board Responsibilities

Historic houses, unlike other objects in a museum collection, cannot be moved except under exceptional circumstances. The White Row board has been troubled by the change in the community around the building, and essentially allowed the building to become an island with no connection to the surrounding community. The board, to fulfill its promise to its preservation mission, must also ensure that the leadership is available to continue the organization now and into the future. The board would be wise to make a concerted effort to identify and invite its neighbors to become actively involved in the life of the organization by participating in relevant new programs and serving as volunteers, members, and board members. Responding to the change in audience or market for the house may be difficult for the current board, which is committed to the status quo. Board leadership, however, has a responsibility to ensure the continued viability of the organization. In this case, that means inviting local residents to participate in programs that have relevance to their lives today.

White Row Solutions

The White Row organization's significance to its community can be strengthened by developing programs that would appeal to the residents, especially students who could be involved in community service projects, and fairly typical educational programming about Major White's military career. The organization could foster citizenship programs to showcase the legacy of the White family and how immigration has created the great nation we all enjoy. Board members not committed to this change in programming probably will resign or be replaced when normal board terms expire. If, after developing new programs that have relevance to the community around them, and actively inviting local residents to participate, the board has failed to engage local residents in the life of the organization, then the board may wish to consider other alternatives mentioned in this book.

CONTAINER OR REAL ESTATE INVESTMENT?

Within the house museum community there is disagreement about whether a historic house is a container for the artifacts in the collections and is therefore the largest artifact that is collected and curated or whether the house museum is simply a real estate investment.

"When a History Museum Closes," the recent AASLH ethics position paper, discusses this issue in an instance where a history museum was dissolved due to bankruptcy rather than as part of an orderly transition to a new use or user. The position paper did not treat historic house museums as part of the broad category of historic museums, leaving future committees to wrestle with this matter.[9]

A historic house museum organization that chooses to formally accession the house as an object does create some interesting legal and ethical issues should the organization later decide to "deaccession," or sell or donate, the house from its collection. The American Association of Museums (AAM) has developed a strict ethical code and standards about how museums should deaccession objects from its collections, as does the American Association for State and Local History. I have found nothing written specifically about the special issues facing house museums that choose to make an orderly transition to a new owner or user. This book will not discuss this issue as the history community has yet to publish discussion papers on the matter. Instead, I refer you to the websites of both the AASLH (www.aaslh.org) and the AAM (www.aam-us.org), and their publications on museum ethics and deaccessioning for information. You and your attorney can determine how these standards would affect your organization if your organization has already accessioned the house as an object in the collection in the past.[10] Organizations that have not accessioned their historic building would not be bound by these standards, and thus have more flexibility as to its ultimate use or ownership.

ATTITUDES TOWARD INVESTMENT

Your board may have treated the site for years or even generations as an artifact to be conserved, rather than a piece of real estate to be used subject to market pressures. Houses used as museums are not subject to the same market pressures as a house owned by a for-profit entity. Privately owned assets like houses are investments that are expected to grow and the profit eventually be harvested by the owner, who may leverage the assets to make additional investments.

House museum stewards, unlike private investors, are unconcerned about sales prices of comparable properties. As an educational and exhibiting organization, the site's value is essentially priceless except as a basis for insurance purposes. The building suffers by this analysis because its upkeep and maintenance become less than paramount considerations.[11] A for-profit entity maintains its investment because it must generate enough cash flow to pay its operating costs, a mortgage, and a profit to the owner. Nonprofits are not so motivated.

Because the house museum's main asset, the historic building, is viewed as a community asset and held in trust for the public, there may be little interest or concern about long-term planning for the building because an unspecified future board would wind up with the responsibility. No current board member may feel any pressure to plan for the building's future, especially if the board is now comprised of energetic and committed people.

FUTURE MAINTENANCE AND RESTORATION

It is incumbent upon inspired board leadership to start a dialogue about the future of the organization and the future of the house, simply because the historic building's well-being demands it. Historic museums (like any old buildings) are constantly deteriorating because of the effects of water, the freeze/thaw cycle, and people—either through wear and tear or vandalism. The historic structure is also entirely dependent on the board to provide for its daily needs: maintenance, restoration, insurance, security, and management.

Importance of Cyclical Maintenance

The building's physical life cycle and maintenance may be easier to confront because most people can easily understand that a roof, water heater, or paint has a useful life. Most house museum organizations start with small budgets and take a "pay as you go" strategy toward costly building restorations and even basic maintenance. The "pay as you go" method may no longer work when expensive parts of the physical fabric of a historic structure inevitably must be replaced.

Routine maintenance prevents larger degradation of the building through an ongoing cycle of small repairs before larger and more expensive ones are needed. Organizations that have cyclical maintenance plans that define specific tasks to be undertaken seasonally for the building ensure that these plans become actions.

A cyclical maintenance schedule identifies all the important systems of a building (for example, roof, gutters, electrical, plumbing, HVAC, security, walls, floors, foundation, etc.), and notes how often the system should be inspected, its useful life, and where the item is in its useful life. For example, a roof replaced twenty years ago needs to be inspected yearly for leaks at the flashing and other points of water entry. An asphalt roof has a useful life of, say, thirty years (depending on the quality); a slate roof 100 years or more. An asphalt roof needs to be replaced much more often, so the organization would be wise to put aside money in a fund as a reserve to replace the roof when the useful life is ended. A qualified architect can prepare a cyclical maintenance schedule for your property, but it is up to the board to follow the advice and make small repairs on an ongoing basis rather than when expensive capital expenses can no longer be put off.

In these cases, the organization has invested in substantive architectural evaluations of the property and is following an annual maintenance schedule.[12] Boards that exercise their overall stewardship responsibilities seriously are good fiduciaries. Regular and predictable expenditures as outlined in a cyclical maintenance plan ensure that the organization's largest asset, its building, is being managed for the generations ahead. In effect, maintenance is preservation.

SUMMARY AND PREVIEW

This chapter focused on the responsibilities of a house museum board and illustrated some common solutions to problems that plague this field today. It also discussed several ethical matters related to house museum disposition and attitudes toward investment in the historic structure.

The following chapter discusses how difficult it is to address change in organizations. The bulk of the chapter deals with setting up a decision-making committee structure, how to organize committees, finding consultants and other help you will need, and advice for handling public relations.

NOTES

1. Marie C. Malaro, *A Legal Primer on Managing Museum Collections*, 2nd ed. Washington, DC: Smithsonian Institution Press, 1998. Care of Collections is discussed 406–17.

2. Marc Smiley, *Board Development for Nonprofit Preservation Organizations*. Washington, DC: Preservation Press, 2000, 2. The American Association for State and Local History and the American Association of Museums have websites with extensive sections dealing with ethics and board member responsibilities. View these at www.aaslh.org (accessed 8 July 2004) and www.aam-us.org (accessed 22 August 2004). Another good resource about board governance can be found online at Board Source www.boardsource. org. See also the chapter in Butcher-Younghans, "Governing the Historic House Museum," 10–23.

3. Malaro, 11 and 19.

4. Malaro, 23–25.

5. Malaro, 25.

6. American Association for State and Local History Standing Committee on Standards and Ethics, "When a History Museum Closes." Ethics Position Paper #2, Final Draft, presented at American Association for State and Local History annual meeting 12–15 September 2006. Thanks are extended to Rich Beard for making me aware of this document.

7. Paul C. Light, *Sustaining Nonprofit Performance: The Case for Capacity Building and the Evidence to Support It.* Washington, DC: Brookings Institution Press, 2004, 15.

8. See Carolyn Brackett, "Why Is Historic Site Visitation Down?" *Forum Journal* 19, no. 3 (2005), 14. See also Colin Campbell, "Sustainability: The Ongoing Challenge for Historic Sites," *Forum Journal* 20, no. 3 (2006), 18–20.

9. "When a History Museum Closes," 1.

10. See the American Association of Museums website for further details about deaccessioning. Available at www.aam-us.org (accessed 18 August 2006).

11. This point is made in Wolf, 319.

12. Two of the best architectural assessments I learned about while conducting research for this book were undertaken on all the properties owned by the Prince George's County Park Department historic properties owned by the Maryland-National Capital Parks and Planning Commission. See the case study on Hazelwood later in this book which talks about the role these assessments played in prioritizing investment at Hazelwood. Another organization that has developed a rigorous maintenance and restoration plan is the Preservation Society of Newport, also known as the Newport Mansions. I am indebted to Terry Dickenson for bringing the Society's efforts to my attention. Terry Dickenson, interview with author, 12 August 2006.

CHAPTER 4

The Decision-Making Process

In order for every one of the fictional house museums noted in the previous two chapters to be successful, they must change the way they do business. Change, as most know, is hard work. Organizational traditions and customs build up over many years, and are hard to disregard even when new realities can no longer be ignored. As we have seen, both White Row and Black's Castle recognize that change is needed, but don't quite know how to implement it. Perhaps they lack information, or perhaps they will need to reallocate scarce dollars to solve their problems. This approach, in turn, can trigger other change issues.

Board members too may wish to hold on to the present, even when there are clear warning signs that inaction will have perilous consequences. The boards of the fictional Brown House and Violet Mansion are left with little choice but to take action, even though it may mean that the institution the individual board members know will be different. Perhaps board members are reluctant to change because "that is how we have always done it."

Part of the clear appeal of house museums to the public is that they do not change. They are beacons of the past that provide stability in communities that often are reeling from change. These buildings, because they are fixed at their location, are easy landmarks, whether in one's memory of the place, or as a symbol of all that has come before.

As much as we would like the historic site and landmark to be permanent, perhaps the organizations that manage them are not permanent, and must change so that they can better suit the building for the coming generation. Nonprofit organizations after all are human creations, made up of caring people committed to a cause and an ideal. All organizations go through predictable life cycles as they serve their mission. For most, organizational change is inevitable. Boards that embrace change are able to prepare for the unexpected and deal positively with life's upheavals.

RESOLVE TO GET STARTED

Change involves risk, and some individuals may be more inclined to take risks than others on your board. But the risk of not changing looms large for our five fictional house museums and perhaps for yours too. It is often easier to procrastinate and to engage in avoidance behavior—focusing on minor details rather than the larger picture of the building and its needs—than to confront the difficult questions posed in these five stories.[1] Ignoring pressing realities, however, does not make them go away. Once the organization understands that there are serious risks if there is no change, the organization can then begin a rational search for alternatives.[2]

Your board leadership may find that confronting change and then getting the board as a whole to act upon it will be perhaps their hardest task. Inertia is a powerful driver in individual lives, let alone an organization composed of many individuals with strongly held beliefs about the nature and function of your beloved historic house. But skilled and dedicated board leadership should not shy away from change that has been thrust upon them by events or from a strategic-planning process to examine the house's needs and respond to them in a measured way.[3] Like the boards of the five fictional houses, all real-life boards can and should take remedial actions to fix their problems before concluding that a new use or user is appropriate.

Part of a Planning Process

Ideally, reuse planning should be one part of an overall review of how the organization is undertaking its basic mission, the preservation of its building and collections. Historic sites that make strategic planning an integral part of their organization will find that planning for the future of their historic site will not be as jarring as those that must respond to a crisis. Organizations that routinely look ahead and make adjustments to respond to events and actions they can or cannot control will fare better throughout a decision-making process for the future of their building.

Even if your organization does not undertake a formal strategic-planning process, you may want to use the annual budget development cycle as a means to identify how much ongoing maintenance costs have risen in recent years. Have the treasurer pull out the budgets and audits (if your organization is large enough to be required to be audited by your state charities agency), and do a simple chart showing how much the organization has invested in the building in the last five years. This will be instructive, because it may show that the costs vary widely from year to year, thus illustrating that the organization is responding only to calamities. Hopefully, you will see that the organization is also spending adequate sums to undertake basic annual or cyclical maintenance such as gutter cleaning, minor exterior painting, routine roof inspections and repairs, and other minor projects.

Your board may want to begin to seriously consider new solutions if you determine that the cost to maintain the building has become an increasing burden on the organization and your good-faith efforts to shore up its finances (as illustrated in the fictional stories in chapter 2) have been unsuccessful.

The Importance of Time

One of the luxuries of strategic planning is that it transpires over a period of time, which allows board members to reflect and respond to ideas presented by their colleagues during the planning process. Strategic planning is a deliberate act that allows for a measured review of many competing objectives and time for a consensus to develop. The decision-making process I describe here also uses time, reflection, and consensus as means to achieving a reuse solution.

Sites that use the decision-making process discussed here should be able to respond to a broad range of "what ifs" without resorting to panic or procrastination behavior. For boards that are responding to a physical disaster at their historic site, such as severe weather damage, they will hopefully have the requisite insurance to pay for at least part of the necessary repairs. While waiting for estimates to come and checks to arrive, there is time to engage in a decision-making process. Having enough time is critical for a good solution to emerge.[4] Sites that are financially unsound and are responding to an emergency will not have that luxury and will be tempted to solve their problem quickly rather than well, which can ultimately undermine the building's security.[5]

Two Masters

Your board will serve two masters during the period when your organization is considering new-use ideas. The normal work of the organization must proceed, while your board will need to be fully engaged in use-change discussions. In this chapter, I will discuss the most important information you will need before discussing alternatives and the kinds of consultants and stakeholders you will need to help you make decisions.

Board leadership must guard against latching onto one particular reuse scenario too early in the decision-making process. Allow enough time to understand the whole range of pros and cons associated with each reuse opportunity before making a final decision. Exploring the feasibility of several options will lead to a richer and more satisfying ultimate conclusion. This advice holds true even if your organization does not routinely plan for its future in a formal way.

GATHERING INFORMATION

To begin to identify new solutions, your board must have all necessary facts and legal documents in hand before starting on this journey. Without all the facts, you may find that people speculate or cast doubt on various reuse ideas because of perceived or long-remembered restrictions about use of the organization's assets, its rules, or its responsibilities.

I recommend that all pertinent legal documents be in your possession before convening any committees. A checklist of information to gather appears on pages 48 and 49. Some of the material may be difficult to track down, but be persistent. Take time to search the files if you don't immediately find the records you need. When other attempts to find these records have failed, then read the board minutes.

Reading the Minutes

You may be able to quickly find the information in the board minutes. It is wise (but also time-consuming) to read all of the board minutes of the organization from start to finish as part of this reuse planning process. The minutes may uncover other stories. You may learn about gifts cited in the minutes that may not be in the accession records. You may also be able to track down the motivations for past changes in bylaws or other board policies that now seem obscure.

Divide up the minute-reading task among several people. First, decide what you are looking for in the minutes and make sure all the minute readers understand their task. Look for resolutions regarding changes to bylaws, endowment policies, information about easements, building purchase or challenges of any kind to the title, gifts of real property, and endowments. Carefully copy all the pages of the minutes for that meeting, highlighting the passages in question, so you have a complete record of the board's actions. Compile the minutes into a notebook, divided by subject, so you have easy access to the facts and can address any concerns expressed.

The Deed for the Property

Look for the deed in the safety deposit box if there is one. Consider paying for a title search by a professional title search firm when the deed is not easily available. The relatively small cost of a proper title search will provide you with complete information about how title for the property is held and reveal if there are any specific encumbrances on the property, such as reversionary clauses (meaning that the property would revert, or go back to, another party if your organization could no longer care for it); utility, preservation, or other easements; mortgages; or liens. There may be additional covenants on the property based on donations accepted long ago or from grants accepted by the organization from governmental entities. After reviewing the deed, note if there are any other legal encumbrances on the property. Be sure to discuss their implications with your attorney.

Current Bylaws

Make sure that you have the most current version of the bylaws. Call a meeting as outlined in the bylaws to restate and vote on any questionable amendments. Your bylaws should be clear about whether the board of directors or the membership is able to sell assets. Hold a special membership meeting to vote on an amendment giving the membership the authority to sell or transfer assets if the bylaws are not clear. It is best to give the membership the authority to decide on asset sales or transfer, rather than the board of directors. This will ensure that the board has made a compelling case to a larger group of people before taking an important vote.

Mission and Vision Statements, Strategic Plan

Have the current mission statement and the current vision statement for the organization (if there is one) available to consult. Organizations that have a strategic plan should review it as objectively as possible, evaluating the outcomes and successes of the overall strategic plan. The strategic plan should then be available to consult during reuse discussions. Ideally, the reuse planning should be part of a broader strategic-planning process.

Planning and Zoning for the Property

Obtain a copy of the current zoning for the property and verify that all board members understand the implications of those restrictions. You must understand if the property is part of any overlay district or in any special taxing district. Your attorney can assist you with any planning or zoning issues that affect the property.

Endowment Policies

If your site has an endowment, identify the endowment instrument and any board policy about investment of the endowment principal, or corpus, plus any interest and dividends. The endowment instrument is a document prepared when the endowment was created. The instrument outlines how the interest and dividends and the principal can be spent. Make sure you have the original endowment instrument—not just a copy—as well as any revisions, board policies, or resolutions that alter the instrument.

Some donations to endowments may have come with restrictions, so gather all documents. You may have to search through decades of board minutes to find these resolutions or changes to board policies for the endowment. Your attorney can help you understand these agreements.

Policy on Any Board-designated Funds

A board-designated fund that functions like an endowment should have a board policy or resolution that spells out how the board can use the principal and interest or dividends from these funds. Make sure you have the current version of any policy for your reuse discussions, as well as any earlier versions. Again, you may have to search through years of board minutes to find these resolutions and policies. Your attorney can help you understand these policies.

Gift Letters

Gift letters lay out the specific terms of a donation of property or significant collections, be they real or personal property. Gift letters may have reversionary clauses that state who is to receive the property if the organization disbands. Check your board minutes as well for references to any gift letters. The donor's intention may be found among the minutes of the board meetings. They may also contain references to gifts made and any particular stipulations about the gift that the board would have to know about before accepting the gift. Your attorney can explain the implications of any gift letter.

Local Historic Landmark or District Designations

You will need to contact the local historic preservation commission to obtain the latest copy of the historic preservation ordinance. The ordinance outlines the process for submitting a certificate of appropriateness. This information will be useful if the organization is considering any changes to the designated property. It will be important to share the current ordinance with any new owner or manager of the site.

Make sure your board understands your landmark designation. There are no formal controls on the site, except if federal funds are being used for properties determined eligible or listed on the National Register (or a contributing part of a National Register Historic District) or a National Historic Landmark. Check with your State Historic Preservation Office if you have questions about the National Register.

Other Information You Will Need

Other items you will want to have on hand for committee meetings include your current operating budget; year-to-date and actual budgets; two or three years of the most recent audits; and interior and exterior photos of the building, landscape, and the neighborhood showing current conditions.

CHECKLIST OF MATERIALS

It will take considerable effort to gather all of these materials, as some may be in safe-deposit boxes (deeds), in minutes from long ago board meetings (resolutions on use of board-designated funds), or old grant files (any term easements or covenants due to receipt of government funds). But it is essential to have all of the information in hand before embarking on committee work; otherwise, committee members may waste time on a potential solution that may be impossible due to a provision of a deed, gift letter, or other governing document.

The following checklist is an expansion of the checklist developed for the Living Legacy Project, a project of the Heritage Philadelphia program working with a small group of historic house museums seeking to make a transition to a new owner or user.[6]

CHECKLIST OF MATERIALS NEEDED FOR REVIEW

____ Mission Statement and/or Vision Statement
____ Strategic Plan, Interpretive Plan, Disaster Plan (any if available), any other planning documents prepared by the organization
____ Bylaws (current version)

____ Audits and IRS 990 forms for two most recent fiscal years

____ IRS letter of tax-exempt status

____ Deed for property

____ Gift letters for the building or significant collections

____ Any easements on the property (utility etc., easements for preservation purposes—some old grants from State Historic Preservation Office may have required a covenant, please review your files)

____ Any restrictions on use or ownership of property

____ Lease for property (if the property is leased)

____ Endowment instrument (all versions)

____ Board policies for investment of endowment (all versions)

____ Board policies for use of any board-designated funds that function like an endowment (all versions)

____ Any previous written plans or efforts to seek a new user or owner for the site

____ Current zoning classification, any planning over lay districts

____ List of current landmark designations (national and local)

____ Historic Structure Report (if completed), Historic Landscape Report (if completed), any other architectural or environmental assessment of the building, grounds or landscape

____ Any other written materials that you feel will help us understand any constraints on the use or the future ownership of the site.[7]

Posting all of this information (as voluminous as it may be) to a private Listserv® or a restricted- access portion of the organization's website will promote transparency in the decision-making process for the committee members. Everyone participating on committees, including all board, staff, and consultants should have full access to the Listserv or the website section and be encouraged to check often for new information. E-mails can be circulated when new information is added to the list serve or website, so that committee members can be kept up to date. The Listserv or website also serves as the archive for the decision-making process.

GATHERING THE PEOPLE YOU NEED TO HELP YOU

Your board of directors will need access to trained specialists to help narrow and focus the myriad of choices available. The board should broaden the group of people deciding on any new use solution. The following pages describe the consultants and groups that should be available to help the board.

Facilitator

Consider whether the board needs an outside facilitator to assist it in decision making. While it may be tempting to have an internal person facilitate the decision making, there are advantages to having an outsider conduct this process. Insiders may offer special insight, but they may lack psychological distance, become embroiled in the process, or have their own agenda.[8] An outside consultant can provide the necessary "tough love" to move the organization forward in times of conflict.

Choosing a facilitator who has worked successfully with nonprofit organizations considering mergers, partnerships, acquisitions, or other major changes can add a dose of reality and urgency to a process that will take months or even years. Like any consultant, he or she works for the board and is hired for a specific scope of work.

To find a skilled consultant who has worked with other house museums or nonprofit organizations in the midst of change, contact your National Trust for Historic Preservation regional office, the program officer of a large, local foundation, or consult a directory of organizational consultants. Ask for, and then verify, references and recommendations. Meet with your potential facilitator to discuss his or her recommendations for how the organization should proceed through the decision-making process. Consider several facilitators before inviting each one to present their qualifications to the board. The board's decision should be based on the consultant's qualifications and experience in similar circumstances, "fit" with the organization, cost, and availability. Determine a schedule in your letter of agreement that spells out the expectations of both the consultant and the board.

Attorney

Your organization will need an attorney to represent the organization's interests in any negotiations, lease, or sale. A local attorney serving on your board may be willing to represent you either pro bono or paid. If the board member is not comfortable with this role, ask him or her to recommend another attorney with the real estate background you need. Seriously consider paying for this legal expertise, even if it is a blend of pro bono and paid work, because negotiations may be time-sensitive and volunteer attorneys may be limited in the hours they can donate. Your board may decide, as it gets further into the decision-making process that an outside attorney with no prior association with the organization may better represent your interests if you plan on entering into complex negotiations.

Other Consultants to Consider

Depending on the range of uses the organization may consider, there are other consultants that may be needed to provide timely advice. These include: architect, realtor, appraiser, commercial real estate consultant, collections consultant, accountant, financial consultant, and marketing or public relations consultant. Begin to gather recommendations from the board for these specialists, so that if the need arises the board will know whom to call.

GATHERING STAKEHOLDERS

Stakeholders are your neighbors, donors, local historians and preservationists, house museum peers, volunteers, and audience. They will all have something to say about the changes you are contemplating. Board leadership should adopt an open and transparent decision-making process. Involve key constituents in the decision making as non-voting committee members.[9] Doing so will add to the discussion and allow you to test ideas in a supportive and non-public setting. While these stakeholders do not become voting members of the board, their opinions should be valued and heard by the board throughout the decision-making process and before voting.

Identify specific people to participate on committees as you begin to discuss the direction with your board. Stakeholder involvement in discussions is critical to the success of the decision-making process since hearing many viewpoints will allow you to make better decisions. Stakeholder participation should occur throughout. If you seek their involvement too late in the decision-making process, such as after the preliminary ideas have been explored, you will lose the ideas and energy that stakeholders can bring to the process. Spread the stakeholders among your committees to ensure that their concerns are not concentrated in a "stakeholders committee," which they may view as being easily ignored.

Confidentiality of Discussions

Board leadership should remind board and committee members of the sensitive nature of their discussions and deliberations and direct all parties not to release confidential information. Discussions at the board or the committee level should remain confidential until the board decides to release the information. Stakeholders should be reminded that they are participating as representatives of their respective organizations or neighborhoods and should keep their organization up-to-date without breaching confidentiality.

Information that is leaked to outsiders—whether unintentionally or deliberately—can spread quickly and create bad press in a matter of days. Leaks can also ruin sensitive negotiations. Those who deliberately leak information are working at cross-purposes to the decision-making process.

Involving Staff

Any and all staff members should be highly involved in the decision-making process as advisors. But staff should not be burdened with the responsibility of managing the decision-making process in addition to their day-to-day duties at the site.[10]

In many cases, the highest-ranking staff member may have advocated strongly for the board to move forward with a formal decision-making process because that key staff member understands the organization's precarious financial future and its impact on the preservation of the historic building. Other staff members may not speak up, fearing they will ultimately lose their jobs if any change is contemplated.

If the board, rather than the staff, is taking the lead in encouraging the start of reuse discussions, board members must address the concerns of staff quickly and forthrightly, and make an effort to engage them in an advisory capacity. Staff may be confused about their role, their employment status, and the overall future of the historic site. Staff in this position must be made aware of the confidential nature of the discussions taking place, whether they participate in the decision-making process or not. Board leadership must remind staff that they must not talk about the deliberations with outsiders.

How to Fund the Advice You Need

In most cases, the board will have to pay for the advice it needs from its own resources. Once the board has committed to making a change, the organization may be able to provide a compelling case to an area granting agency or other funder for assistance to pay for needed consultants. Discuss this prospect with area foundations or with key donors to the organization, because you will probably get some keen advice during these conversations, whether or not you are successful in obtaining additional funding.

I recommend that the board set aside money at the start of the decision-making process for commemorative activities and events to be held at the end of the process. Donating the organization's papers and archives, or making the record of the building's preservation available to the new leaseholder or owner, is an important part of the transition process. Commemoration ideas and information about philanthropic activities appear in chapter 5.

Advice for Board Leadership

Literature abounds about organizational transitions, be it in the for-profit or nonprofit sectors. The role of the leader in guiding a board through a transition, whether it is a capital campaign, a founder leaving their organization, or a top staff member leaving for another job, should stress the human element in the transition.

The decision-making process discussed below acknowledges that not all board members will embrace change. Some may actively thwart any change to the status quo by passive or active means. Board leadership must be prepared for objections and actively engage the dissenters or resisters and stress the positive elements of the potential change.[11] Unlike a work situation where leaders can reassign or fire employees who do not go along with the change agenda, you, as a board leader, must actively involve your volunteer peers on the board and spend extra time trying to persuade dissenters on the merits of the change.

Those that resist the changes that the board as a whole seeks to make may have real complaints that should be taken seriously. Their association or involvement with the organization as evidenced by their role in the organization may be lost if the board decides to no longer manage the historic house museum. Some resisters may believe that their social status in the community may be fundamentally altered if the house is no longer open and interpreted to the public. Board leadership must understand that some board members may end up negatively affected. New roles must be found for these individuals that mitigate the negative impact and focuses on the positive future.

For-profit change literature stresses rewards as a means to encourage compliance with a change agenda. For board members, rewards will not be monetary. Rewards in a nonprofit context might be a better or more prestigious committee assignment, a leadership role or an honorary title or position that has meaning to the resister. Board leadership will need to be creative and have an excellent understanding of the motivations of the resister to find rewards that have meaning for him or her. Not every resister will respond willingly to these entreaties. Some may resign from the board; others may stay to the bitter end. It is incumbent on board leadership to move the whole of the board forward with a change agenda, knowing that not everyone will agree.

Transition literature stresses that change is a process, not unlike grieving that Elisabeth Kübler-Ross wrote about in her pioneering work *On Death and Dying* in 1969. Leaders should acknowledge that everyone will respond to change differently because there is some sense of loss. Loss of routine, loss of status, loss of a specific role in the community might be cited by board members when asked about how the change directly affects them. Good relations among the board members themselves may be the key to making the transition less rocky. Board relationships may be longstanding and individuals may have lived through other perhaps larger organizational changes in the past.

Leadership should acknowledge that change is an adjustment. Time and empathy can go a long way toward making the loss less stinging. Leadership should stress the gains to be made to the organization, to the building, and to the preservation movement in general through the decision to transition the historic building to a new owner or user.

I emphasize the commemorative element of the decision-making process because it can help everyone, but especially passive resisters, to move through their losses toward a brighter future. The summing up of the organization's past, through oral histories, pamphlets, and other forms, gives board members the opportunity to properly acknowledge the debts of today's board to those from the past who set aside the historic site as a museum. Honoring founders and key leaders can help make the transition more meaningful, and therefore less troublesome.

Envisioning a New Future

Critical to the change process is discovering the new identity for the future organization. The transition may necessitate a whole set of new actions for the organization to complete the change and launch the new endeavor. Mission statements may need to be changed, bank accounts closed, new committees formed to provide oversight for the leasee, or a capital campaign mounted to convert a building to a new use. If the sale of the building is the ultimate decision, then the organization may need to wind up its affairs, pay bills, and dissolve. The board, through its leadership, must articulate the new future to the organization's members, its constituency, and the public.

A MODEL DECISION-MAKING PROCESS

The following pages offer some preliminary advice for your decision-making process and are based on interviews with other house museum stewards making use or ownership changes.

Establish a Committee System

Information-gathering and a thorough investigation of alternative uses will require time. Do not expect the entire board to participate in this process. Institute a committee structure to help expedite information gathering. These committees should make recommendations to the board as a whole for voting. Some committees may be short-term; others may work throughout the change process. The board chair should appoint committee chairs but each committee chair should be allowed to add committee members, especially from stakeholder groups, with the concurrence of the board chair. Committees may include:

- Consultant qualifications
- Reuse goals
- Preliminary alternatives and preferred alternatives
- Public relations and community outreach
- Commemoration and philanthropic activities

Distribute board members and stakeholders evenly among each committee. Do not allow any group to concentrate on any one committee.

Keep Minutes

One way to ensure that the organization is not making "secret" decisions is to involve stakeholders in the process. A "slow and deliberate, open and transparent decision-making process" will go far toward assuring the community that the organization is making an ethical, good faith effort to find a new use to ensure the building's long-term preservation.[12]

Keep accurate minutes of all committee meetings and share these minutes with all board members and committee chairs in a timely manner. The minutes do not have to be elaborate, as long as they succinctly itemize all issues discussed at each meeting, the text of any resolution, and all votes taken. Be sure to share any relevant reports prepared on behalf of the organization with the committee chairs so that everyone has access to the same information.

Goal-Setting for the New Use

House museum boards should consider the overall goals of the potential conversion and decide which architectural elements must be retained at the start of the decision-making process. How much of the uncompromised historic fabric, interior and out, and the setting, including the landscape and ancillary buildings, should be retained?[13] There may be specific features such as significant historic woodwork or original ornamentation that should be considered inviolate, because these features provide the essential architectural character of the house and the reason it was initially saved for posterity.

Some organizations may be willing to allow much of the interior to be altered for a new use because the original historic fabric has been compromised over time or solid documentation is lacking. Board members can start these discussions by reviewing *The Secretary of the Interior's Standards for Treatment of Historic Properties.*[14] This document can be used as a baseline for judging how proposed changes will impact the features of the house. Check with the historic preservation commission first to determine their guidelines for change for both the interior and exterior of any landmark property.

Your board may want to allow less flexibility than contained in the *Standards*. Regardless of how tightly you wish to regulate any new user, you should set these goals at the start of any reuse planning process. Without overall goals for the preservation of the building in a reuse project, the board will not be able to judge the impact of the specific uses on the architectural fabric of the building and its overall preservation.

Review Preliminary Uses, Decide on a Preferred Alternative

Once the organization has a working committee system set up, and reuse goals have been established, these committees should work closely with the facilitator to test the board-chosen alternatives for feasibility. The board as a whole should choose specific ideas to test, but let the committee undertake specific review. A thorough evaluation of each potential use, and its legal and financial feasibility, should be reported to the board as a whole in brief written reports by the committees or the consultants. Keep the board up-to-date on information throughout the process, rather than expecting them to absorb the material all at once.

Care must be taken to fully investigate the broad financial implications of each alternative, as there may be unintended consequences. A "back of the envelope" assessment of the relative costs to convert the house into a bed and breakfast, for example, may later haunt the organization because no one investigated the costs and the building code implications of such a conversion. Perhaps the board would have abandoned this use possibility early in the process, had they known of the excessively high construction costs to meet the building code for this use. Take the time, crunch the numbers, and compare real and tested costs by independent experts before deciding on a preferred alternative.

Your organization may choose to identify reuses that will require zoning or other use changes, even though these typically require a costly and lengthy governmental approval process. Decide if the organization will undertake the approval process itself, or leave this to the potential leaseholder or new owner. The new zoning category may increase the value of the building. The committee should investigate the costs to gain these approvals, how long it would take, and balance whether the time and effort merit the financial outlay. Expect a lower lease value or sale price when the approval process is left to the new owner or user.

Board meetings should be reserved for questions to the committee members and any consultants retained. Special working meetings may be necessary as the organization draws closer to a preferred alternative. Board leadership may want to wait to appoint the preferred alternative committee members until all alternatives have been reviewed, as committee members may emerge that have unique skills or viewpoints.

It may be difficult for the organization to involve itself in reuse planning while undertaking their normal day-to-day activities, as reuse planning requires considerable time for both board and staff. Expect that there will be some normal activities that will be given short shrift during the reuse planning process and plan for this accordingly.

The board should be kept informed of the committee's work at least on a monthly basis. Minutes of all reuse committee meetings should be kept, posted, and circulated. The preferred alternative committee is charged with exploring in considerable detail the financial, market viability, and legal ramifications of the specific use change. This committee should be able to engage consultants to provide necessary advice with budgeted funds, with the permission of the board. The committee should be allowed and encouraged to return to the board if the alternative is flawed and needs to be reconsidered.

When the preferred alternative is still determined to be viable after careful study, the committee and any consultants should present their findings to the board, accompanied by a written report. When the board agrees that this alternative makes sense, then the larger group of stakeholders who have not participated in committee work should be invited to hear this presentation soon after the board meeting. It is likely that after this stakeholder meeting there may be additional information needed before the board can vote to recommend the alternative to the membership for a final decision.

Tell Your Story and Dealing with the Media

Throughout this process the relationship with the media should be actively managed by a public relations or communications committee.[15] Early in the process, this committee should develop their media plan and be ready to implement it immediately. Most of their work will be done when the organization begins to identify possible uses and then again when a preferred alternative is developed. This committee should receive all press inquiries. The board should choose one spokesperson, which can be the board chair, another board member, or staff. This individual should be generally available to take press inquiries and to sit for interviews as needed. Scripted answers or talking points should be prepared, approved by the board, and practiced in advance of any public appearance.

This committee needs to actively communicate what is happening to the membership throughout the process. The membership should not be hearing about this process when a preferred alternative has emerged, or else they may feel that it is already a "done deal."

The membership should be aware that the board is considering a variety of use options, because the public relations committee is also communicating with the membership. Information about proposed alternatives should appear in the newsletter, via letter, website, e-mail messages, or other vehicles as appropriate. The public relations committee would be wise to conduct several small meetings with members in the form of focus groups to gain reaction to ideas being discussed. A trained facilitator should be used for the focus groups to ensure that the organization gets the information it needs. Focus groups should not substitute for frequent communication with members about the changes being contemplated, however. The membership should not hear about a vote of this magnitude at the last minute as it may be doomed to failure.

Make the Decision and Vote

Once a preferred alternative has emerged and been tested for validity, and the board feels that they can answer most, if not all of the questions raised by constituents about the preferred alternative, then consider scheduling a meeting with the membership. Some organizations may prefer to have informal informational meetings throughout the decision-making process to share the facts they have gathered with members. Other boards may choose to schedule a special meeting specifically for a vote. Your board will have to decide how to approach this meeting after careful deliberation.

At this point, it is critical that the organization follow the specific instructions in the bylaws for special meetings, including any timing and notice requirements. Follow the instructions of the bylaws "to the letter" to prevent challenges to the validity of the meeting. Months before this meeting, review your membership list carefully and understand who is eligible to vote. Rumors in the community about an impending change may lead to a run-up of people becoming members so they would be eligible to vote (and probably defeat) your proposals. Discuss with your attorney any questions about how members should be treated for voting purposes before sending the meeting notice.

The preferred reuse should be the only issue on the agenda for the membership meeting to focus the attention of the audience. Know what constitutes a quorum to conduct business at this meeting, and ensure you have one. Make sure that there are enough well-informed people in attendance who can ask informed questions. Review this process with your attorney.

Have the consultants and the preferred alternative committee members present their findings with visuals, including plans and photographs, at this meeting. Have a tight agenda that includes adequate time for questions from the membership. Propose the resolution and ask for a vote. The vote should pave the way for a new future for your historic site if you have done your homework.

Implement the Decision

In many ways, the theatrical vote by the membership is only the start of the change process. The board must then take action to put the decision in place. Depending on the choice, this may include dissolving the corporation and transferring its assets (the house or the collections) to another organization or to the local community foundation. In other cases, the organization has found a willing partner and leased the site to someone else to manage. For those who choose to reprogram the site for a mission-based use, the board will still remain intact and implement the new use itself (see figure 4.1).

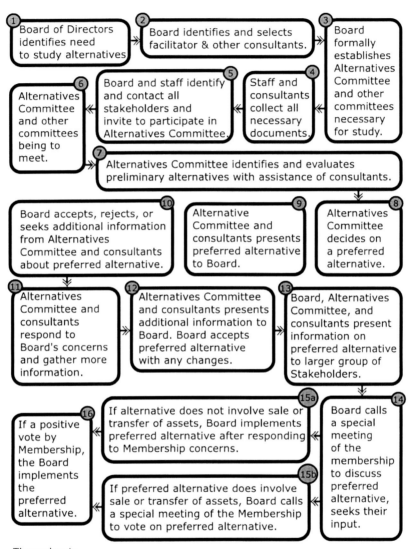

1 Board of Directors identifies need to study alternatives

2 Board identifies and selects facilitator & other consultants.

3 Board formally establishes Alternatives Committee and other committees necessary for study.

4 Staff and consultants collect all necessary documents.

5 Board and staff identify and contact all stakeholders and invite to participate in Alternatives Committee.

6 Alternatives Committee and other committees being to meet.

7 Alternatives Committee identifies and evaluates preliminary alternatives with assistance of consultants.

8 Alternatives Committee decides on a preferred alternative.

9 Alternative Committee and consultants presents preferred alternative to Board.

10 Board accepts, rejects, or seeks additional information from Alternatives Committee and consultants about preferred alternative.

11 Alternatives Committee and consultants respond to Board's concerns and gather more information.

12 Alternatives Committee and consultants presents additional information to Board. Board accepts preferred alternative with any changes.

13 Board, Alternatives Committee, and consultants present information on preferred alternative to larger group of Stakeholders.

14 Board calls a special meeting of the membership to discuss preferred alternative, seeks their input.

15a If alternative does not involve sale or transfer of assets, Board implements preferred alternative after responding to Membership concerns.

15b If preferred alternative does involve sale or transfer of assets, Board calls a special meeting of the Membership to vote on preferred alternative.

16 If a positive vote by Membership, the Board implements the preferred alternative.

Throughout:
Board communicates to Membership about progress of search for preferred alternative. Board manages communication with Stakeholders and the public through a spokesperson.

Figure 4.1   Decision Making Flowchart

Closure

Regardless of the new use chosen, the board should make an effort to commemorate the work of the volunteers, former board members, or staff who for so long cared for the building and its contents. Commemoration ceremonies or activities can be varied, and be formal or informal. Boards can develop scrapbooks, histories, exhibits, brochures, or gather other physical remnants of the organization. Events should be held to honor donors and volunteers, past and present, who were responsible for the initial and continued preservation of the site. Tasteful plaques can be affixed to the building prior to transfer that describe the building's history and the organization's involvement in its preservation. A party celebrating the new future of the property should be held to honor those who have served.

SUMMARY AND PREVIEW

This chapter described the people and the documents that the board will need to help with decision making. A model decision-making process was briefly outlined.

The next chapter describes how to commemorate the work of the organization and gives advice about establishing permanent, educational, and legacy projects to mark the transition.

NOTES

1. Irving L. Janis and Leon Mann, *Decision Making: A Psychological Analysis of Conflict, Choice, and Commitment*. New York: The Free Press, 1977, 171–200.
2. Janis and Mann, 179.
3. Janis and Mann, 180.
4. Janis and Mann, 50–52.
5. Janis and Mann call this behavior hypervigilance, in other words, panic.
6. Visit the Heritage Philadelphia Program web site at http://www.heritagephila.org.html/.
7. Donna Ann Harris, "Materials Needed for Attorney Review, Living Legacy Project," Heritage Philadelphia Program, Philadelphia, 2005.

8. Information about organizational change can be found in Thomas Wolf, *Managing a Non-profit Organization in the Twenty-first Century,* New York: Simon and Schuster, Inc, 1999.

9. John J. Gabarro, *Managing People and Organizations*, Cambridge, MA: Harvard Business School Press, 1992.

10. Feeney, 113. Also see La Piana, 181–225.

11. Harvard Business Essentials, *Managing Change and Transitions.* Boston: Harvard Business School Publishing Company, 2003, 70–81. This book compresses Kübler-Ross' five grief stages down to four: shock; defensive retreat; acknowledgment; and acceptance and adaptation. William Bridges, *Transitions: Making Sense of Life's Changes.* Reading, MA: Addison Wesley Publishing Company, 1980. Bridges states that a transition occurs in three phases: endings, the neutral zone, and making a beginning.

12. Thompson M. Mayes, interview with author, typescript of telephone conversation, Washington, DC, 13 May 2003.

13. Samuel Y. Harris, "Alternate Use as a Preservation Strategy: The Eastern State Penitentiary Case Study, *Forum Journal* 9, no. 1 (1994): 2.

14. *Secretary of the Interior's Standards for Treatment of Historic Properties*, 1995. www.cr.nps.gov/hp/tps/secstand1.htm.

15. Richard L. Thompson, "Contingency and Emergency Public Affairs," in Tracey Daniel Connors, *The Non-Profit Book: Management,* 3rd ed. New York: John Wiley and Sons, 2001, 471.

CHAPTER 5

Making the Transition

At the very start of the decision-making process, the board spent a good deal of time talking about when the organization was founded, the initial goals, and how far the organization had come from its simple beginnings. The following suggestions will help you integrate your stewardship mission into the reuse planning process. Any transition to a new use or ownership deserves an appropriate set of activities to mark the occasion. While many may put little emphasis on the commemoration element of the transfer process, it is an important transition that deserves some discussion.

CELEBRATING THE TRANSITION

How you choose to mark the transition occasion will depend on how traditions are observed in your organization already. Have you hosted a Founders Day, or other anniversary of the site or the organization? Has the organization developed an exhibit or general interest publication about the house or site? Events, publications, and other reminders of the work of the organization are all keys to making a successful transition.

Events and Celebrations

Events should be held to honor the donors and volunteers, past and present, who were responsible for the initial and continued preservation of the site. A party celebrating the new future of the property should be held to mark the occasion.

Symbolic Events

Host symbolic events to mark the change in management or owner-ship of the property. Events to mark the transfer of the building to new users or owners can be formal or informal. An informal picnic or lunch-eon to celebrate with the new stewardship organization that will be tak-ing over maintenance and management responsibilities can be held with the combined boards. Sale of the building may warrant a more for-mal occasion, with a ceremonial presentation of the keys to the build-ing, for example. How your organization chooses to remember and honor the work of generations of volunteer stewards should reflect the customs of the organization itself.

Celebrations

Celebrations should focus on the passion that drove the initial and current board to take action to save the site. Their selfless work should be honored. Even today, when we know that there are other options for maintaining historic homes than turning them into house museums, the celebrations should champion those who made the effort long ago to save your magnificent building.

Board leadership should determine which events are appropriate to celebrate the transition based on the tenor of the last several months of negotiations. Some board members may feel the transition of the house museum to a new use or owner is a personal or organizational failure. This is an unfortunate and unfounded response. Instead, the board is acting on its fundamental preservation mission.

Encourage your board to focus on the greater preservation mission of your organization and fit the transition into that context. A dignified and sensitive ceremony can be both cathartic and inspirational to the people who have loved the historic building. Plan at least one celebra-tion during the transition that has meaning for the board as a whole. A lunch or dinner may be all that is needed to gather everyone together to mark the transition occasion.

Ideally, the board will plan several different types of commemorative activities because settling on one activity may not be meaningful to the broad spectrum of board members, stakeholders, and other constituents who have shared in the history of the building or in decision making for its future. I recommend one activity in each of the following categories.

- An educational component
- A permanent reminder
- A living legacy for future generations

Here are some suggestions for activities in each of these categories.

AN EDUCATIONAL COMPONENT

The board can decide that a publication or journal article about the house and the organization is a worthy memorial. Produce exhibits, brochures, compact discs (CDs), websites, pod-casts, histories, and other documentation of the organization's stewardship of the property or the organization as a whole. Consider sharing your updated interpretive information at a local history venue.

Learning about the Past to Inform the Present

The commemoration process should start with an understanding of the organization's past. Update any articles or books written about the history of your organization in the past. Remember that a good researcher will always confirm even the most basic facts by going back to the original historic documents. For nonprofit organizations, this often means the minutes of the board meetings.

Read Your Minutes

Board minutes embody the history of the organization, but that history is in raw form. The minutes need interpretation to have any real relevance to tell the story of your group or the building. Even though it is time-consuming, it is wise to read all of the board minutes of the organization from start to finish as part of this reuse planning process. The alternatives committee may already be reviewing the minutes to find facts and resolutions regarding changes to bylaws, endowment policies, any information about easements, building purchase or challenges of any kind to the title, gifts of real property, and endowments.

Do not expect the alternatives committee readers to also gather facts about the history of the organization, as they are reading the minutes for a very different purpose. The committee charged with commemorating the history of the building/organization should read the minutes as well.

Divide up the minute-reading task among several people if the organization is more than ten years old and there is much reading to be done. Perhaps group the minutes by decade, then ask each person to summarize the most important events in the form of a timeline. The minutes may uncover other stories or reveal trends that would otherwise be obscure. The names of key board members will emerge from the minutes, in addition to the founders of the organization. The minutes will also show how the organization reacted to change at other times in its history. This knowledge may be instructive for any history-related project. Collect the information about when the building was acquired, any restoration undertaken, and produce educational information as part of the transition.

Collect Your Papers

Collect and deposit the organization's papers in an appropriate archive or repository if the building is being sold or the organization merged. Collecting your archives is an important activity as you transition the organization or building to new ownership. Gather everything. Do not attempt to "clean up" your archives or purge selectively. History comes alive for people most often in the smallest detail, and future historians who want to know about the organization will need to see the entire scope of records. Selective destruction of documents will not help future historians. Do not even reorganize the file drawers; leave this to the professional archivists.[1]

Organizational Records to Collect

Collect all of the organizational documents including bylaws, incorporation papers, minutes of meetings of the board of directors, brochures of any kind (especially older ones), special event publications, articles written about the house, newspaper clippings (especially if you have a clipping file), the range of strategic plans completed by the organization, mission and vision statements, newsletters and reports, and all financial statements and reports (including audits and tax returns). Sensitive information such as donor records, membership lists, and personnel records can be protected by restricting access to them. Discuss this issue with the potential repository. The status of the organization's papers should be discussed as part of the merger agreement.

Approach the archive or repository that makes the most sense to house the organizational and restoration records. See the head librarian or archivist about donating your archives. Discuss the donation process, if they would accept the organization's papers, if funds are needed to catalog the papers, and how they would like the papers boxed and delivered. Review how the public would have access to your papers and sign any necessary agreements.

Scrapbooks

Create scrapbooks about the organization's stewardship experiences. Scrapbooks about the history of the organization are an excellent way to collect information in one place about the building and the organization that saved it. Remember to use only copies of original documents in the scrapbook. The originals will go with the archive to the local historical society or library so that others have access to the history of the organization.

Oral Histories

Conduct oral history interviews with the organization's founders or key leaders. Transcribe the interviews, and then deposit them with an appropriate repository.[2] Oral history of the organization's founders or prominent donors can help future historians understand the history of the building, and the organization that saved it.[3] You may want to ensure that the people involved with the organization at its founding, important donors, and others in the life of the organization are properly honored or memorialized.

Building Records to Collect

Collect all the records about the building's preservation and maintenance. It is very important to gather all the old records about the building, even if they are now outdated (including drafts of reports and duplicates) because future historians will want to see this important part of the historical record. Preservationists will want to know what happened in the nineteenth, twentieth, and twenty-first centuries.

Gather all the maintenance logs and records; bills; invoices and warranties for equipment; histories written about the building; reports about the condition or restoration of the building; historic structure reports; and conservation reports and assessments that you can find, even if outdated. All of these documents will provide clues for future historians.

You will want to make copies of all the records about the building for the new owner if you are selling the property. The party that will maintain the property will need access to these records and may want copies for their files. Another property stewardship organization taking over the day-to-day management and maintenance of the site will need a copy of the property maintenance and restoration records. Originals of these materials should be donated to an appropriate public archive. If the property will be going to new owners or managers, they will also need a copy of the records about the building.

A PERMANENT REMINDER

Plaques and Interpretive Signage

Tasteful plaques can be affixed to the building prior to transfer that describe the building's history and your organization's involvement in its preservation. Also consider volunteer and donor acknowledgment in the form of a plaque or interpretive signage for the site in the public right-of-way. The plaque could tell about the house's history and the organization's role in saving it.[4]

Easements

Easements are the best method to assure that the work that your organization has done over the years to restore and maintain your property will not be undone by future owners. An easement is a voluntary legal agreement in the form of a deed between a qualified easement-holding organization and a historic property owner. In the easement agreement, the historic building owner agrees not to demolish or subdivide the property and to affirmatively maintain it forever.

Easements are an effective tool to ensure maintenance of an historic property over time, as the agreement runs with the land and is difficult to extinguish. Easements bind the current and any future owner of the land. The building is inspected by the easement-holding organization regularly and the terms of the easement are enforced by the easement-holding organization if there are violations. The easement-holding organization has an obligation to inspect the property and enforce the easement restrictions against demolition and insensitive alteration.

Most easements are donated for the exterior of buildings, and occasionally to protect historic interior features if they are significant to the property. Open space easements are used to assure the preservation of open space and can be utilized to ensure that the grounds, gardens, or other landscape features, if they are significant to the setting of an historic building, are maintained. An easement between two nonprofit organizations generates no federal tax incentives.[5]

The easement document is negotiated and is site-specific. No two easement documents are alike. The easement document outlines in writing and through photographs the current condition of the building, and describes the condition to which the property should be maintained. The document states that the building is to be kept in good repair, structurally sound and substantially in the form and condition on the date of the closing. The new owner cannot make additions, remove, or alter the existing features named in the document, build temporary structures, or add signs, awnings, and satellite dishes without the express prior written approval of the easement-holding organization.

The easement-holding organization may have specific criteria for accepting donated easements and may or may not agree to accept your building. The easement-holding organization can work with any realtor representing your organization in the sale to educate any potential buyer about the obligations placed on the new owner and any future owners to maintain the property forever.

The easement may diminish the value of the building for the organization selling the property. The organization will not receive the full fair market value for the sale to a new owner, and the easement may affect any future sale price because of the restrictions. Potential buyers may object to the easement restrictions or try to become involved in negotiations with the easement-holding organization about elements of the document. Do not allow this to happen. The final draft of the easement should be available as part of the listing agreement so that all potential buyers are aware of the terms of the easement agreement before a sales contract is signed.

There are often costs associated with placing an easement on a property. The easement-holding organization may charge fees for preparation of the easement document and will probably require an endowment contribution to ensure that the easement-holding organization has funds to enforce the terms of the restrictions. Some of these fees may have to be paid up front, while others could be paid out of proceeds from the sale of the house.

The house museum organization itself could accept the easement donation should there be no easement-holding organization nearby or if the local easement-holding organization declines to accept your building. This is less desirable because it would require that the organization exist in perpetuity to administer the inspection and enforcement of the easement agreement. Some governmental entities may be willing to hold easements.

There are about 100 easement-holding organizations across the country at the local or statewide level. The National Trust for Historic Preservation also accepts easements. Contact your National Trust regional office to locate the nearest easement-holding organization.

BE A LIVING LEGACY FOR FUTURE GENERATIONS

Establish a grant fund with the remaining assets of the organization at a local community foundation as a donor-advised or restricted-fund to benefit specific preservation organizations or preservation activities.

What to Do with the Sale Proceeds?

Sale of the house should release large sums of money to be donated to other preservation organizations or spent on historic preservation activities in the community that could not be realized any other way. A sale will release the board from its continual obligations to maintain the structure after debts are paid. If the building's market value is nominal due to deterioration, and you believe that the sale will not generate enough money to pay the debts of the organization, work with your attorney before listing the property for sale to discuss how to dissolve the organization and pay your creditors.

Nonprofit organization bylaws direct how the organization's assets are to be distributed should the organization dissolve. Most often the organization will seek to place its assets with a nonprofit organization with a similar mission. Proceeds after expenses must be distributed to these entities after the sale is concluded.

A less-preferred option would be for the organization to continue to exist to manage grant making with the sale proceeds. This arrangement is not recommended because of the additional expense of staffing and managing the assets. This arrangement does not allow the organization to complete its affairs and dissolve after the sale of the building. Another concern is that the intentions of the dissolving board may be muddied over time as to the purposes of the distribution of the assets.

Finally, the board could place the proceeds in a restricted fund at a local community foundation or bank trust fund to benefit local historic preservation efforts or other mission-related activities. The house museum organization could determine the criteria for how these funds would be spent. This arrangement allows the organization to complete its affairs and direct its assets to other worthy projects in the future.

Options to Consider

After the board has paid its remaining bills, and if it has remaining assets left to donate, the board should decide whether to donate these directly to a similar organization or to create a grant fund at the local community foundation. Consult your bylaws and attorney. An outright donation to that entity is another possibility, if the organization has a like-minded nonprofit entity that it would like to support with the remaining assets. The opportunity to create a lasting legacy for the preservation movement by contributing the remaining assets to worthy causes, at the same time as ensuring that the building is well-cared for in the future, is the fundamental reason for making this effort.

Community Foundation Options

Donating the remaining assets of the organization to a community foundation can continue the organization's legacy by offering grants for worthy projects in the future. There are specific benefits to donating the remaining assets to a community foundation rather than setting up a private foundation to distribute the funds, as costs are steep to establish and administer a private foundation. Each community foundation can explain the relative merits and costs of donating to that entity.

Most community foundations offer a variety of opportunities that allow the donor, your board, to specify how the income or principal are to be used for the benefit of specific causes or organizations.

These funds are called donor-designated because the donor states specifically the organizations or types of activities they wish to support with their philanthropic dollars. Here your board can decide if several members wish to serve on the grants committee, recommend people to serve, or allow the community foundation staff to serve in this role.[6]

Another community foundation option is the donor-advised fund where the community foundation or a committee of advisors appointed by the donor recommends eligible charitable recipient for grants from the fund. The community foundation has the ultimate decision-making power and can reject the committee's recommendations.[7]

In both cases, the donor can name the fund to honor or memorialize the organization or building and set up eligibility criteria, while the foundation professionally manages the fund as part of the larger community foundation endowment.

The local community foundation in your area may have other options where the donor's gift can be pooled with others or restricted to a specific field of interest. Contact your local community foundation to learn more about these funds.

Create a Named Fund

You may also donate the remaining assets outright to a like-minded organization as a named fund. Your bylaws may dictate which organization will receive the assets of the organization should it disband. You could create a named fund at the new organization to honor the work of your organization. Your organization could endow a staff position; purchase an object or name a room with your assets. Begin discussions with the like-minded organization about how your board would like its gift to the new organization to be memorialized well in advance of making your gift.

Revolving Loan Fund

With the sale proceeds, establish a revolving loan fund in your community to buy threatened historic sites, place easements on them, and sell to private owners.[8] Revolving funds will need to be administered by a competent organization skilled in historic preservation. Seek the advice of the nearest National Trust Regional Office about starting a revolving fund, or work with the local preservation organization to expand their services to start a revolving fund in your community with the assets from the sale of your site.

Other Options

A trust can be created and administered by a local bank if the remaining assets are substantial. The bank will charge fees for administration and will require a trustee to be appointed. The organization's attorney can provide advice about which option makes the most sense given the size of the remaining assets and the overall intentions of the board to honor founders and donors.

WELCOME HOME!

The transition of the historic house museum to a new use or owner is an opportunity to welcome both the building and its volunteer stewards back into the preservation movement. So many house museums got their start as threatened buildings saved by citizens who wanted assurances that their efforts would not be undone by the next unsympathetic property owner. These once-threatened historic houses seldom witness or demonstrate the process or philosophy of the preservation movement when turned into house museums.

Somehow, these sites got separated from the preservation mainstream when they were converted to museum use.[9] As house museums, they became "don't touch," "backward looking," or even "elitist," according to Frank Sanchis, the former Vice President for Stewardship of Historic Properties at the National Trust.[10] He also commented "how counterproductive that there is a rift between historic sites and the rest of the historic preservation community."[11]

The preservation community will heartily welcome these sites back into the fold for several reasons. First, these houses are most often seminal examples of our country's historic patrimony and a source of community pride. Second, a new owner or new use will ensure for the foreseeable future that the property will be restored and well-maintained, which was the original preservation objective of the organization. Now, through easement donations or maintenance reserves funded by rental income, good repair of the site will be assured. Finally, if sold, the historic building's sales proceeds can infuse the local preservation community with new funds to continue the organization's preservation mission for future generations.

SUMMARY AND PREVIEW

This chapter discussed how house museum organizations should celebrate the transition of the historic house to a new owner or user and recommended that organizations create a permanent reminder, an educational component, and a living legacy for future generations. The chapter also discussed a variety of philanthropic opportunities to ensure that the house museum organization's original mission to preserve the house lives on after the property changes hands.

The next chapter discusses the initial motivations of the organizations profiled in the case studies beginning in chapter 7. It also issues a call for action to house museum boards struggling with insufficient funds or people power to sustain their site to the level that their historic building needs and deserves.

NOTES

1. Archdiocese of Boston, "Parish Closing Manual, Version 1.0," 25 May 2004, from *Boston Globe* online, from Church Offers Guidance on Closings, 28 May 2004, available at boston.com/ news/specials/parishes.html (accessed 19 July 2004). See the *Boston Globe* website mentioned above for further information. Also, Elisabeth Kübler-Ross, *On Death and Dying.* New York: Scribner, 1969.

2. The Oral History Association has a variety of publications about starting a local oral history program. Contact them at Oral History Association, www.dickenson.edu/organizations/oha. Also excellent is Barbara W. Sommer and Mary Kay Quinlin, "A Guide to Oral History Interviews." Technical Leaflet No. 210. Nashville, TN: American Association for State and Local History, 2000.

3. Willa K. Baum, *Oral History for the Local Historical Society*, 3rd ed. Rev. Walnut Creek, CA: AltaMira Press, 1995.

4. The American Association for State and Local History has several technical leaflets about starting a plaque program or interpretive signage. See Richard Bamberger, "Establishing a Plaque Program: Bringing Local History to the Community." Technical Leaflet No. 168. Nashville, TN: American Association for State and Local History, 1989.

5. Easements can offer substantial tax benefits if donated by a private individual to a qualified organization. See the National Trust for Historic Preservation's website, explaining their easement program and the tax benefits available to individuals and corporations, available at www.nationaltrust.org/law/easements.html (accessed 2 November 2004).

6. Lincoln Nebraska Community Foundation, Inc. "Agreement Designated Fund, March 2004," found at Lincoln Community Foundation Inc. website, www.lincolncommunityfoundation.org.htm (accessed 2 June 2004).

7. Lincoln Nebraska Community Foundation Agreement.

8. Preservation North Carolina, the statewide preservation organization, has an old and well-established revolving fund, which they call their endangered properties program. With $5 million in assets they have purchased 450 buildings and resold them with preservation restrictions to owners who will restore and maintain the building. Learn more about their program at www.presnc.org.html (accessed 4 June 2005).

9. Frank E. Sanchis III, "Looking Back or Looking Forward? House Museums in the 21st Century." A paper presented at American House Museums, an Athenaeum of Philadelphia Symposium, 4–5 December 1999, philaathenaeum.org/sachis.htm (accessed 4 June 2005).

10. Sanchis, "Looking Back."

11. Sanchis, "Looking Back."

SOLUTIONS AND CASE STUDIES

CHAPTER 6

Eight Solutions Explained

This chapter describes a variety of possible ownership and reuse solutions that historic house museum boards of directors have successfully tackled. The solutions are organized on a continuum from the smallest change or intervention to the most significant change or intervention.

Before your board can begin to consider new uses, here are some key issues to consider.

A Use that Fits the House

The first challenge to house museum stewards facing a reuse decision is finding a use that fits the house, rather than to fit a use into the house. Destruction of the historic fabric will be less severe if your board chooses a use that is well-suited to the home's condition and location, and respects the original architectural character and historic fabric of the site.[1] The previous chapter discussed why it is necessary to determine which character-defining elements of the building and landscape must be preserved at all costs at the start of any reuse decision-making process.

Small Size

A domestic-sized building will have limited reuse options based on its historical location pattern, especially if it remains within a residential planning and zoning context. The small size of a domestic building will limit potential uses. Sites that possess outbuildings, vacant land surrounding their buildings, or are on large lots have additional potential to realize economic gain. The marketability of the building may be increased significantly when the board makes some land surrounding the house available for reuse, especially for parking. However, a home on a domestic-sized lot has severe limitations on reuse possibilities.

Condition and Setting of the Building, Planning, and Zoning

The physical condition of your historic building will drive many of the reuse options, along with zoning, location, scale of the project, and the amount of usable square footage available in the building. A matrix, in the form of a table, appears at the end of this chapter to help narrow down the range of options available, based on the current condition of the building. Common sense dictates that a building in good condition in a good location has many more alternatives than a site that is not currently habitable or in a remote location.[2]

Two Fundamental Choices

The following is an overview of the range of alternatives that other historic house museum stewards have successfully implemented. Your board leadership has two options to consider: to retain ownership of the site or sell or donate your site. Each alternative will be discussed in more detail in the coming pages. The chapters that follow contain a dozen case studies of organizations that successfully made the transition to a new management agreement, user, or owner.

RETAIN OWNERSHIP OF THE HISTORIC BUILDING

The organization retains daily management control or shifts this responsibility to a new entity while retaining ownership. Here are five options being used by house museum stewards today.

1. Continue to manage the site but reprogram it as a study house with limited visitation.
2. Continue to manage the site but reprogram it for another mission-based use.

3. Give up daily management, and enter into a formal co-steward-ship or cooperative relationship with another house museum or-ganization to operate and manage the house museum.
4. Dissolve the corporation and merge with another nonprofit to manage the property as a house museum.
5. Give up daily management, and enter into a long-term manage-ment or lease agreement with another nonprofit or for-profit that manages the property for a house museum or another adaptive use. Several variations on this option are included in this section.

Each of these solutions will be discussed in turn.

1. Creation of a Study House with Limited Visitation, House Museum Use

What Is It?

A study house is a historic house museum that is fully furnished (or not) and completely restored using collections with certain provenance to the building.[3] The site is open to scholars or to the public to visit on a limited basis, usually by appointment only. The house museum or-ganization continues to own, manage, and maintain the property.

Why Do It?

This option might be appropriate for a house museum that is isolated from other properties and receives limited visitation or is too fragile to withstand even moderate visitation. Consider this option for properties that are already well-restored and maintained, and have significant his-toric features or collections that deserve to remain in the public trust and in nonprofit ownership, but cannot withstand heavy visitor traffic.

When Does It Not Work?

This option will not work if the organization does not want to con-tinue to own, manage, secure, insure, and maintain the property. The house is essentially put into storage.

How to Do It:

The board would make an internal decision to reprogram the site as a study house. The organization should then inform local tourism agencies of its decision.

Costs:

While staffing costs are reduced because the property is only open by appointment, the property remains in the organization's inventory. The organization may see its revenues decline if the property is not open for tours on a regular basis, but this may be mitigated by the lower costs of overall operations. This option reduces only slightly the attendant costs to the organization, mostly in personnel, but certainly not in maintenance or insurance. Insurance costs may increase because the house is not used or inhabited regularly.

Who Can Make the Decision?

This decision can be made at the board level and should be communicated to the members, local residents, and tourism agencies. No other entities need to be consulted.

How Long Will It Take to Make a Decision?

The decision-making process can go quickly once the board reaches the conclusion that change is needed.

See chapter 8 for a case study about Historic New England's study houses.

2. Reprogram the Site for a Mission-based, Non-house Museum Use

What Is It?

The house museum board decides that the museum property no longer needs to be interpreted to the public as a house museum, but still wants to use the site for a mission-based purpose. There are a wide range of operational uses for these properties, including staff housing, library, guest house, museum shop, organizational offices, educational setting, artifact storage or other storage. The house museum organization continues to own, manage, and maintain the property.

Why Do It?

The board no longer wants to interpret the site to the public, but still wants to retain ownership, and have some use that is related to the organization's overall mission.

When Does It Not Work?

This option will not work if the board does not want to continue to own, manage, secure, insure, and maintain the property. The new use may necessitate insertion of modern enhancements, equipment, or features to meet the local building code for the new use.

How to Do It:

The board would make an internal decision to reprogram the site for a mission-based use. Local tourism agencies should be informed that the organization will no longer offer tours at the site.

Costs:

Staffing costs may be reduced because the property has another use, but the property remains in the organization's inventory. There may be additional costs to change the use of the building, including bringing the building up to local building code standards for the new use. Depending on the use chosen, considerable restoration or rehabilitation costs may be required.

Who Can Make the Decision:

This decision can be made at the board level and communicated to the members. Consultation with the community at large before the decision is made to reprogram the site is advised to make a smooth transition.

How Long Will It Take to Make a Decision?

The decision-making process can go quickly if the board seeks to retain the property and is motivated by the continued care and preservation of the property as its ultimate objective.

See chapter 9 for a case study about how the Nantucket Historical Association reprogrammed the 1800 House for a mission-based use.

3. Enter into a Formal Co-Stewardship, Cooperative Relationship, or Lease with Another House Museum Organization to Manage the Property as a House Museum.

What Is It?

A cooperative or co-stewardship arrangement brings additional resources, both financial and human, into the existing historic house museum organization.[4] The organization seeks a partner to take over management of the house on a short- or long-term lease basis, but still retains ownership of the property. The use of the building does not change, but the daily management is undertaken by another house museum organization. The building is still used as a house museum.

Why Do It?

The organization may be motivated to enter into a cooperative or co-stewardship agreement because the property would become part of the larger entity that could draw more financial support or have more cachet with potential donors, volunteers, or board members. A cooperative agreement would not bind the parties to permanent change. Since the agreement is flexible and subject to negotiation by both parties, it can be customized to meet specific needs.

This solution may be worth considering if the ownership of the house, the building's endowment, or the collection has specific covenants that make a sale or another use untenable. The co-stewardship organization takes on all or partial responsibility for maintenance, restoration, and management of the property, as spelled out in the agreement. The economies of scale of operating more than one site might be the main motivator for each party. This arrangement may be worth considering if one party owns the historic building and another owns the collections. Both parties have an equal interest in ensuring that the whole of the historic site, the building, and the collections are well-maintained and preserved. Both parties in a co-stewardship agreement should have parallel goals to ensure the preservation of the historic site.

When Does It Not Work?

This will not work if the organization is focused on its own autonomy and does not want outsiders involved in management of their site. Developing joint programs or sharing personnel might be incremental steps toward a formal co-stewardship relationship. A short-term or easily renewable agreement may be a good way to test whether a longer-term agreement might work between the two parties.

Considerable energy must be expended at the front end of the negotiation to ensure that each organization understands its obligations to the agreement. Negotiations will have to be undertaken again in the not-too-distant future with all the attendant costs should the agreement be short-term. The organization seeking a co-stewardship partner may have a minimal role in the day-to-day management of the property, but it does not go out of business because it still owns the underlying real estate.

This solution may be attractive for a property that is locally significant, does not have significant collections, or is not a large tourist draw. The property must be in very good condition for another organization to take on maintenance burdens as well as operate the property. Financial inducements might have to be offered to a potential partner for them to accept the responsibility of managing the building as a house museum, especially if the building is not in excellent condition.

The main motivator is the desire of the partners to manage the site as part of a larger tourism network. Often the cooperative or co-stewardship terms are renewable, but the terms need to be long enough for the new manager to amortize any costs related to maintenance and restoration. The house museum will not realize a windfall from leasing the property to the new managers, because it is still in house museum use. There will be a great difficulty attracting a likely partner if the property is remote or there is not likely a co-stewardship partner to take on this function.

How It Works:

Most cooperative/co-stewardship agreements are formal documents with limited terms, often renewable in five years, that set out specific responsibilities for each party. No organizational merger occurs and no new organization is formed. This might be agreeable to an organization that still seeks to retain ownership of its site, and to ensure that the site remains in museum use, but does not want to actively manage the site any longer. This arrangement may be especially useful if one entity owns the building and another owns the collection.

Costs:

There may be costs to negotiate the agreement and to upgrade the site to meet operating standards of the co-stewardship partner. Operating subsidies may be required or other financial incentives may be required to create the partnership. Organizational costs can be significantly reduced, as the only function the board would play would be is as titleholder. Annual maintenance costs, restoration obligations, insurance, or other operating costs may still be in effect, depending on the agreed-upon terms. The organization will need an attorney to help negotiate the agreement terms.

Who Can Make the Decision?

The board of directors makes this decision, but consulting with the membership before the agreement is signed is advised. A transparent decision-making process helps ensure a complete public understanding of the motivations for entering into the agreement.

How Long Does It Take?

Finding a new house museum partner or manager may be impossible, unless one already exists locally. A larger heritage tourism effort such as a scenic byway or heritage area or a new destination management organization could be formed, but this might take years. Even with a destination management organization interested and available, this arrangement could take months or even years to negotiate if both parties do not see the immediate benefits to cooperating. Because it is a partnership, the other party cannot be compelled to take on the management burden of the house. Both parties must see the benefit to their cooperation.

See chapter 9 for two case studies on co-stewardship agreements: Historic Adams House in Deadwood, South Dakota, and Frank Lloyd Wright Home and Studio as co-stewards of the Frederick C. Robie House, Chicago, Illinois.

4. Formal Merger with Another House Museum Organization

What Is It?

Formal mergers of nonprofit organizations create a successor organization and one or more dissolving organizations. The new entity created encompasses both missions. All the assets, including buildings as well as liabilities of the dissolved organization, become the property of the new or merged entity.[5]

Why Do It?

The leadership of the house museum must believe that the merged entity can achieve more than the two organizations operating independently. A formal merger may be warranted when there are clear synergies or economies of scale that can be created. A merger would work best if neighboring sites agree to join forces to create a larger unit to better serve and expand the tourist market. One site may be far larger than the other, so care must be taken to ensure that the subsumed or smaller organization is treated with respect during merger discussions. Outside forces, especially funders, may encourage organizations to merge. Hostile or unfriendly mergers are rare in the nonprofit field.

When Does This Not Work?

A merger is unlikely to create a better organization if two small, struggling nonprofits with limited resources are merging. A merger will not work for historic sites that insist on autonomy.

How to Do It:

Informal and preliminary discussions can occur between key board or staff members. The board of directors would need to be involved in all discussions and negotiations, especially during due diligence information gathering, before any merger can be concluded. The boards of each organization would make their decision about merging independently. Once they commit to a resolution to merge, they can share an attorney to develop the merger document, transfer of assets and liabilities, and dissolution of the subsumed organization(s). Formal action may be required by the state's attorney general. Organizations may find it challenging to merge if they are from different states.

There is a winding-down period for the dissolving organization, when the board oversees that the final bills are paid; all necessary notices are given; proper reports are filed with funders, the IRS, and state charity agencies; formal merger and dissolution papers are signed; and the final transfer of assets are made to the merged entity.[6]

Who Can Make the Decision?

The board can propose the merger, but the incorporation papers and bylaws must be reviewed to determine whether the board or the membership has the final decision on merger and voluntary organizational dissolution. The organizations should involve any staff, as well as the community, if the use of the building(s) will change. Both organizations will need legal assistance during negotiations and perhaps during the discussion and dissolution phase. It is important to seek the advice of competent professionals in the field before major board discussions take place. Often historic house museum consultants will have much more information about the state of the house museum field and can inform the board of many other cases where mergers have been successful.

How Long Will It Take to Make a Decision?

Thoughtful decision making for a merger can take months or even years. Once the agreement is reached, the formal merger process and property transfer can occur quickly. Stakeholders and members should be informed of discussions and when an agreement is reached, a general membership meeting should be held to explain the benefits of the merger.

Costs:

Both entities will need legal counsel. There will be pre-merger costs to consolidate the organizations, including: integration of information technology; personnel/human resources issues (severance if necessary); selling of real estate or breaking leases (if any); moving; design/printing; pension obligations (if any); and other costs.

See chapter 10 for two case studies on the merger of two organizations. The Margaret Mitchell House and Museum merged with the Atlanta History Center, Atlanta, Georgia, and Cliveden merged with the Historic Upsala Foundation, Philadelphia, Pennsylvania.

5. Long-Term Lease to a For-Profit Entity for an Adaptive Use, Along with Two Variations on This Solution

What Is It?

The house museum organization retains ownership of the property but actively seeks a new user for the property from the private marketplace. The organization's role is reduced to being a titleholder, collecting rental fees (if any), and interacting with the leaseholder. The organization can seek a wide variety of potential uses, subject to any local planning or zoning restrictions.

The board can choose to structure a long lease term so that the leaseholder is able to obtain financing for the rehabilitation of the property's adaptive use, or have a shorter term, which would force the tenant to undertake restoration using the tenant's own resources.

Why Do It?

The board retains its preservation mandate by using this solution, as it still retains title to the property. The private marketplace will determine the highest and best use of the property, if the organization offers the property with few restrictions. The highest lease payment will be offered for a site with fewer restrictions on use and interior alternations. The physical condition of the property will drive many potential uses as well as the classic rule of real estate: location, location, location. Incentives may have to be offered if the property is in poor condition. Organizations can offer the property with either a wide or narrow range of potential uses, but constraints will lessen the potential value to the lessor.

The variety of adaptive uses is almost endless, but most house museum stewards seem to be attracted to hospitality or office uses such as bed and breakfasts, vacation and holiday retreats, and other professional office uses that allow the public some kind of access.

When Does It Not Work?

Boards concerned about allowing the property to be used for any purpose a private owner can imagine may not want to consider this option. This is not a good solution for properties that have particularly significant interior and exterior features that should not be compromised by a tenant. This may not work for properties that are in less marketable locations or are not in good condition. Developers are most often seeking properties that require little work for turnkey operations.

How to Do It:

A formal Request for Proposals (RFP) process can assist your board in making choices among potential bidders. The board may need assistance to prepare a quality RFP document and should be advised by someone knowledgable about the local commercial real estate market. The house museum organization will need assistance in structuring the solicitation to ensure that the new use(s) are viable in the marketplace. The organization would retain ownership to ensure that the property is maintained, and should dedicate rental fees to preservation of the building first, then allocate funds not needed for maintenance to other aspects of its mission.

Who Can Make the Decision?

The board of directors can make the decision to change the use of its building, because it still retains control of the real estate. However, the board should consult and involve the community and other preservation partners in the area. Community involvement in decision making will help tremendously in preventing adverse publicity.

The organization needs to make the case to the community that its ultimate objective is the preservation of the historic building. More information about telling your story is located in the previous chapter. Leasing the site for a new use is a way to ensure the organization's continued ownership as well as the long-term maintenance of the property by the leaseholder. The organization would receive rent from the new user, but the organization's only function in relation to the historic house is as titleholder of the property and as landlord.

How Long Will It Take to Make a Decision?

Persuading the board to consider leasing the property for a non-museum use may take a long time. Finding an acceptable lessor could still take months, even if the property is in good condition and in a good location. The private marketplace will drive use options, not the organization.

See chapter 11 for a case study on how the Maryland-National Capital Park and Planning Commission signed a long-term lease for Hazelwood, one of its many properties. See chapter 12 for a case study on how the Heritage Branch of the British Columbia government signed short-term leases for a number of properties, and a short case study about how the City of Philadelphia, through the Fairmount Park Historic Preservation Trust, found reuses for over forty historic buildings on park land.

SALE OR DONATION OF THE PROPERTY, WITH PROTECTIVE EASEMENTS

House museums considering the sale of their properties have three alternatives based on the research conducted for this book based on the experiences of historic house museums around the country.

- Sell the house to a private owner with easements;
- Sell to a nonprofit stewardship organization with easements; or
- Donate the site to a governmental or other nonprofit entity.

6. Sale to a Private Owner with Easements

What Is It?

The outright sale of the historic house museum's real estate to a private owner or for-profit business for any use as the private owner sees fit. It is recommended that any sale be subject to easement restrictions (in some states called conservation restrictions) to permanently protect the property from demolition and insensitive alteration. Chapter 5 discussed how an easement can ensure the permanent protection of a historic site.

The sale is a permanent change that cannot be undone. Some may believe that a sale to a private owner is the ultimate abrogation of the organization's stewardship duties to the public, but in most cases the new stewards will have the resources necessary to ensure the preservation of the building well into the future.

It is recommended that the board place an easement on the building concurrent with or before the sale to prevent demolition or insensitive alteration of the protected features forever. An easement-holding organization must be identified early in the process and the sale must be contingent on signing an easement agreement concurrent with or before the sale. The easement should not be optional for the new owner. The easement must be mandatory. In this case, easements would not be a tax deductible donation for the new user, since the easement must be a freely given gift, not a condition of sale.[7]

Easements are the only permanent legal protection that your board has that the historic building will be maintained forever. Even if your site is designated as a local landmark and must undergo review for any alternations, an easement is still necessary because it ensures perpetual preservation, while landmark laws can be changed at the whim of local elected officials. National Register listing or designation as a National Historic Landmark provides no protection whatsoever against additions, alternations, or even demolition. Easement donation is the best method to protect your historic house after it leaves your ownership.

Why Do It?

Returning the historic house to a residential use may be the best solution if the board feels that a new owner will have greater financial resources to maintain and restore the building than a struggling nonprofit organization. When the easement restriction is placed on the property prior to sale, the board is assured that the property is preserved forever. The house museum organization could then be dissolved after the sale, if the organizational mission is solely the preservation and interpretation of the property.

How to Do It:

The sale of a historic building may be a good option for properties that are in good or stable condition, and in neighborhoods that have strong real estate value.

The board should make its decision to sell widely known, and seek offers from other nonprofit organizations for a period of time before placing the property with a realtor to sell to the private sector. The goodwill you will engender by informing the community that the board has decided it can no longer care for the site properly and are seeking its help to find a responsible buyer will more than outweigh the time spent reviewing proposals. The bylaws of your organization will spell out how the organization's assets are to be transferred to another nonprofit or governmental entity if the organization is dissolved. Consult your attorney about any questions regarding your bylaws or the sale process.

Sale proceeds must be dedicated to mission-based uses such as historic preservation or educational uses, and not benefit anyone (called private inurnment) associated with the organization.

Setting up a preservation or educational grant or loan fund at the local community foundation may be the best way to ensure that the public purpose of the organization's sale of its major asset, the historic building, benefits the broader preservation or museum community. Further information about using sale proceeds for mission-based philanthropy is discussed in the previous chapter. An attorney should represent the organization and the attorney should consult with the state's attorney general before a final decision is made to sell the property or list it with a real estate broker.

Who Can Make the Decision?

The board of directors may not have the right to sell the property without the express consent of the membership and the state's attorney

general. Consult your attorney and bylaws to determine whether the board
or the membership has the final say in the sale of assets. Further information about planning for this meeting appears in the previous chapter.

The board leadership must consult an attorney to represent it on any
sale, whether the organization chooses to sell to a private individual or
to another nonprofit organization. The organization's attorney should
contact your state's attorney general's office, the charities registration
officer, or the museum chartering office to discuss the sale well in advance of listing the property. Also discuss with the attorney general's
office how the organization will transfer any remaining assets if the organization is dissolved.

Community and local preservation partners should be apprised of
the organization's interest in selling in the private marketplace and
they should be given ample time to submit offers along with other interested parties. Review the deaccessioning standards of the American
Association of Museums (www.aaam-us.org) when there are collections that need to be placed with other institutions and consult your attorney.

How Long Will It Take to Make a Decision?

There may be a long time lag, sometimes years, between the time the
board makes an initial proposal to the membership about a possible sale
and an actual sale of the site to a new owner.

*See chapter 13 for a case study about how Elfreth's Alley Association
in Philadelphia sold some of its properties to private owners with easements.*

7. Sale to Another Nonprofit Stewardship Organization with Easements

What Is It?

The house museum organization sells the real estate to another
nonprofit organization that is better able to manage the site. An existing or a new stewardship organization may be set up to take title to
the building.

Why Do It?

Sale to another nonprofit may be the only acceptable alternative if the property was donated with specific restrictions on use or ownership. This kind of sale is often a bargain sale, meaning that the new owner does not pay full market value. Another variation is to sell the house and contents to the new stewardship organization for only a nominal sum (i.e., $10.00). The former ownership organization could be dissolved upon transfer of the real estate. Despite its sale to another nonprofit organization, it is wise for your organization to place an easement on the property prior to its sale, so you can ensure your good work will not go undone in the future.

How to Do It:

The house museum sells its real estate assets to a new nonprofit organization. The existing house museum organization is dissolved, after paying all remaining bills and filing legal documents for dissolution. The new organization would receive any endowment or other maintenance funds from the dissolving organization to help maintain the property over time. How the property is used in the future would have to be part of the negotiation with the new organization. Sale proceeds should be donated to a community foundation or a bank trust fund created to serve as a maintenance endowment to benefit the property.

Who Can Make the Decision?

The board of directors should consult with the community and local preservation partners to determine if there are other viable options. An attorney should represent the organization and the attorney should consult with the state's attorney general prior to sale.

How Long Will It Take to Make a Decision?

This decision could take months or years, assuming there is an appropriate nonprofit that has the resources to purchase, operate, and endow the property.

See chapter 14 for a case study on how the National Trust for Historic Preservation sold Casa Amesti to another nonprofit stewardship organization, the new Casa Amesti Foundation in Monterey, California. Another short case study is included in this chapter about the Heurich House in Washington, D.C., and its efforts to create a new stewardship entity.

8. Donation of the Property to a Governmental or Other Nonprofit Entity

What Is It?

The organization donates the historic house museum to a governmental entity—a state, county, or municipality—or another nonprofit organization that has the financial resources to maintain and perhaps restore the building.

The property would have to be a major architectural or historic landmark in the community and the house museum board would need many influential friends to convince the accepting organization or government to take on the burden of ownership.

Why Do It?

This may be seen as a desperate move, perhaps the last step before the property is abandoned by the organization. Given the budgetary crises of most governmental entities, it may be very difficult or even impossible for the organization to interest government or another nonprofit to take a building, especially if it is in poor condition.

How to Do It:

Contact elected government leaders as well as the government staff to discuss the donation informally before making a public case for the government or nonprofit to accept. Since it is a donation, the government or other nonprofit can decide NOT to accept the property under any circumstances.

Who Can Make the Decision?

The board of directors or the members can make this decision, according to the organization's bylaws. An attorney can advise the organization on the merits of this solution.

How Long Will it Take to Make a Decision?

Trying to convince a government unit to accept the donation of a landmark in poor condition may take years, if it is ever successful. An elected official will have to serve as the champion for this proposal for there to be any hope of the governmental unit accepting the property.

See chapter 15 for a case study on how the Adel Historical Society donated the Adel Historical Museum to a governmental entity, the City of Adel, Iowa.

HOW TO USE FIGURE 6.1

The condition of the historic house museum will drive which options are realistically available to your board. The majority of new users or new owners will not treat the historic house as a museum property to conserve. Rather, they will view the building as a real estate investment that has economic value based on its location, use, and condition.

This transition from treating the building as an object to be conserved to a real estate asset may be extraordinarily jarring for your board, which has lavished attention on the house museum for generations. Consultants experienced in working with house museums facing these issues can add a dose of reality to the discussions. In addition, a trained facilitator can ensure that the board does not waste time on options that are unrealistic due to the building's poor condition or undesirable location.

Boards seeking new uses or new owners must be open to a wide variety of options based on the true market for the historic house based on its location and condition.

House Museum Reuse Solutions	Study House (HHM use)	Mission-Based use. (non-HHM use)	Co-stewardship Agreement. (HHM use)	Merge with new HHM (HHM use)	Lease for Adaptive Reuse (non-HHM use)	Sale to Private Sector with Easement	Sale to nonprofit with easement	Donation to govvernment or nonprofit with easement
Building Conditions								
Restored/ well maintained	***	***	***	***	***	***	***	***
Restored/ some Deferred Maintenance	**	***	**	**	**	**	**	**
Restored/ major Deferred Maintenance	*	**	*	*	*	*	*	*
Partly restored/ well maintained	*	**	**	**	**	**	**	**
Partly restored/ some Deferred Maintenance	*	**	**	*	*	**	*	**
Partly restored/ serious Deferred Maintenance	*	*	*	*	*	*	*	*
Unrestored/ well maintained	*	**	*	**	*	**	*	**
Unrestored/ some Deferred Maintenance	*	*	*	*	*	*	*	*
Unrestored/ serious Deferred Maintenance	*	*	*	*	*	*	*	*

KEY: ***excellent solution   **possible solution   *unlikely solution.
Determine the current condition of your house museum by reading down the left hand column of this chart. The various options are listed along the top of the page. The more stars pictured in each box, the more feasible this choice would be.

Figure 6.1   Reuse Options Based on the Condition of the Historic House Museum Building

SUMMARY AND PREVIEW

This chapter discussed a variety of solutions that were successful for other historic house museum stewards. Boards and members of organizations interviewed for these case studies made difficult decisions after serious and lengthy discussion to consider the most desirable and sensible change for their organization.

Some organizations toy with a use change for more than forty years, like Elfreth's Alley Association (see chapter 13), before reaching the conclusion that the historic site would be better served by having a new use that would protect it long-term. These decisions should not be made in haste. These decisions will provoke great emotion and possibly bad press. It is recommended that the board make the community aware that it is being an active and responsible steward by planning for the future of the building according to the organization's preservation mission.

The next several chapters in Part II provide case studies to illustrate each of the eight solutions discussed in this chapter. Some of the case studies are quite long and have exhaustive detail. Others are short and give an overview of both how and why the house museum organization decided to undertake change. For some of the solutions, there are several short case studies to show a range of experiences.

The five longer case studies were prepared during a Mid Career Fellowship I received in 2003 from the James Marston Fitch Charitable Foundation in New York City. Through this fellowship, I was able to visit each of the sites and speak to the principals involved in the transition of the historic property to a new owner or user. All of the individuals cited in the case read and reviewed drafts of the case to ensure that it described why the organization made the change and how it came about. These five long cases were chosen because the issues the organization addressed were common to many institutions and thus could be replicated by organizations seeking new options for their historic sites.

NOTES

1. Samuel Y. Harris, 4.
2. See chapter 11, the case study on Hazelwood, for a discussion about reuse options for an uninhabited building.

3. Drayton Hall, located in Charleston, South Carolina, is a co-stewardship property of the National Trust for Historic Preservation and probably the most famous historic house museum that is empty.

4. Suzanne C. Feeney, "Governance, Collaboration and Mergers," in Tracey David Connors, *The Non-Profit Book: Management,* 3rd ed. New York: John Wiley and Sons, 2001, 108. Also see David LaPiana, *The Non-Profit Mergers Workbook: The Leader's Guide to Considering, Negotiating, and Executing a Merger.* St. Paul, MN: Amherst H. Wilder Foundation, 2000, 6.

5. Most of the information for this section on mergers was gleaned from David LaPiana, *The Non-Profit Mergers Workbook: The Leader's Guide to Considering, Negotiating, and Executing a Merger.* St. Paul, MN: Amherst H. Wilder Foundation, 2000. This book is an excellent source of information about nonprofit mergers. See also the chapter on organizational mergers in Tracey Daniel Connors, *The Non-Profit Book: Management*, 3rd ed. New York: John Wiley and Sons, 2001.

6. Each state has different rules for dissolving nonprofit organizations. Contact your attorney for information about your state's requirements.

7. Easement-holding organizations can advise your organization on structuring the terms of the easement document and explaining why easements as a condition of sale are not tax deductible.

CHAPTER 7

Case Study:
Study Houses

HISTORIC NEW ENGLAND, HEADQUARTERED IN BOSTON

The concept of a study house was pioneered by the Society for the Preservation of New England Antiquities (SPNEA) in the late 1970s in response to the increasing costs of maintaining their inventory of sixty-five historic structures. SPNEA, founded in 1910 by William Sumner Appleton, recently changed its name to Historic New England. The organization, initially focused on saving historic buildings of architectural value for future generations, is still dedicated to the entire six-state New England region.[1]

Appleton did not believe that all the structures he saved should become museums or period homes. SPNEA became the "owner of last resort" when there was no local group to take the lead in saving the structure. Some of the rescued buildings were turned into tea shops, or rented to tenants for residential purposes. Houses came to SPNEA through gifts and purchase and, starting in 1920, through bequests of significant sites accompanied by endowments.

Appleton encouraged donors to place few restrictions on their gifts, allowing the Society considerable flexibility to determine how to maintain, interpret, or restore the historic buildings. By the time of Appleton's death in 1947, SPNEA owned more than twenty-five properties and routine maintenance was beginning to slip.[2] During the years after Appleton's death, the Board decided to sell some properties to pay for repairs on others in the inventory, but this was viewed as a stopgap measure.

By the late 1970s the organization's inventory had grown to sixty-five properties spread all over New England. These houses were "open if you sought them out, typically in the afternoons and by appointment."[3] To deal with the accelerating deterioration, SPNEA took aggressive action and pruned the number of sites from sixty-five to a more manageable forty through a formal process of deaccessioning sites.[4] Fifteen of these properties were sold to private individuals with restrictive covenants (also called easements in some states) to preserve the house forever. The organization further focused its interpretive mission, turning some of the remaining forty properties into study houses during this period. Five additional sites have been sold since the late 1970s, leaving the group's holdings at thirty-five.

Historic New England continues today to reassess these thirty-five houses to determine whether every one of the homes should remain open for public visitation. Eleven of its houses are study houses. Eight are open as house museum. Sixteen are open for Private Heritage Tours, meaning they are only open the first Saturday of the month.[5]

Recently, the board made the decision to remove the Gilman-Garrison House (c. 1709) in Exeter, New Hampshire from its active inventory to become a study house. This property is one of several historic house museums in the area, and has had very limited visitation over the years. Historic New England decided to move this property into the study house category after assessing that this property had limited appeal to tourists visiting other sites in the community. Members of the organization are encouraged to visit these study houses during the summer season to become reacquainted with these important examples of American architecture.[6]

How to Use This Case

A study house could also be created from a completely intact, but yet unrestored, historic house, assuming the structure is safe to enter and interpret. The house could be furnished or not. Active maintenance and monitoring must occur regularly to ensure the building envelope is weather tight. This option essentially mothballs the structure and may be of special interest to site owners who have outbuildings with extensive original fabric.

A study house solution could be either a permanent solution or a temporary transition for a historic site, depending on the needs of the organization, its mission, and whether the site is an active tourist draw. The property still remains in the organization's inventory and is fully furnished and insured, but is not actively staffed except for tours planned well in advance. A study house solution could be an excellent temporary option while additional strategic planning takes place around the programming or disposition of the historic site.

NOTES

1. Hosmer, *Presence of the Past*, 240–45.
2. Robert Campbell, "Making Properties Pay Their Way," *Historic Preservation* 34, no. 1 (1994): 24–28.
3. Campbell, 24.
4. Campbell, 27.
5. Historic New England website www.spnea.org.html/ (accessed 22 October 2004).
6. Historic New England website.

CHAPTER 8

Case Study:
Reprogram for Mission-Based Use

NANTUCKET HISTORICAL ASSOCIATION,
NANTUCKET, MASSACHUSETTS

Since its founding in 1894, the Nantucket Historical Association (NHA) has been a historic property steward. The NHA acquired its first building, the old Quaker Meeting House, from a dwindling congregation for $1,000 during its first year. The organization has been most interested in collecting and interpreting the era from 1740 to 1840, when Nantucket was the world's largest whaling port. Mary Eliza Starbuck, the NHA's first secretary, in her address to the members in 1894, encouraged islanders to "make an active search for all sorts of relics, particularly manuscripts, before it is too late and these valuable mementos are carried away from the island as trophies or by progressive housewives 'cast as rubbish to the void.'"[1]

Like so many historical societies founded in the late nineteenth century, the NHA was seen as "one way to preserve ties to a seemingly simpler past, while also providing a touchstone for longtime residents, as tourists began to arrive in droves."[2] In 1897 the group bought the Old Mill on Mill Hill.

In 2000, board president Dorothy Stover described the evolution of the organization in her annual letter to members:

The first period of the association from its birth in 1894 until the 1980s was primarily a period of acquisition. . . .As the association neared its hundredth birthday, attention was turned from acquisition to conservation and restoration with increasing emphasis on interpretation, exhibitions, and programs. The association then turned to its properties and rented three of its buildings to provide a revenue stream for restoration and maintenance of its twenty-two other properties. . . .The Nantucket Historical Association has now turned its energies to the future, to address the way it can better fulfill its mission and serve the community.[3]

Today, the NHA owns twenty-five properties ranging from open spaces and fields, memorial tablets, stones and benches, nineteenth-century warehouses, the Old Gaol (jail), the Hose Cart House (for fire hoses), a Greek Revival mansion, an eighteenth-century livestock barn converted in the 1930s to a summer home, a museum, and rare—as well as humble—domestic buildings dating from the seventeenth to nineteenth centuries.

During its 110-year history, these properties came to the NHA by various means: purchase at auction; by deed of gift; through private sale; and by bequest. Some of the NHA properties arrived in pristine condition; others were rescued from the wrecker's ball. All but one was acquired without an endowment or maintenance fund. Arie Kopelman, Board President in 2002, commented, "We're rich in properties. We accepted properties with no way to take care of them."[4]

As can be expected of a venerable institution with such a rich variety of historic properties, there is extreme sentimental attachment to these tangible reminders of the past on the "faraway island." Nantucket, a relatively isolated "elbow of land" located beyond Martha's Vineyard off Cape Cod in Massachusetts, is now home to 10,000 year-round residents. The summer-time population increases each year to 60,000 as vacation-home owners (called off-islanders) and 60,000 annual visitors come to the NHA's renowned Whaling Museum. But with an annual operating budget of $2.8 million, and an endowment of just $1.98 million, the NHA could no longer maintain and operate every historic property it owned, especially those that did not fit within the overarching story that it sought to tell.

A new executive director, Dr. Frank Milligan, arrived in Nantucket in January 2000. A Canadian who began in the museum field as an interpreter, Milligan's most recent assignment was in New Brunswick, Canada, as director of a well-regarded maritime museum. Just six months prior to Milligan's arrival, Niles Parker, the chief curator, had come on board. His experiences at the New York State Historical Association in Cooperstown directing exhibition planning, coordinating seminars, and overseeing the quarterly magazine were a unique fit.

Other staff positions were vacant and the board president was expected to change that summer.[5] "With the addition of new staff with new skills, Niles in particular, the staff had the people and plans in place to execute new programming," Milligan said. He added that the "chemistry of the people who were hired, and who embraced the new opportunities, that is what made the difference."[6]

Interpretive Plan Shapes Decision

Milligan recommended that the board begin a strategic-planning process to encompass new mission and vision statements as part of an overall strategic plan. The Board agreed and Harold and Susan Skramstand were engaged as consultants for the strategic-planning process. The new documents were completed and approved in spring 2001. Work on the interpretive plan began soon after.

According to Milligan "it was just time" to do a new strategic plan and the organization's first ever Interpretive Plan.[7] Although the organization had just begun a five-year, $15.4 million dollar capital campaign, its first phase of two million dollars was fully funded.[8] This project entailed conversion of the 1904 Fair Street museum building into a state-of-the-art library and archive for the organization's celebrated collection of Nantucket documents, photographs, artifacts, and whaling manuscripts. The two million dollar renovation of the old poured concrete Fair Street museum building opened in 2001.[9]

Milligan explained, "Initially there were some skeptics on the board about the need for an interpretive plan. Since the organization had never had one before, there were some initial reservations, but once it became clear that the plan would help broaden the interpretive story of the organization, the museum, and its properties, the plan was embraced. It took a year to develop, and the staff was assisted by a group of local historians and community members to identify the common themes and then develop the themes presented. The entire board was involved in review and enthusiastically embraced the new interpretive plan."[10]

The interpretive plan identified five overarching themes that the organization would use as its core content to "shape the Association's agenda of acquisition, deaccession, preservation, programs, and activities."[11] These themes are: Ebb and Flow: Peopling the Island; Making a Living; Living in the Light: Island Ideologies; Whaling; and the Island Resort. Whaling would still be a central story, but the additional themes would "expand to include the broader story of Nantucket Island and its inhabitants."[12]

The interpretive plan identified properties that did not fit into the five themes.[13] "At the time, how the properties were divided into the themes was not at first controversial, but there were some questions about what it all meant," said Milligan. "How the houses fit into the stories that the organization wanted to tell through the interpretive plan generated discussion by the board. Instead of trying to be all things to all people, the organization would interpret the history of the island based on the themes developed through the interpretive plan."[14]

A news article later in the year described the interpretive plan. "The plan researched and drafted by NHA staff identified specific NHA historic properties especially important to convey historical themes. As a result of the plan, officials said they decided to devote the bulk of their restoration budget to restoring and operating properties deemed central in the plan, including the Hadwen House, the Old Mill, the Old Gaol, the Hose Cart House, the Quaker Meeting House, the Oldest House and the Whaling Museum. But officials said they have nowhere near enough money to do what they deem essential."[15]

Mill Hill Controversy

Three properties were called out as "nonessential to the interpretive plan." The first, a 1.5-acre vacant parcel of land known as Mill Hill, was said to provide a setting and context for the Old Mill, the last remaining working windmill in America. The second, the 1800 House, is a shingled saltbox house of that date that had been shuttered since 1997. Finally, Greater Light, a former eighteenth-century livestock barn, had been converted into a summer home in the 1930s by two sisters who were members of the island's artist colony in the early twentieth century. Greater Light, with its collection of knickknacks collected by the Mongahan sisters from their travels around the world, had also been closed to visitors since 1997. Both of these houses needed considerable restoration and rehabilitation work before they could be interpreted and again opened to the public.

In spring 2002, the NHA properties committee was given the responsibility of discussing various options for the three properties. "The properties committee was charged with brainstorming ideas for the sites deemed non-essential to the mission," said Milligan. "All ideas were on the table."[16]

During their deliberations, the eight-member properties committee had questions about the value of the 1.5-acre Mill Hill parcel. Milligan said, "The committee's questions led to statements like 'Well, we need a plot plan' to see how many sites could be developed on that land." As part of their mandate, the committee contacted the island's leading conservation groups, the Nantucket Land Bank and the Nantucket Conservation Foundation about the Mill Hill property, but neither organization was willing to buy the land. Committee discussion continued, but without reaching a conclusion.

Newspaper articles in advance of the annual meeting in July 2002 gave the erroneous impression that the board was seriously considering the sale of the Mill Hill land. Describing the controversy about the sale of the Mill Hill land, Milligan said, "In the end, it was a short-lived idea. It was very hot for a short time, but it focused at a community meeting after the newspaper stories broke that the properties committee was considering options for the Mill Hill land." There was no mechanism for the board to decide, because the committee had not made a recommendation to them. "It was still in committee," explained Milligan. Like most nonprofits, any sale of land would require approval by both the board and the membership.

Following the annual meeting, the NHA called a special community meeting in August 2002 in response to the newspaper articles. The newspaper reported, "The Board of Trustees of the Nantucket Historical Association voted last Friday to shelve for three years any plans to sell a parcel of land behind the Old Mill, so that the funds can be raised to keep the land 'forever green', said Arie Kopelman, president of the NHA."

"We would far prefer that this land remain as open space," said Kopelman, "But we must grow our current endowment; it is badly under funded. . . . At the same time we can't allow our properties to fall apart," he said. "The funds raised through the forever-green campaign will go directly to the endowment for the preservation and restoration of ailing historic sites."[17]

Growing the endowment was a key piece of the capital campaign then underway. "The meeting allowed the board to explain the needs of the organization and how the capital campaign would help," said Milligan.[18] At the annual meeting, Kopelman described the need for a larger endowment. "We have an operating budget of $2.8 million with a general endowment of $2 million. . . . Our endowment supports only 4 percent of our operating budget."[19] Milligan added: "We have a restoration budget under $200,000 and we have 13 buildings that need truthfully $2 million to 3 million."[20]

One hundred people attended the August 2002 meeting, according to Milligan. "We had a good discussion. It showed that the organization listened to what our members said. In the long run, the Mill Hill controversy was good for the organization, as it focused our priorities. It brought the needs of the organization for money to maintain the properties out in the open."[21]

Lifelong Learning Idea Takes Hold

Barely two weeks after the August special membership meeting, two staff members, Kirstin Gamble, the newly hired education and public programs coordinator, and Ben Simons, the assistant curator, began working with Parker and Milligan on a proposed reuse scenario for both the 1800 House and Greater Light. Their proposal, to reuse these properties for a lifelong learning program on Nantucket decorative arts and crafts, got an enthusiastic response from the management team.

To further refine the idea, Milligan engaged island architect Chip Webster to undertake an analysis of the 1800 House and Greater Light to determine the feasibility and potential costs of reusing these buildings for the proposed lifelong learning program.[22] Meanwhile, as they had promised their members, the board started "Mill Hill and Beyond," a fundraising initiative to establish a $3 million endowment for the Mill Hill land.[23] This campaign goal was later folded into the overall capital campaign goal, making it $21 million.

"The Mill Hill controversy also helped to accelerate the [reuse] effort," recalled Milligan. "The lifelong learning proposal was developed in the fall of 2002 and presented to the board at the winter retreat held in February 2003. It got a good, but calculated, response from the board, as the board as a whole was focused on the campaign, which was for the museum, endowment and library and not the historic properties."[24]

The proposal recommended developing lifelong learning programs on Nantucket social and cultural history with a focus on three centuries of island decorative arts and crafts. It was hoped this programming would bring in significant new income through registrations for the programs. "The timing for this proposal was great," said Milligan, "as the new use would allow restoration of the site, and make the whole island happy that the property would be used again."[25]

Milligan explained, "I have always believed that everyone wants to learn throughout their lifetime. The organization had lots of collections and rich traditions such as Nantucket baskets, sailor's valentines, handicraft and hand work, samplers, quilts, etc. And in the museum-education field this was the buzzword: lifelong learning. We just found out how to apply it to Nantucket's unique attributes."[26]

During a January 2003 board retreat, the staff received approval for the lifelong learning program, and the board allocated $250,000 toward restoration of 1800 House from unrestricted gifts to the already-successful capital campaign. The lifelong learning programs will be hosted in the 1800 House, which will be rehabilitated to accommodate the modern requirements of contemporary learning workshops while preserving their unique architectural features.

New Life for 1800 House

The trustees, in assigning $250,000 from the capital campaign, understood that the restoration of the 1800 House would cost well in excess of this amount. "The group felt they had to walk before they could run, and start 1800 House, and expand the effort to Greater Light later but see if it worked first."[27] Initial costs for restoration and programming for the 1800 House were in excess of $887,000 (see figure 8.1). According to Milligan, "The board contributed about a third of the cost. The balance would have to be raised for the restoration and the new use."[28]

Figure 8.1   1800 House, Nantucket, Massachusetts

In 2003, Nantucket residents voted to increase the real estate transfer tax by 1 percent to support the Community Preservation Act (CPA),
a fund to support open space, restoration, and affordable housing programs on the island. The NHA successfully tapped this source for
$337,000 for the restoration of the 1800 House. An additional $150,000
came from a contribution to the endowment specifically for this building, and $150,000 came from other sources. These funds matched the
$250,000 that the board contributed via the endowment.[29]

In its application for CPA funding, staff wrote:

The demands of maintaining these [historic buildings] and performing
the necessary restoration work is considerable. During the past year
NHA has worked hard to develop a properties plan that creates a strategy for not only preserving these building but finding uses for each one
that will increase the public's accessibility to them and enhance the educational role that is at the heart of the NHA's mission. The 1800
House is perhaps the most significant example of this new approach. It
also happens to be the structure that demands the most resources and

immediate attention. The structure has been closed to the public for the past seven years, and is in serious need of extensive work. However, when completed, the building will become the center for the NHA's new "lifelong learning" series of educational programs. . . .The classes and workshops will focus on traditional Nantucket decorative arts and crafts within the context of an early nineteenth-century house. It will offer hands-on learning for people of all ages on a year-round basis. By taking the approach of blending preservation with education, the NHA will not only re-open one of the island's historic homes, but will also increase accessibility to it while creating a new resource for the community.[30]

The restoration of the 1800 House included both interior and exterior work. Exterior work included: new shingle siding and cedar roof; replacement of missing trim, gutters, and downspouts; rebuilding chimneys and flashing; installing a handicap access ramp; and installing off-street parking. Interior restoration included: repair of the historic paneling in the first floor rooms; removal of non-historic partitions; installation of a kitchenette and two bathrooms (one handicapped-accessible); refinishing floors; replacing missing elements; and adding new lighting for workshop use.[31]

Before the organization could close on the grant from the community preservation committee, the organization needed to place a preservation restriction (called an easement in some states) on the property. Board president Peter Nash described the restriction to the members: "The restriction prevents any changes to a building's exterior that impairs or interferes with a building's historic fabric. Permission would be needed from the holder of the restriction for any work that affects the exterior of the buildings."[32] Mr. Nash's letter went on to say:

The NHA bylaws state that any transaction involving the giving of an easement or restriction affecting real property owned by the Historical Association requires majority votes of both the trustees and the members voting at a duly called meeting. . . .The NHA's Trustees voted unanimously to grant preservation restricts to a third party for. . .the 1800 House. . . .Therefore, in order to enact such restrictions and pave the way for the NHA to receive CPC funding, a membership meeting must be called for the purpose of voting on this matter. . . .This is an important preservation tool that will ensure the architectural integrity of these buildings. We ask for your support in this matter.[33]

The vote to place preservation restrictions on the property was favorable. The opening of 1800 House, timed to the start of the summer tourist season, was planned for July 2005.

A series of community meetings was conducted throughout 2004 to help with programming ideas and identify teachers and workshop leaders. "There was an overwhelmingly positive response to this idea," said Parker. "We received unsolicited proposals from other educational groups on the island to use the space for teaching crafts."[34]

Reflecting back on the work to prepare the house for its new use, Niles Parker noted, "it was important for us not to create yet another house museum, but to arrive at a vision for the house that would offer exciting possibilities for educational instruction while being historically sensitive. Uppermost in our minds was striking a balance between creating usable instructional space that evoked a nineteenth century dwelling and preserving the house and revealing elements of the architecture that remained intact."[35] Parker also noted, "although we wanted to work carefully to remain true to the preservation ethic, at the same time we knew that we weren't painstakingly restoring a house as a house museum, but for use as an instructional space, a functional working environment with active student participants."[36]

Nancee Erickson, a local volunteer, was critical to the successful development and programming of the 1800 House. Of the 1800 House, Ms. Erickson said, "I knew it could be put to better use and the answer was a home for eighteenth and nineteenth century Nantucket crafts education."[37] During the first season, the 1800 House offered instruction on wide-ranging types of crafts including reverse painting on glass, silhouettes, embroidery, stenciling on velvet, and crewel embroidery. Other classes held during the first season included bent wood furniture, lampshade design, canvas work, sailor's valentines, rug hooking, and miniatures.[38]

Besides decorative arts and crafts education, the 1800 House hosts other educational events such as the Nantucket Girl Book Cub and programming tied to Native American legends and Black History Month. Most of programming is offered around themes such as "Skills on

Shore" where candle making, rope work, sewing sailcloth, and silver-smithing are taught and "Early American Home Life," which included butter churning, weaving, and quilting classes. Ms. Erickson explained that the house was designed to be a "meeting place where people make new friends, share and learn and have a joyful experience."[39] The facility is also available for seminars, retreats, and conferences.

Conclusion

For the Nantucket Historical Association, finding a new and compelling use for the shuttered 1800 House was not part of a long-term plan, or active and deliberate decision making. Rather, the staff listened to the organization's membership and successfully responded to an unusual opportunity after the controversy over the possible sale of the Mill Hill land. Today, both the board and staff are pleased that this historic site, so long in the organization's inventory, will be open again to host captivating, year-round public programs for residents and visitors alike.

How to Use This Case

Adaptive use is not a new concept in the preservation field, but here the house museum organization changes the house museum use to something viable to meet the organization's mission. This option might be appropriate for your situation if the collection in your house has little direct provenance to the site, the house is still habitable but perhaps unrestored, or there are other pressing organizational needs that the house, as a piece of real estate, can be used to solve.

NOTES

1. Aimee E. Newell, "'That Pride in Our Island's History': The Nantucket Historical Association," *Nantucket History* 49, no. 1 (2000): 9–12.

2. Newell, 10.

3. Dorothy Stover, "Letter from the President," *Nantucket History* 49, no. 1 (2000): 5.

4. Stephanie Saunders, "NHA's Kopelman takes case for land sale to annual meeting of members," *Inquirer and Mirror*, Nantucket, MA, 2 July 2002, 6a.

5. Harold and Susan Skramstand, "Goals and Strategies 2001–2003," Spring 2001. This document, called the Strategic Plan, was critical to setting the stage for the creation of the Interpretive Plan. The "Goals and Strategies" identified which of the NHA's historic properties were key to the organization's educational mission. The Goals and Strategies document recommended: "Make necessary changes in the NHA organizational structures to provide more appropriate lines of functional authority and decision making; major functional categories would be: Collections; Public and School Programs; Institutional Advancement and Administration." At the time this case was written the management team consisted of an Executive Director, Chief Curator, Manager of Properties and Grounds Maintenance, Director of Development and Membership, and Manager of Finance and Human Resources. In May 2002 Ben Simons was hired as Assistant Curator, reporting to Niles Parker. In June 2003 Kirstin Gamble became the Education and Public Programs Coordinator, reporting to Parker. Gamble, Simons, Parker, and Milligan were the key figures in developing the plan to reuse the 1800 House. Milligan, Gamble, and Parker have since left the Association.

6. Dr. Frank Milligan, interview with author, 9 October 2004.

7. Milligan interview.

8. Nantucket Historical Association, "The Campaign for the Nantucket Historical Society, Starting with History, Starting Now," 2001. The Campaign began in 1998 under a previous Executive Director. The goal of the campaign was: "to build a Museum Center that links the Peter Foulger and the Whaling Museum, both of which will be restored and renovated to provide new gallery space; to increase significantly the permanent endowment so that the interest income supports its mission of restoration, preservation and education; and to construct a Research Library in the former Fair Street Museum that securely houses the library and archival documents, a goal that was realized in 2001." The initial capital campaign goal was subsequently expanded twice as budgets for the new Museum Center were further developed and endowing the Mill Hill land came to the fore. The organization successfully completed the now $21 million dollar capital campaign in 2004.

9. The 1904 Fair Street Museum, one of the first poured concrete structures ever built in Massachusetts, is attached to the side of the Old Quaker Meeting House. Since 2001, the former museum building houses the NHA's renowned archives and manuscript collections.

10. Milligan interview.

11. Nantucket Historical Association Interpretive Plan, Approved by the Board of Trustees with Question and Answer Supplement, 25 May 2001.

12. Nantucket Historical Association Interpretive Plan.

13. Nantucket Historical Association Interpretive Plan, 30–33.

14. Milligan interview.

15. Saunders.

16. Milligan interview.

17. Milligan interview.

18. Milligan interview.

19. Marianne R. Stanton, "NHA decides to delay action on Mill Hill land," *Inquirer and Mirror,* Nantucket, MA, 3 August 2002.

20. Staunton.

21. Milligan interview.

22. Chip Webster, CWA-Architects, "1800 House Rehabilitation Study for the Nantucket Historical Association," November 2002, and Chip Webster, CWA-Architects, "Greater Light Rehabilitation Study for the Nantucket Historical Association," November 2002.

23. Kirstin Gamble, interview with author, 23 May 2003.

24. Milligan interview.

25. Milligan interview.

26. Milligan interview.

27. Niles Parker, interview with author, 8 October 2004.

28. Milligan interview.

29. Milligan interview.

30. Nantucket Historical Association, "Community Preservation Committee Application for Funding FY 2005," 11 September 2003.

31. Nantucket Historical Association, Community Preservation. Cost estimates for restoration were developed by Norton Preservation Trust, a local preservation builder.

32. Peter Nash, Letter to NHA members from the President, regarding placement of preservation restrictions on Quaker Meeting House and 1800 House as condition of accepting Community Preservation Act funding, 7 August 2003.

33. Nash letter.

34. Parker interview.

35. Ben Simons, e-mail message to author, 6 October 2006. Ben Simons, "Early American Arts and Crafts," *Nantucket Home and Garden,* Summer 2006, Nantucket, MA: Anderson Publications, 2006.

36. Simons, Arts and Crafts, 3.

37. Simons, Arts and Crafts, 3.

38. Simons, Arts and Crafts, 4.

39. Simons, Arts and Crafts, 5.

CHAPTER 9

Case Studies: Co-Stewardship Agreements

HISTORIC ADAMS HOUSE, DEADWOOD, SOUTH DAKOTA

The Historic Adams House, located in Deadwood, South Dakota, is a handsome Victorian building that retains virtually all of its original furnishings. Built in 1892, it was described in the press of the time as "the grandest house west of the Mississippi."[1] Today, according to Mary Kopco, the site's executive director, the house has been returned to its former glory after a $1.5 million restoration under a co-stewardship agreement between the City of Deadwood and the site's board of directors.[2]

This Queen Anne-style property was built by one of the area's pioneering families, the Franklins. Son Nathan Franklin bought the property in 1905, followed by the Adams family in 1920.

Kopco explained that W. E. Adams was an early mayor of Deadwood and was keenly interested in the history of the Black Hills. In 1930, he built a local history museum in town and filled it with artifacts and objects whose "exhibits capture the mysteries, the tragedies, the bawdiness, and the dream found in the history, art and natural history of the Black Hills."[3] In building his museum, a memorial to his first wife and two daughters, he decided that the City of Deadwood should own the building, but not the museum collections. He established a separate nonprofit corporation with trustees appointed for life to oversee the collection, an early example, according to Kopco, of a public-private partnership.[4]

Adams eventually married again, to a much younger woman who would outlive him by decades. At his death in 1934, W. E. Adams bequeathed $20,000 to support the museum collections. These funds were invested and still generate income for the museum.[5]

Two years after Adams' death, Mrs. Adams shut the Historic Adams House and left the house and all its contents intact, and that is how it remained for nearly fifty years.[6] She later remarried and moved to California, but continued to vote in Deadwood, visiting the house from time to time. But she did little to maintain it or change the interior in any way.[7] Finally, in 1987, Mary Adams Balmat sold the property to a couple who used the Historic Adams House as a bed-and-breakfast inn for several years.[8]

Gambling Arrives in Deadwood

Since 1989, South Dakota has permitted gambling in Deadwood, with a percentage of the tax revenue earmarked for historic preservation purposes. This revenue stream produces almost $6.8 million a year, said Kopco. The influx of casinos and casino visitors has allowed significant new investment in historic resources in the community.

One of the beneficiaries of this largesse has been the Historic Adams House. Kopco explained that the bed and breakfast proprietors were good stewards, but they were faced with unrelated personal issues that compromised their ability to maintain the building. The City of Deadwood, with the new gambling revenues, was able to purchase the property in 1992 and operate it as a bed and breakfast until 1995, when the heating system failed.

Restoration Begins

The City of Deadwood hired experts to undertake a historic structure report, which in turn guided the restoration of the property with a goal of house museum use since it was wholly intact. Restoration began in 1998 and cost $1.5 million. Half of the funds came from the city's historic preservation commission (which administers the historic preservation funds from gaming) and the rest from a charitable organization begun by Mary Adams Balmat with funds left to her by her second husband.[9]

The historic house is a superb reminder of the past. The conical tower on the front of the house has metal shingles that match the original, thanks to the restoration. The 1892 color scheme of the exterior was reproduced. The foundations and basement were stabilized. The walls on the inside of the house were covered with hand-painted canvas; these were cleaned during the restoration. Decorative tiles, stained glass, and other features were restored. Reproductions of wallpaper were located, and paint colors were matched. The iron fence that surrounded the property was reproduced from historic photographs. A new structure was added to the rear of the house for an ADA-accessible entry and restrooms, a gift shop, and a new orientation area.

The Management Agreement

By the time the restoration was complete, the City of Deadwood had worked for more than seventy-five years with its unusual management structure, in which the city owned and maintained the museum building, while a separate board of directors was responsible for the collection.[10]

According to Kopco, this arrangement resulted from W. E. Adams' experience as mayor. He believed cities were good at managing facilities: repairing roofs, cutting grass, and the like. He was less certain of their skill at maintaining collections, fearing that at some point a financially stressed municipality might wish to sell or dispose of the collection if it became a financial burden. The decision to place the care of the collections in the hands of a separate board of trustees made a great deal of sense in 1930 and this arrangement continues today at the museum.[11]

In setting up the new Historic Adams House museum, the City of Deadwood decided to use a similar arrangement to the one that had worked so well for the Adams Museum. For the Historic Adams House, a separate board of directors would own the valuable collection in the historic building and run the operation, while the city would own and maintain the building and grounds.

This management arrangement, which they call a co-stewardship agreement, placed both the city and the Adams House board on equal footing regarding the overall preservation of the house and its contents. The city provides half of the funds to operate the site each year, and the Adams House board must raise an equal share.[12] The house opened to the public in 2000. Since that time, the Adams Museum has been reorganized to create a single institution called the Adams Museum and House, Inc. Formerly appointed for life, the directors now have term limits.[13]

The entire operation's annual budget is $636,000, according to Kopco. Support for the museum and historic house comes from a single board of directors that oversees the collections at both facilities.

The board is responsible for raising half of the operating budget each year. This sum comes from a variety of sources: admissions, shop sales, online gift catalog, interest income, grants, donations, weddings and facilities rentals, endowment interest, a year-long calendar of events, memberships, and business sponsorships.

Visitation to the museum is about 65,000 yearly; at the house it is about 15,000. Kopco believes that summer visitation at the house is close to the building's maximum. Additional visitation could be handled only during the shoulder seasons and during the winter. As stipulated by Adams, there is no admission charge at the museum, although there is a suggested donation. Last year $68,000 was collected from visitors to the museum. At the Adams House, admission is charged at $5.00 for adults and $2.00 for children.

The Adams House and Museum are on a trolley route that brings visitors up from downtown and the casinos. Since visitors are deposited on the doorstep each day during the summer season (and every day but Sunday and holidays during the winter season), the museum and house respond to this continuing demand.

Deadwood, the recent television series on HBO, has also generated increased interest in the sites. Series producers used both Kopco and research curator Jerry Bryant as resources for authenticity. Both staffers received an EMMY Award Certificate in recognition of contribution to the "Emmy Award Winning Achievement for Outstanding Art Direction for a Single-Camera Series." Specifically, Kopco and Bryant were recognized for their work on three episodes: "Requiem for a Gleet," "Complications," and "Childish Things."[14]

Organizational Expansion

The Adams House and Museum is about to significantly expand and diversify its operations. It has received the papers of the Homestake Mining Company, a prominent local business in the area during the nineteenth and twentieth centuries. The company's papers, consisting of more than 10,000 cubic feet of archival materials, are being catalogued and prepared for researchers. According to a press release, "The Homestake collection includes thousands of historic photographs and glass negatives, architectural drawings, maps of the mine and area, blueprints and patents, geological records of the Black Hills, original correspondence, daily journals, Homestake operation and production records, original artwork, the illustrious Noble geological specimen collection, equipment manuals, and scientific records. These extensive records are exceptionally valuable as they interpret the intellectual and cultural heritage of a significant mining business and the communities it supported. This phenomenal collection is complete, rare and intact."[15]

Homestake's parent company, Barrick Gold Corporation, donated the collection to the Adams Museum and House Inc. In early 2006, the City of Deadwood purchased the former F. L. Thorpe building to house the collection in a climate-controlled, secure facility. When completed, the new Homestake-Adams Research Center will provide a resource center for historians and scientists from all over the world.[16] The city and the board plan another co-stewardship agreement to operate this research facility.[17]

How to Use This Case

The City of Deadwood does not have a traditional landlord-tenant arrangement with the Historic Adams House, in which the landlord, as property owner, is the dominant party. This co-stewardship arrangement allows both parties to finance and run their respective aspect of the museum which, when examined as a whole, is a well-interpreted and staffed historic house museum. Deadwood is fortunate to have access to gambling revenue used exclusively for preservation purposes. However, like any other tax revenue, it can decline over time.

It is not uncommon for historic sites to be owned by a governmental entity, with a separate board of directors established for fundraising purposes. What makes a co-stewardship agreement so appealing is the common purpose of both parties, to ensure that the two elements that make a good house museum—the building and the collection—are well-maintained.

FRANK LLOYD WRIGHT PRESERVATION TRUST, CHICAGO

The Frederick C. Robie House, Frank Lloyd Wright's masterpiece of Prairie School architecture, has long been owned by the University of Chicago, in Chicago, Illinois.[18] Over many years, the university completed repairs and commissioned a historic structure report to identify needed restoration of the building while opening the site for tourists. The Frank

Lloyd Wright Home and Studio Foundation, the operators of the Frank Lloyd Wright Home and Studio in Oak Park, Illinois, negotiated to obtain a long-term lease from the university so they could operate and manage the restoration of this seminal Wright home. The university believed that the Home and Studio understood how to manage a restoration project. Both parties worked for two years to negotiate a thirty-six-year lease.

The lease had several performance provisions to ensure that money was being raised to restore the building. The Wright organization committed to raise $2.8 million during the first five years. A second phase, lasting ten years, will include the balance of the fundraising and restoration. The Home and Studio Foundation assumed the responsibility for maintenance, liability, and operational control of the building. Robie House is a major tourist attraction on the campus, drawing visitors from the Hyde Park neighborhood and around the world, with timed tours, a high-quality museum shop, and well-regarded docent program.

The organization assumed management and restoration responsibility in February 1997, and the Robie House, like the Home and Studio, became a National Trust co-stewardship property. The organization changed its name to the Frank Lloyd Wright Preservation Trust in 2000 to better reflect the organization's stewardship of both houses.[19]

How to Use This Case

This option may be worth exploring if there are several historic house museums in the general vicinity and the boards see advantages to sharing costs. Houses could begin to work toward a co-stewardship arrangement through joint programming or marketing their sites together. Economies of scale can be gained through joint purchasing, sharing staff members, maintenance crews or consultants who would get larger contracts and therefore be more inclined to offer a better price to several co-operating organizations.

Funders may find cooperative projects appealing because synergies between sites can be developed over time, leading to greater collaboration, trust, and inventiveness. Formal co-stewardship agreements like the one between the University of Chicago and the Frank Lloyd Wright Preservation Trust can grow from even the simplest form of cooperation between sites (see figures 9.1 and 9.2).

Figure 9.1   Frank Lloyd Wright Home and Studio, Oak Park, Illinois

Figure 9.2   Frederick Robie House, Chicago, Illinois

NOTES

1. Overview Historic Adams House, available at www.adamsmuseumandhouse.org/overview.html (accessed 30 August 2006).

2. Mary A. Kopco, interview with author, 30 August 2006.

3. Adams Museum Overview, available at www.adamsmuseumandhouse.org/overview.html (accessed 30 August 2006).

4. Adams Museum Overview.

5. Kopco interview.

6. Overview Historic Adams House.

7. Kopco interview.

8. "Historic Adams House Restoration" News Article, 30 November 2003, available at www.adamsmuseumandhouse.org/house/article.php?readit=2.html (accessed 30 August 2006).

9. Kopco interview.

10. Kopco interview.

11. Kopco interview.

12. Kopco interview.

13. Kopco interview.

14. Local Museum Receives Nod from Emmys, available at www.adamsmuseumandhouse.org/awards.html (accessed 30 August 2006).

15. Homestake-Adams Research Center Overview, available at www.adamsmuseumandhouse.org/harc.html (accessed 5 September 2006).

16. Homestake Overview.

17. Deadwood City Commissioner Meeting, Regular Session 1 August 2005.

18. Joan Mercuri, interview with author, typescript of conversation, Oak Park, IL, 21 July 2003.

19. Mercuri interview. See also www.wrightplus.org.html/ (accessed 20 July 2003).

CHAPTER 10

Case Studies: Asset Transfer and Merger

MARGARET MITCHELL HOUSE AND MUSEUM AND THE ATLANTA HISTORY CENTER, ATLANTA, GEORGIA

Margaret Mitchell, famous for her novel *Gone with the Wind*, lived in Atlanta, Georgia, at the Crescent Apartments at 990 Peachtree Street, a single-family house that had been converted in 1919 into a ten-unit apartment building.[1] Here, between 1925 and 1932 in Apartment #1, Mitchell began to write her novel of the South during the Civil War and Reconstruction. The novel was published in 1936, winning the Pulitzer Prize in 1937. The novel's already-considerable fame was cemented by the 1939 motion picture starring Clark Gable and Vivian Leigh.

The house itself has had nine lives. Constructed in 1899, the two-story house was repositioned on the lot forty feet back from the Peachtree frontage in 1913–1914 and then subdivided into apartments by 1919.[2] At this point, the front porches were removed and porches added on the back of the house on the Crescent Street facade.[3] Three brick stores were constructed at the Peachtree frontage where the original building had been located.

Mitchell and her husband, John Marsh, moved into a one-bedroom unit when they married in 1925. A succession of building owners during the late 1920s and into the 1930s sold the house or went bankrupt after the start of the Depression, and maintenance slipped. Mitchell characterized the place as "the Dump," and by 1931 the Marshes lived in one of only two occupied apartments in the ten-unit building.[4] They eventually moved out in 1932. A new owner renovated the house and it remained an apartment building until after World War II. Falling into disrepair again, the property was rehabilitated as the Windsor Apartments in 1964.[5]

Up from the Ashes

In 1977, a new owner planned a major redevelopment of this part of Midtown Atlanta and evicted the tenants, but little evolved from those schemes save for a large new office building at Tenth and West Peachtree.[6] In 1989, the property was designated a City of Atlanta Landmark, the first building to be accorded that status in the city.[7] However, a fire on the southwest corner of the building in the late 1980s, and another, more devastating, fire in September 1994 destroyed much of the building.[8]

Margaret Mitchell House and Museum founder Mary Rose Taylor began her work in 1987 to prevent the demolition of the building. With a $5 million dollar contribution from Daimler-Benz, the German auto manufacturer, the museum was able to purchase the property. Restoration began in 1995.[9] At the time, it was decided to restore the building to its 1914 appearance, as the commercial buildings on Peachtree were gone, and to restore the Tudor Revival front and porches.[10] In May 1996, with fewer than forty days before it was to be opened to the public, an arsonist struck and the building was nearly gutted by fire. Amazingly, Apartment 1 suffered only minor damage.[11] Another restoration project ensued, and the house was finally opened to the public in 1997 to showcase where Mitchell lived and worked while writing the famous work.[12] Today, the apartment is furnished with period pieces.

The Mitchell House organization further expanded their scope by purchasing a bank building across the street on Crescent and opening the *Gone with the Wind* Movie Museum in late 1999. The Museum tells the story of the making of the 1939 movie through original objects, correspondence, and artifacts from the movie's production, including the doorway to the set for the mythic plantation, Tara. Correspondence between Mitchell and producer David O. Selznick's movie studio show her "keen desire that her book be accurately portrayed" in the film.[13]

A visitor and orientation center located at Peachtree Street and 10th Street is a 4,000 square-foot exhibition facility with a small orientation theater where the short film *Before Scarlett: The Writings of Margaret*

Mitchell is shown. The visitor center has a small shop with collectible items related to the film.[14]

The Center for Southern Literature

Perhaps the most ambitious program organized by the Mitchell House and Museum is the Center for Southern Literature, designed to "preserve the legacy of Margaret Mitchell through weekly literary events, creative writing classes for adults and youth and the administration of the PEN/Faulkner Writers in the Schools program."[15] The Center hosts authors and journalists to discuss their recent books and host book signings. More than 300 people attend many of these weekly talks.[16] Bestselling authors, as well as local journalists, have spoken based on themes designed to spark debate about both local and global events.

Adult writing classes are held year round with instruction, critique, and short lectures. Youth writing camps are held each summer. The creative writing classes for young people were recently expanded to include offerings about short fiction, writing for stage and screen, and fantasy writing.[17]

Change on the Horizon

In late 2003, Taylor, then in her sixteenth year as Executive Director of the Margaret Mitchell House and Museum, approached Jim Bruns, the Executive Director of the Atlanta History Center to talk about joining together.[18] Taylor had been a board member of the Atlanta History Center for several years and was very familiar with the organization and its programs. Bruns said at the time of the initial talks about joining forces, the Mitchell House and Museum were profitable, and the organization was able to cover its costs each year and break even, but the small size of the organization and its staff prohibited further expansion.

Prior to the initial meeting, said Bruns, Taylor had received consent from her board to begin conversations with Bruns about a possible alliance between the organizations. He explained that a merger with the much-larger Atlanta History Center would make a compelling partnership and ensure that the current programs and offerings of the Mitchell House and Museum could continue and even expand.[19]

Getting a favorable initial response, both boards agreed to share their documents and financial information to determine how the Mitchell House and Museum could be absorbed into the workings of the Atlanta History Center. Joining the Atlanta History Center would mean that the Mitchell House and Museum would have access to the Center's top-notch development staff, as well as other professionals skilled in collections storage, curatorial assistance, archives, exhibition planning, curriculum development, capital repairs, and maintenance.[20] The staff would also get improved employee benefits.[21]

At the time of the initial conversations, said Bruns, the Mitchell House and Museum had about $300,000 in a line of credit used to pay for the launch of the *Gone with the Wind* Museum. In addition, there were some deferred maintenance issues on the house that amounted to about $250,000, and the funding to make the necessary repairs would be needed before the History Center would accept the property.[22] Prior to finalizing the deal, pledges were received to cover the estimated repair costs. All of the essential repairs were completed during the first year of operation as part of the Atlanta History Center.[23]

Bruns said that the attorneys at Allston and Bird were the first to suggest that joining the organizations might best be accomplished through an asset transfer. This would mean that the assets of the Margaret Mitchell House and Museum would go to the History Center, while the liabilities would remain with the Mitchell House Board of Directors until such time as all the liabilities were satisfied.[24]

David La Piana describes an asset transfer in his book *The Nonprofit Mergers Workbook* as "transactions in which the corporations remain separate, but the valuable assets of one corporation, which may include money and real property, as well as a name or other intangibles, are 'purchased' by the other. This purchase may be for cash, but is commonly for some other consideration, such as a commitment to continue the organization's mission, to preserve its archives or art works, or to raise money for its programs."[25]

Asset Transfer Garners Wide Support

In preparation for the transfer, the development staff at the Atlanta History Center made inquires to the area's philanthropic community, and they responded enthusiastically to the proposed joining of the two institutions through an asset transfer.[26] Nearly $1 million was raised from individuals, family foundations, and corporations to pay off the line of credit, make all the much-needed repairs to the house, and pay for the integration of information and business systems needed to make the transfer successful.[27]

Just before signing the transfer agreement on August 1, 2004, the line of credit was paid off. At this point, the Margaret Mitchell House and Museum Board became an advisory council to the Atlanta History Center to principally assist in the development of the programming at the house and museum and in fundraising. [28]

Bruns said that one of the first orders of business was to establish an integration plan and a series of operating protocols to govern how the Mitchell House and Museum would join with the History Center. These documents, dealing with personnel, programming, and operational issues, were written and adopted, he said. New exhibitions were designed for the Visitor's Center and an endowment campaign was launched.[29]

In his initial conversations with Taylor, Bruns said that she insisted that the house needed a large endowment to ensure its continued preservation and a goal was set to try to raise $5 million.[30] Bruns noted that the Atlanta History Center, which is an operating division of the old Atlanta Historical Society, was then in the midst of launching a large endowment campaign, so the $5 million dollar goal for the Margaret Mitchell House was incorporated into the broader overall campaign.[31]

Conversations with area developers identified an overlooked historic preservation planning tool that would permit the landmarked Mitchell House to sell the development rights or air rights to another location where a taller building might be appropriate. Atlanta is one of fifteen cities in the United States that has an historic preservation Transfer of Development Rights program.[32]

The Atlanta Transfer of Development Rights program was started in 1980, and permits city designated landmarks on highly zoned parcels to sell their unused floor area ratio to a multifamily residential use or mixed use (with residential at least 50 percent), via a special permit process.[33] The idea of selling the Mitchell House air rights was explored further and the Atlanta History Center issued a Request for Expressions of Interest to the development community in early 2006, yielding several real prospects for sale of air rights in the coming year. It is hoped that the air rights sale will result in a several million dollar endowment to guarantee the future of the historic house.

Bruns calls the asset transfer of the two organizations a win-win situation for both. While the memberships for the organizations have remained separate because there are many people who belong to both, a plan is being discussed to develop a premium level membership in the coming year to provide membership benefits to both organizations. All staff members from the House and Museum became employees of the History Center immediately.

In the intervening years, some staff realignments have occurred. A seasoned manager from the History Center, Diane Lewis, was appointed to take over Taylor's former daily responsibilties as Executive Director at the House and Museum. Bain and Company is assisting in the development of a long-range strategic plan for the house and the History Center has included the Margaret Mitchell House and Museum in its re-accreditation plans with the American Association of Museums.[34]

With the anticipated sale of the development rights to create an endowment, the future for the Margaret Mitchell House and Museum seems assured.

How to Use this Case

Initial conversations between executive directors are often the start of any merger or asset transfer discussion, only because executive directors have intimate knowledge of the organization's finances and future potential. Merger partners are often unequal in size, but both directors must see benefits to joining together for merger discussions to advance to the board level.

Here, the asset transfer solution allowed the Atlanta History Center to move quickly before all the Mitchell House debts were satisfied, leaving those issues to be handled when funds became available. Board members of the Mitchell House still play an advisory role at the home. The Mitchell House's mission complements the broader mission of the

Atlanta History Center and brings additional resources that would be unavailable otherwise to a beloved historic property.

The consolidation of the Margaret Mitchell House and Museum with the Atlanta History Center had another beneficial result in that it allowed the leadership of the History Center to broaden its view and standing. With two campuses, the senior management took on a more corporate management model, where Bruns became the President and Chief Executive Officer of the long-dormant parent organization—the Atlanta Historical Society—with separate executive directors running each of the Society's campuses.[35]

MERGER OF CLIVEDEN OF THE NATIONAL TRUST AND HISTORIC UPSALA FOUNDATION, PHILADELPHIA, PENNSYLVANIA

Cliveden, the grand Georgian-style home owned since its construction (1763–1767) by descendents of Chief Justice Benjamin Chew, is the site of the famous 1777 Revolutionary War Battle of Germantown.[36] The property and its Colonial furniture were donated to the National Trust for Historic Preservation by the Chew family in 1972 for use as a historic site.[37] As a co-stewardship property, Cliveden is managed by a local board of directors, Cliveden Inc., which is responsible for maintenance and day-to-day management of this fine home, barn, and land.[38] Situated in a six-acre, park-like setting, and up a long driveway set back from Germantown Avenue, a traditional neighborhood commercial street, the home is one of a dozen historic house museums within a one-mile-radius that interprets some aspect of Colonial or Federal history in Philadelphia.[39]

Across the street from Cliveden is Upsala, a fine Federal-style historic house that has been open to the public since 1944 by the Historic Upsala Foundation volunteers. In 2000, the board of Upsala, concerned about its small operation, continued financial viability, and lack of any endowment, approached Cliveden about a possible merger. Both sites saw benefits to joining together. After several years of discussion, the two boards agreed to formally join. Upsala would be programmed for meetings and events and would house staff offices. Cliveden would continue as a historic house museum.

In 2004, the merger was finally concluded when the Historic Upsala Foundation was dissolved, transferring the house, assets, and liabilities to Cliveden, Inc., the co-stewardship entity that manages the house. It is hoped that Upsala will become a centerpiece for revitalization programs, including commercial district revitalization, in the northwest section of Philadelphia.[40]

How to Use this Case

Formal mergers occur after a lengthy period of discussion. Both parties must believe that there are benefits to the union, knowing that one of the organizations will likely dissolve. Some mergers occur between similarly sized organizations, but most often one party is smaller. This option is not often used in the house museum community, but deserves to be seriously considered more often by sites that are in close proximity. Joint programming and co-stewardship agreements are excellent preliminary tasks that can lead to formal organizational mergers.

Figure 10.1   Cliveden of the National Trust, Philadelphia, Pennsylvania

Figure 10.2   Historic Upsala, Philadelphia, Pennsylvania

NOTES

1. "The House and its History," available at gwtw.org.html.
2. "The Margaret Mitchell House: Its Historical Significance," available at gwtw.org/mitchellhouse.html.
3. "Mitchell House: Its Historical Significance."
4. "Crescent Apartments," Atlanta: A National Register of Historic Places Travel Itinerary, available at www.cr.nps.gov/travel/atlanta/cre/htm (accessed 9 November 2006).
5. "Crescent Apartments."
6. Windsor House Apartments (Crescent Apartments) available at atlanta.gov.citydir/URBAN/Windsor.htm (accessed 9 November 2006).
7. "Mitchell House: Its Historic Significance."
8. "Mitchell House: Its Historic Significance."
9. "Mitchell House: Its Historic Significance."
10. "The Dump is Reborn, Mitchell House Rises From the Ashes," *The Atlanta Constitution*, 15 May 1997, F12, available at nl.newsbank.com/nl-search/we/Archives?paction=doc&pdocid=0EADA31B22367777F&P (accessed 9 November 2006).

11. "Mitchell House: Its Historic Significance."

12. "Mitchell House: Its Historic Significance."

13. *"Gone with the Wind* Movie Museum," available at www.gwtw.org/tour.html.

14. *"Gone with the Wind* Movie Museum."

15. "Center for Southern Literature," available at www.gwtw.org.csl.html.

16. James Bruns, interview with author, 21 September 2006.

17. The Center for Southern Literature.

18. Bruns interview.

19. Bruns interview.

20. "A Letter from Mary Rose Taylor," available at gwtw.org/taylorletter.html.

21. Mary Rose Taylor Letter.

22. Bruns interview.

23. James Bruns, e-mail message to author, 26 September 2006.

24. Bruns interview.

25. David La Piana, *The Nonprofit Mergers Workbook: Part I The Leader's Guide to Considering, Negotiating and Executing a Merger*. St. Paul, MN: The Fieldstone Press, 2000, 17–18.

26. Bruns interview.

27. Bruns e-mail.

28. Bruns e-mail.

29. Bruns e-mail.

30. Bruns interview. Bruns e-mail.

31. Bruns interview.

32. Donna Ann Harris, "Survey of Landmark Transfer of Development Rights Programs, Interim Report for the City of Miami." Unpublished report for the National Trust for Historic Preservation, Preservation Development Initiative program, April 2006.

33. "Survey Landmark Transfer of Development Rights Programs."

34. Bruns interview.

35. Bruns e-mail.

36. Hosmer, 87. See also www.cliveden.org.html/.

37. Mayes interview.

38. Vaughn interview.

39. Silberman interview.

40. Vaughn interview. Mayes interview.

CHAPTER 11

Case Study: Long-term Leases

HAZELWOOD, MARYLAND-NATIONAL CAPITAL PARK AND PLANNING COMMISSION, UPPER MARLBORO, MARYLAND

Andy and Pam Cooper are the new resident curators for Hazelwood, a deteriorated but historic home surrounded by land owned by the Maryland-National Capital Park and Planning Commission (M-NCPPC).

Hazelwood sits amid 148.3 acres in a rural part of Prince George's County in Maryland, near Washington, D.C. The house and land were acquired in 1976 by the M-NCPPC to add to the Patuxent River Park System to protect the valuable natural resources along the river and add to the existing greenway.[1] Acquisition of lands along the Patuxent River began in the 1960s with the passage of the Patuxent River Watershed Act, whose funding came from the Program Open Space Land Preservation program from the State of Maryland.

The entire Hazelwood site had been acquired primarily for its open space values. As such, funding was not made available to protect and preserve the historic home located on the property. At the time the property was acquired, the former residents left Hazelwood. A series of rent-free tenants then monitored the house until it was later mothballed.

The Commission was deeply concerned about the deterioration of the house and sought alternate solutions to restore and rehabilitate Hazelwood. A public-private partnership was created through the Resident Curatorship program to bring non-tax funds and resources to pay for restoration, rehabilitation, and maintenance of selected historic structures owned by the M-NCPPC. "Our goal for the project," says

Barbara Funk, Chief of the Arts and Cultural Heritage Division of M-NCPPC, "is the preservation of this historic property for future generations."[2]

About Hazelwood

Hazelwood, listed on the National Register of Historic Places, is a large, three-part frame structure representing three distinct building periods (Colonial, Federal, and Victorian). It was constructed in three phases between 1750 and 1860. It has twenty-one rooms and features a large center hall, double parlors, foyer, dining room, and kitchen on the first floor. The second floor has six bedrooms and two bathrooms with connecting hallways. The third floor has two bedrooms and an attic.[3]

The Hazelwood site includes a number of historic outbuildings, including a tobacco barn, two livestock barns, an icehouse/dairy, modern pump house, modern garage, and a historically significant smokehouse/privy (see figure 11.1).[4]

Figure 11.1   Hazelwood, Upper Marlboro, Maryland

About the Commission

The Maryland-National Capital Park and Planning Commission is a bi-county agency established in 1927. It is responsible for parks, recreation, and planning in Montgomery and Prince George's Counties and owns and operates more than 51,000 acres of parkland. The Commission's Parks and Recreation Department is charged with managing a comprehensive park system and acquiring land for parks, developing park and recreation facilities, maintaining and policing park property, and conducting a wide array of leisure activities.[5]

The Commission's Prince George's County Park and Recreation Department owns 23,000 acres and twenty-four historic properties. These historic sites range from monuments to mansions and span more than 300 years of Prince George's County history.[6]

1997 Study

In 1997, the Department of Park and Recreation of the M-NCPPC undertook a study of all of the historic buildings in their parks to "evaluate the historic structures of the M-NCPPC for their present condition and future potential."[7] This yearlong study concluded that "conditions varied widely." It was noted that "when historic structures were secondarily included in the acquisition of large tracts of land acquired for multiple purposes, the historic structures on those sites had little public use potential and they received little or no restoration funding."[8] Hazelwood was one of the sites that stood empty and had not received any maintenance or restoration funding over the years.

In 1997, the study noted that Hazelwood was located on a 148.3-acre parcel that had been acquired for $314,800.[9] The house was not usable at that time but had been stabilized, according to the report. Extensive renovation would be required before it could be used, as previous water and insect damage had not been repaired. At the time, further stabilization of the structure was estimated to cost just under $60,000. To partially restore the building would cost in excess of $1.1 million. Full restoration for public access and to comply with Americans with Disabilities Act accessibility guidelines would cost in excess of $1.6 million.[10]

The 1997 report concluded that "Hazelwood has considerable potential for a public/private partnership arrangement that could preserve this significant historic structure while reducing the tax supported costs."[11] The report finally suggested that the Commission "advertise Hazelwood for long-term lease to a responsible individual, organization or business that would enter into a contract with the Commission to restore and utilize it within guidelines and terms to be established by the Commission."[12]

The Resident Curatorship Program at M-NCPPC

Another report was prepared as a follow-up to the 1997 study of the twenty-four historic sites managed by the department. The purpose of the second report (completed the next year) was to "review the best historic marketing and preservation practices in the nation with the intention of improving marketing and preservation of M-NCPPC historic sites and increasing private-sector support for historic preservation and marketing in the county."[13]

Among the report's recommendations was to implement a Resident Curatorship program for "those historic structures that are deteriorating and for which there is little or no funding for restoration."[14] The report recommended that historic sites meeting specific criteria and those that could attract potential curators be advertised for restoration for residential and commercial tenancy.[15] A department team was formed to develop a curatorship program. It identified Hazelwood as the first property for a curatorship, and released a request for proposal (RFP) and began to advertise Hazelwood to prospective residents in July 1999.[16]

Curatorship Programs around the Country

Resident Curatorship programs are not new. They were pioneered in Massachusetts for deteriorated historic properties on publicly owned land.[17] Several other states and county parks programs on the East coast have started programs recently or are in the midst of planning programs. Close to home, the State of Maryland's Department of Natural Resources (MDNR) has a well-regarded and longstanding program.

This is the program used as a model for the M-NCPPC's Resident Curatorship program.

The MDNR Resident Curatorship Program

The MDNR's Resident Curatorship program now has about fifty historic sites that collectively represent more than $8 million in donated restoration services to state-owned properties since it began in 1982.[18] Promotional literature about the MDNR program states "The Resident Curator program of the DNR secures private funding and labor for restoration and maintenance of historic property, but for which neither the state nor DNR has the means to preserve in the public interest."[19]

The MDNR program's website acknowledges that:

DNR owns far more historically significant buildings than it can maintain itself. It is the largest landowner (400,000 acres) in Maryland; it finds itself the proprietor of hundreds of structures deemed historically significant. While many are in good condition, and serve public uses, others are in poor condition and require extensive assistance that DNR cannot provide.

Many of the Resident Curator properties are farmhouses, some with complexes of historic barns and other outbuildings. Most are located in state parks, in state forests or natural resources management lands, in natural environmental areas, wildlife management areas, and the like.

The public benefits from the program because publicly owned historic structures are restored and maintained at no cost to the public. From a dollars and cents standpoint the value of Maryland's natural resources and public lands appreciates as a result of private involvement, rather than depreciates from neglect.

Resident Curators benefit too. Though old house restoration is expensive, dirty and often exasperating; curators reap the benefit of long-term residency in a restored structure for which they take great pride. Aside from restoration and maintenance expenses, curators are not burdened with rental or mortgage payments or with property taxes.[20]

The MDNR Curatorship program administrators note that

The ideal curator has experience in historic restoration, has the financial resources to undertake a particular restoration and presents a superior proposal. You must demonstrate that you have the financial resources to meet the bottom line value of your proposed schedule of work. For an average Curatorship program, a candidate with steady employment, adequate cash flow for their circumstances and moderate assets (say a net worth of $50,000) may qualify. Because Resident Curators do not own their Curatorship properties, they can't use the property as security for improvement loans.[21]

The MDNR program administrators are "interested in high quality work that preserves as much of the historic fabric as possible with the least modern intrusion. Of course modern kitchens, bathrooms, heating and air conditioners and so forth are permitted."[22]

The M-NCPPC relied heavily on the MDNR program to shape its own. There are minor differences between the two, the most significant being the term of years of the curator's lease, with M-NCPPC deciding on a term of forty years, the maximum allowed under state law.[23]

Marketing Hazelwood

The press release announcing the availability of the Hazelwood's Resident Curatorship described it as "a new and innovative program [that] promotes public/private partnership investment in endangered public properties. . . .[The Commission would] enter into a long-term lease with a curator/tenant in exchange for the restoration, rehabilitation, renovation and maintenance of the property."[24]

The press release went on to say "responding to widespread community concerns about the loss of historically significant properties through neglect or inappropriate development, the Historic Curatorship Program represents a unique opportunity to restore Hazelwood to its former beauty and significance."[25]

Yasmin Anderson-Smith, regional manager for the Commission's historic rental properties program, was the project coordinator for the Resident Curatorship program. According to her, "the Commission advertised the availability of Hazelwood widely in the Montgomery and Prince George's County *Journal* (the community newspaper); RAPID, the online listing of bids managed by the Montgomery County office of procurement; *Maryland Contract Weekly*; the Washington D.C.-based *Afro-American* newspaper; *The Old House Journal* and in *Preservation* magazine published by the National Trust for Historic Preservation."[26] Word of mouth proved the most effective method, as the eventual Resident Curators learned about Hazelwood from someone active in the community.[27]

Request for Proposals Solicitation

The Request for Proposals (RFP) noted that "Hazelwood offers the potential for an exciting opportunity in the preservation of a unique architectural treasure and a chance to restore what was a significant structure in the former town of Queen Anne on the Patuxent River. The Commission is committed to the preservation of the property and to identification of a use that will be complimentary to the surrounding community while paying tribute to the history and legacy of Hazelwood."[28]

The M-NCPPC would enter into a Curatorship agreement or long-term lease in exchange for the restoration as a professional services contract. There was no specific dollar amount expected to be spent on the building in the RFP. It would be up to the potential Curator to describe to the Commission in their bid how they intended to pay for the restoration and maintenance of Hazelwood during the forty-year lease term.[29]

According to the RFP, "the Curator would provide the restoration, rehabilitation, and maintenance of Hazelwood as a 'gift' to the Commission. The amount of which shall represent a minimum dollar-value based on the proposed schedule of work."[30] The contribution would be in the form of both payment for materials and services purchased by the curator/tenant and their time and labor used in the restoration, rehabilitation, and maintenance of Hazelwood.[31]

After restoration was complete, the Curator would maintain "the premises and grounds as necessary during the term of the Curatorship agreement lease" without charge and as long as the Curatorship was in effect. The gift to the Commission of the Curator's time and money to restore and maintain the property during the lease "shall be effective and complete regardless of the tax consequences. The tax liability, if any, arising from any part of Curatorship/lease shall be solely the Curator/tenant's responsibility."[32]

Restoration Activities in the RFP

The RFP stated that "the Curator agrees to thoroughly document all restoration and rehabilitation work with photographs or video records, retain complete records of funds expended and time/labor spent, so they can be examined by Commission staff upon request."[33]

As part of the agreement, the Commission would inspect and approve all restoration and rehabilitation work and provide written acknowledgment to the curator/tenant of the value of their contribution to the Commission upon final acceptance of each phase of the schedule of work.

The Curator was expected to establish residency in the main house no later than six months after signing the agreement and complete the restoration work within five years. The M-NCPPC specified that all restoration and rehabilitation work must meet the *Secretary of the Interior's Standards for Historic Preservation*. The Curator also agreed to open the grounds and house to the public four days each year, as arranged in cooperation with the Department.[34]

Open House and Evaluation Team

A pre-proposal conference was held at the site on November 15, 2003. Proposals were reviewed by an evaluation team of eight people. The evaluation team, according to Anderson-Smith, consisted entirely of Commission staff members, including an architect, historian, archeologist, historian/preservationist, architectural historian, park planner, purchasing representative, and attorney.

Included among these were Barbara Funk, the Chief of the Arts and Cultural Heritage Division, and Chris Wagnon, Chief of the Natural and Historic Resources Division. Yasmin Anderson-Smith served as the project administrator/planner for the project, as well as on the evaluation team. The evaluation team judged each proposal against the selection criteria listed below, and then made a recommendation to the Commission.[35]

Selection Criteria

The evaluation team used the following criteria to judge the proposals.

- 35 points: Nature of the proposed use that provides for long-term preservation of property, that is compatible with its historic character, and a use that is compatible with parkland;

- 20 points: Experience to complete work in proposed schedule based on qualifications and experience to implement and manage rehab and maintenance of the property. Specialized skills in historic preservation, awareness, and understanding of the technical, legal, financial, and environmental issues associated with the project;
- 20 points: Estimates of cost of work/services;
- 15 points: Financial resources to implement the schedule of work, reliability of financial proposals, adequate project financing methods, and adequacy of information on expected project costs; and
- 10 points: Minority, female, or disabled status.[36]

After the proposal was submitted, selected applicants would be invited to make oral presentations for thirty minutes, followed by a question-and-answer session with the evaluation team.

Third Time Is the Charm

The Department of Park and Recreation made three public requests for Curator proposals between December 2001 and February 2004. The first time the proposal was made, according to Barbara Funk, the department received no responses. The RFP was issued again and the M-NCPPC staff entered into negotiations with a bidder, but they could not come to an agreement and the negotiations were abandoned.

The third time the proposal was issued, the Cooper family submitted a proposal. It was reviewed favorably by the evaluation team and negotiations commenced immediately. "Throughout the evaluation phase of the Curatorship process," said Anderson-Smith, "we faced the challenge of finding a curator that had a passion for preservation. We feel we have found that in the Coopers."[37]

The First Curators

The M-NCPPC's winter 2005 quarterly newsletter announced the signing of the Curatorship agreement. "With their love of history and the environment, demonstrated sensitivity to historic preservation and significant experience in preparing grants and fundraising, the Coopers are ideal curators for Hazelwood. Prior to the approval of the Curatorship program, Mrs. Cooper began working as a volunteer at Hazelwood. Her love of history and preservation is reflected in the restoration and renovation work she has performed to date. Although there is still much work to be done, the Coopers completely hand finished the old wood floors in the main part of the house to their former shining glory, an indication of the wonderful transformation yet to happen." [38]

The news story went on to say, "As curators for the house. . .the Coopers. . .would fully fund the building's restoration—estimated in 1996 at $1.6 million. They would also maintain it. In exchange, they would be allowed to live in the property rent free for up to forty years. The property would then be turned back over to the county."[39]

"This is great that there are people like them that have the vision and want to take this on," said Chris Wagnon, Chief of the Natural and Historical Resources Division for the Maryland-National Capital Park and Planning Commission. Wagnon has been helping to orchestrate the Curatorship, which will be the first time the county has tried that approach for preserving a historic home.[40]

"We just fell in love with the house" said Pam Cooper. "It has a sense of community and sense of protecting our cultural and historical heritage." She acknowledged though, that she still sometimes wonders what she is getting herself into. The restoration project will be arduous, given the mansion's extensive water damage, dry rotted structural beams, and missing patches of ceiling.[41] "A lot of it you don't have to be a rocket scientist to do, but it is hard work," said Cooper. "Most people think we are insane."[42]

After working at the site as a volunteer, and now as the approved Resident Curator since the agreement was signed in April 2005, Mrs. Cooper noted, "there were a lot of hidden costs and problems that we found out about after we submitted our proposal, so it's not a simple project. We plan to address the structural issues first. Our advisors told us they felt this was a doable project."[43]

Lengthy Approval Time

Because Hazelwood was the first property to be processed under the Commission's new Resident Curatorship program, there were a series of delays in the approval process, as procurement, legal, planning, and legislative bodies had to become familiar with the program and then review the Curatorship agreements for the first time. Given the unique nature and length of the lease (forty years), it was critical that all parties involved were in full agreement on all the terms and extensive reviews contributed to unanticipated time delays as terms and conditions were reviewed and approved to meet all parties' satisfaction. Although the Prince George's County Council approved the lease in November 2004, the lease was not fully executed until April 2005, when the Coopers and the Commission signed the Curatorship agreement.[44]

Restoration Plans

The Cooper's agreement included the scope of work for the multi-year restoration project, and their restoration plan, timetable, and budget. In addition, a project team was outlined that included a historic preservation consultant, architect, archeologist, electrician, and plumber.[45] Skilled preservation contractors and tradesmen are being used or consulted for advice on carpentry, plumbing, electrical, roof repair, HVAC, and lead paint abatement.[46] Mrs. Cooper is hoping to work with the historic preservation program of the University of Maryland to have some of their preservation students use Hazelwood as a place to learn practical preservation skills such as paint analysis, tuck pointing, and materials analysis.[47]

The work the Coopers plan for the site will address structural damage and other serious threats to the house first. Then they will establish a modest living area so residence can be established and work can continue. Work will be paced by funding available through grants and personal funds and the Coopers expect to spend a significant amount of time and money on Hazelwood. All told, the Coopers plan to spend a minimum of $50,000 to $100,000 on Hazelwood during the first five years of their lease, an amount that would be several times that if the Coopers were not performing a significant amount of the work themselves on the property.[48]

Each year the Coopers will present to the M-NCPPC their accounting of the work done that year, along with photos and videos taken to document the work at least every six months and when completed.[49] In turn, the M-NCPPC will inspect, approve, and acknowledge the work completed.[50]

The Coopers are donating a significant portion of the work in the form of sweat equity and must record both the hours and work performed throughout the entire restoration process.[51] When restoration is complete, the M-NCPPC will issue a letter acknowledging completion of the restoration work.[52] While there may be some tax advantages to the Coopers to restore a property they are leasing, the M-NCPPC provides no advice about tax treatment to potential curators.[53]

Speaking about the Coopers in the news report, Wagnon said, "They have the knowledge and the resources to pull off the restoration. . . . Hopefully we'll have a beautifully restored site which has amazing architecture and is an important part of the town of Queen Anne for future generations."[54]

How to Use This Case Study

The Resident Curator program, while geared toward historic sites on parkland owned by government, also has excellent applicability for privately owned historic house museums. This solution may be especially appealing to historic property stewards who do not want to give up ownership of their site, but have reached the conclusion that they do not have the funds to restore or maintain it and would prefer a lease with a sympathetic person willing to restore the building. In exchange for a long-term lease, a private individual who is preservation minded may be willing to invest significant sums into a site that they do not own.

Unlike the government-managed Resident Curator programs, a private house museum Resident Curator would not be exempt from property tax, but would be able to reap any tax benefits available for donating time and restoration costs to a nonprofit organization. The house museum organization could not disband, as it would still be the titleholder and hence obligated to inspect the property at least yearly to ensure that the Resident Curator was living up to the terms of the agreement.

This case demonstrates the difficulty of identifying the "perfect" curator and the need to be patient until such a curator is identified. The Maryland-National Capital Park and Planning Commission released the RFP for Hazelwood three times, and waited more than two years before a qualified individual came forward with a credible proposal.

Advertising in various publications was not inexpensive, but in the end, word of mouth proved the best form of advertising. Local people are more likely to be interested in the property as they are already familiar with the area. The Coopers learned about the property from someone active in the community.[55]

There was considerable staff time needed to manage inquiries, host the open houses, call an evaluation panel, and then review submissions, even for the early RFPs that did not result in a contract. A similar time frame might be necessary for a nonprofit-owned venture.

The house museum organization will have a much easier time finding a resident curator for the property if it is already habitable. Hazelwood was in poor condition when the Commission began seeking a Curator, which might account for the long time needed to find someone willing to take on the project.[56]

Finally, the nonprofit organization would receive no payment from the Curator, who lives at the site rent-free in exchange for making a significant investment. Over the years, the Curator may in fact behave as if they own the site (when indeed they are merely tenants) unless the house museum organization actively manages the site and has an ongoing relationship with the Curator.

NOTES

1. Maryland-National Capital Park and Planning Commission, Request for Proposals (RFP), 24–137, "Historic Curatorship/Lease of Hazelwood," Scope of Services, 4 November 2003.

2. Barbara Funk, interview with author, Upper Marlboro, MD, 5 May 2005.

3. Pamela Cooper, e-mail message to author, 5 August 2005.

4. RFP. Cooper e-mail.

5. Richard Dolesh, interview with author, typescript of telephone conversation, 27 June 2003.

6. Prince George's County Department of Park and Recreation, "Report to the Prince George's County Council on the Historic Sites of the Maryland-National Capital Park and Planning Commission in Prince George's County," 1997.

7. Dolesh interview.

8. Dolesh interview.

9. 1997 Report on Historic Sites in Prince George's County, 46–48.

10. 1997 Report.

11. 1997 Report.

12. 1997 Report.

13. Department of Park and Recreation, "The Marketing and Management of the Historic Sites of the Maryland-National Capital Park and Planning Commission," January 1998. Volume 1 of 3, 1.

14. "Marketing and Management," 4.

15. "Marketing and Management."

16. "Department of Park and Recreation Announces Historic Curatorship/Lease Availability," Maryland-National Capital Park and Planning Commission, News release, 30 July 1999.

17. Rachael S. Cox, "Resident Curators: Private Stewards of Publicly Owned Historic Houses," *Forum News* 5, no. 1 (1999), available at forum .nationaltrust.org/subNTHP/displayNews.asp (accessed 18 July 2004). Delaware has just begun a program "Delaware State Parks Signs Up First Resident Curators," DNREC *News*, 12 January 2005, vol. 35, no. 7, available at www.dnrec.state.de.us./dnrec2000/Admin/Press/Story1.asp? (accessed 29 July 2004). Several counties in Pennsylvania are considering programs, see "Historic Curatorship program draws criticism from idea's proponents," *Delaforum*, News, 10 September 2004, available at www.delaforum.com?2004/ Jul-Sep/ARTICLES/Resident%20Curator%20(9-10).htm (accessed 22 July 2004).

18. See the Maryland Department of Natural Resources website for further information about their Resident Curator program, available at www.dnr.state .md.us/publiclands/curatorship/html (accessed 22 July 2004).

19. Maryland Department of Natural Resources website.

20. Maryland Department of Natural Resources website.

21. Maryland Department of Natural Resources website.

22. Maryland Department of Natural Resources website.

23. Anderson-Smith interview. Cooper, e-mail, 5 August 2005.

24. News release.

25. News release.

26. Anderson-Smith interview.

27. Pamela Cooper, interview with author 5 September 2006.

28. News release.

29. RFP.

30. RFP.

31. RFP.

32. RFP.

33. RFP.

34. RFP.

35. Anderson-Smith interview.

36. RFP.

37. Anderson-Smith interview.

38. Maryland-National Capital Park and Planning Commission, "Planning Board and County Council Approve Residential Curatorship for Historic Hazelwood" *Views*, newsletter of Maryland-National Capital Park and Planning Commission, Department of Park and Recreation, Prince George's County, MD, Winter 2005, 2.

39. *Views*, 2.

40. *Views*, 2.

41. *Views*, 2.

42. "Hazelwood Curator selected by county," *Gazetteer* (Upper Marlboro, MD), 12 August 2004.

43. Pamela Cooper, interview with author, Upper Marlboro, MD, 5 May 2005.

44. Funk interview.

45. Cooper e-mail.

46. "Resident Curatorship Agreement between Philip Cooper, Pamela Cooper and Philip and Pamela Cooper as Guardians of Ethan Cooper a minor and the Maryland-National Capital Park and Planning Commission," 22 March 2004. Cooper e-mail.

47. Cooper e-mail.

48. Cooper e-mail.

49. Curatorship Agreement, 8.

50. Curatorship Agreeement, 9.

51. Cooper interview. Cooper e-mail.

52. Curatorship Agreement, 10.

53. Cooper interview. Cooper e-mail.

54. *Gazetteer*.

55. Cooper interview, 5 September 2006.

56. Cooper interview.

CHAPTER 12

Case Studies:
Short-term Leases

HERITAGE BRANCH, BRITISH COLUMBIA MINISTRY OF COMMUNITY, ABORIGINAL AND WOMEN'S SERVICES, VICTORIA, BRITISH COLUMBIA, CANADA

In 2001, Rhonda Hunter had just taken a new job as the Director of the Heritage Branch of the British Columbia Ministry of Community, Aboriginal and Women's Services.[1] The Heritage Branch, equivalent to a state historic preservation office in the United States, managed the historic preservation program for the Canadian province and administered thirty historic sites throughout British Columbia.

Hunter, an accountant and former assistant deputy minister for finance for the Ministry, was a nonpartisan civil servant. She was well-known in government circles throughout Canada as the past president of the Certified Management Accountants of British Columbia. Her senior colleague at the Heritage Branch, John Adams, was a teacher and historian who had just completed twenty years with the Branch and was a past president of the British Columbia Museums Association.

Both were seasoned administrators, one in finance and management, the other in heritage preservation and programming. Little did Hunter and Adams know that their well-honed administrative skills would be taxed to the maximum after a new political party took office in British Columbia in May 2001.

A New Era and Change Ahead

In 2001, after being out of power since 1933, the British Columbia Liberal party won the election on their "New Era" platform. Their plan was heralded as a way to balance the Province of British Columbia's spiraling budget and renew economic investment in the province. Critical to balancing the budget was a Core Review of each Ministry, to determine which services should remain within government and which could be privatized or outsourced to other entities.[2]

The Ministry of Community, Aboriginal and Women's Services, in which the Heritage Branch was located, was a vast agency that managed a broad and diverse range of programs affecting every British Columbian. The Heritage Branch is now located in the Local Government Department, and the broader agency has changed its name to the Ministry of Tourism, Sport, and the Arts. In 2000, the Branch had a budget of $6 million and staff of fifty-five. By 2002, the annual budget had been reduced to $4.5 million. By 2005, the budget had been further cut to $3.8 million, with only ten staff remaining to manage the province's heritage programs, including its thirty historic sites.[3]

British Columbia Acquires its Historic Sites

Starting in 1939, the British Columbia government began acquiring historic sites.[4] First to be acquired was Helmcken House, located in Victoria and opened to the public two years later. When the Province held its Centennial in 1958, the government purchased additional sites. Barkerville Town, a gold mining town located in the central interior portion of the province, became a historic site during this period.

Throughout the 1960s and 1970s additional sites were acquired. Fort Steele, located in the southeastern portion of the province, was acquired in 1962. Another site, the Kilby Store and Farm in the Fraser Valley of British Columbia, became a government-operated site in the 1960s. Point Ellice House, located in Victoria, British Columbia, and operated as a private house museum, was purchased by British Columbia in 1974.[5] Two other sites, Craigflower Manor and Craigflower Schoolhouse in suburban Victoria, were soon opened to the public under government stewardship.[6]

The collection of British Columbia historic sites grew randomly, with no coherent philosophy about which properties should be acquired and why. The sites range from small homes to ranches, gold mining villages, an Indian long house, a church, and a school, as well as archeological sites. These properties were scattered throughout urban, suburban, and rural portions of the vast province.

In 1977, the province passed the Heritage Conservation Act and created the Heritage Branch. At the time, the historic sites were managed by various provincial agencies. Consolidation under the Heritage Branch gradually took place until the mid-1990s, when the Heritage Branch owned and managed thirty sites. Of these, thirteen were operated as historic sites for public visitation, most on a seasonal basis. Other sites, mostly archeological, remained undeveloped and did not encourage visitation.

Throughout the late 1980s and 1990s, the government reduced funding to the Heritage Branch. Government funding for heritage seemed to rely more on the personal whims of respective ministers than on sound philosophy, according to Adams. Occasionally, special funds were established that enabled essential conservation work to take place, but generally the sites' overall funding diminished. Given these uncertain times, Adams and his colleagues at the Heritage Branch began to experiment with a variety of funding alternatives and management models that encouraged private-sector involvement with the sites.[7]

Experimenting with New Management Models

Starting in 1987, Adams said that "friends groups" or nonprofit societies were created specifically to help manage public programming and visitor services at certain sites. Day-to-day operations, collections management, and overall conservation remained a government function. Adams recalled that the nonprofit organizations were much better at getting governmental and foundation grants for programming and educational activities, although there were some Provincial grants for restoration in these years. While Provincial government still owned the sites and provided security and maintenance for the site and collection, less and less funding was available.

Since the 1970s the two largest sites, Barkerville Town and Fort Steele, had used multiple park use permits for visitor services such as restaurants, gift shops, and parking. These parks use permits that were publicly bid for five-year terms. Anyone could bid on these concessions. Permitees turned back 5 percent of their gross revenue to the government annually in exchange for the permit. Permitees at the large sites generally were small, incorporated businesses or sole proprietorships.

Heritage Branch staff initiated a new policy for the smaller sites in the mid-1990s that borrowed on the concept of the park use permits. Instead of issuing multiple permits at a site, only one permitee would be involved in programming, tours, and visitor services. The provincial government would retain ownership and continue to be responsible for buildings, security, and collections management. Park use permits would be issued to third parties for five years. At the smaller sites, permits were issued to a variety of entities including Indian tribes, school districts, nonprofits, or sole proprietors to provide visitor services.

This system was considered successful, according to Adams, because it "got government out of providing specific services to the public while opening these services to private businesses to be run as businesses. Operators got minimal day-to-day direction from government while opening these services to private businesses or nonprofits."[8] However, by the late 1990s, the province's funding had been reduced to such an extent that more and more was being expected of the permitees. Successful permitees were those who learned how to manage their budgets and operate in a businesslike manner.[9]

The park use permits at the smaller sites demonstrated that enterprising parties, whether sole proprietors, nonprofits or others, could successfully operate a site, according to Adams. Though a modest income could be earned under a park use permit, the most successful ones relied on the personal dedication and lifestyle choices of the permitees.[10]

EMILY CARR HOUSE, VICTORIA, BRITISH COLUMBIA, CANADA

Typical of the sites that the Heritage Branch managed is the Emily Carr House, a handsome Gothic Revival home on a residential street about four blocks from the Inner Harbour of Victoria, behind the Parliament building and Government Centre. This site has been managed for over eight years by Jan Ross and her husband Michael. The couple was attracted to the Emily Carr House because Carr was a well-loved Canadian artist and writer active at the turn of the nineteenth century. The

Carr house, saved from the wrecker's ball in 1967, had been restored over thirty years by the Branch, and was bid out for private management in 1996 under a park use permit.

Unlike most of the park use permit operators, Jan Ross has an extensive education and background in conservation and museum programming, having worked at virtually all of the Victoria area museums and historic sites as an employee or contractor over the years.[11]

Ross and her family reside in the caretaker's apartment on the second floor and open the site daily from 9 a.m. to 5 p.m. for visitors during the summer tourist season and again throughout December for holiday events. As a park use permit operator, the Rosses manage the site as a historic house museum, but still had access to Branch contractors for help with curatorial and conservation concerns, and other Branch staff including landscapers, plumbers, and architects. The Branch paid for heat, light, security services, and ongoing and routine maintenance.

The permitees could charge fees for admission or other programming at the site based on Heritage Branch guidelines. They could also determine whether they would be open beyond the minimum hours specified in their five-year permit agreement.

Figure 12.1   Emily Carr House, Victoria, British Columbia, Canada

Devolution Begins

In May 2001 the Liberal party made a clean sweep in the election. When the Ministry, through the Core Review process, made the decision to devolve all the historic sites within three years, Branch staff was told there was no recourse. The government wanted communities, through nonprofit organizations or the private sector, to assume responsibility for managing all the historic sites owned by the province.

Hunter and Adams were given the responsibility to carry through on this task with little specific direction. Adams did a thorough search in Canada, the United States, and elsewhere, looking for models he could use for devolving the sites to private management. Finding little of relevance, he concluded that "we had to make it up as we went along."

First among the tasks that Hunter and Adams undertook was ranking the sites based on their story to tell, physical condition, and location. The small historic sites, four of which are located in and around Victoria, the provincial capital, were deemed the easiest to manage, so these would be the first sites to be devolved.

In March 2002, just as plans were being formulated to devolve the historic sites, George Abbot, then Minister of Community, Aboriginal and Women's Services, was asked by a legislator to explain the devolution plans during the Debates of the Legislative Assembly.

> The first thing I want to emphasize is that we are not undertaking the devolution of management of these sites to enjoy cost savings. We are undertaking the devolution of management of these sites so that we have stronger local management of the sites and better management of the sites generally than is possible with the government doing it directly. However, we do expect savings probably in the area of about 30 percent—or across the Province perhaps $2 million or $3 million in terms of those savings—but it is not the reason we're doing it. We are doing it because we believe it provides a better management regime.[12]
>
> These . . . sites are located all over British Columbia and staff find it awkward and cumbersome attempting to manage those geographically widely scattered and diverse sites from Victoria. The new model will provide for regional and local management of these resources. . . . As government operates these sites directly there are not the same opportu-

nities for flexibility and innovation in terms of management as we would have with third-party contractors.[13]

We will be building on what have been actually some very successful contractual arrangements with private-sector interests, but we are quite willing, certainly, to expand that to communities. We're happy to talk to municipalities. We're also happy to talk to nonprofits, as well as other potential private sector contractors.[14]

We are looking at the devolution of management of these sites. That means that in virtually every instance, we would not be involved in the day-to-day oversight of the facilities. Rather, we would set out the standards and parameters for the operation and management of the sites. Presumably, as in other contracts, there would be performance measures, audits, and so on, at appropriate points to ensure that the contractors were undertaking the responsibilities they contracted to undertake.[15]

Management Agreement Term

In planning for the devolution process, Hunter and Adams understood that the provincial government was not interested in selling the historic sites outright. Rather, the Ministry wanted to retain ownership of the land, buildings, and the artifact collections at the sites, and establish a long-term business arrangement with third party managers to run the sites on a day-to-day basis.[16] While a term of forty or ninety-nine years would allow the leaseholder to better finance business investments and repairs, some felt that if the manager defaulted, the government's ownership of the site would be threatened. A compromise was struck at a fifteen-year license term, because Hunter felt it was a long enough term to allow a site manager to have stability, but not long enough to create an ownership interest in the site, or allow the manager to mortgage the property.

Devolution Is Announced

For their 2002 service plan, the Ministry of Community, Aboriginal and Women's Services proposed the "devolution of management of all provincial heritage sites to nonprofit societies or local organizations (e.g., local governments, businesses, or individuals) by 2004."[17] A three-step procurement process was devised, which would take two years to find new managers and operators for its thirteen operating historic sites.[18]

The first step was the Request for Expressions of Interest (RFI) to explain the three-step process, to interest people in the possibilities, and to gain feedback. The RFI stage would be followed by a formal Request for Qualifications (RFQ) process to identify qualified bidders who would be invited to move on to the final phase, a Request for Proposals (RFP). This final phase, in which qualified teams scrutinized during the RFQ would be invited to identify which property they wished to bid on and prepare business and operational plans for the site, as specified in the RFP.

The Ministry's plan was not without controversy. The Heritage Canada Foundation, the country's largest nongovernment organization dedicated to preservation and heritage issues, passed a unanimous resolution at its September 2003 annual meeting denouncing the devolution process in British Columbia, the reduction in Heritage Branch staff, and termination of the British Columbia Heritage Trust (an agency of the Province responsible for several grant programs.)[19] The City of Victoria's Heritage Advisory Committee passed a similar resolution that they later sent to the Ministry.

Expectations for Devolution

The Ministry envisioned that there would be a variety of entities that would respond to their call for new managers of their historic sites, including individuals, couples, private businesses, nonprofit societies, First Nations (tribes), school districts, or combined entities. Proponents interested in multiple sites were welcome, but the Ministry expected most interest would be for individual sites. One nonprofit organization expressed interest in taking on all of the sites, but did not follow through the process, according to Adams. The Ministry was aiming for entities that could "meet or exceed the Ministry's current standards for heritage conservation and collections management issues for heritage structures, landscapes and artifacts in keeping with specific needs of the site."[20]

While the park use permit operators paid 5 percent of their gross revenues to the Branch, the site managers of the devolved sites would not be required to share any of their profits since the Ministry would no longer provide any services to the sites as they had before. New operators under the devolution plan would have considerable flexibility to set fees, develop and deliver interpretive and other heritage programming, and operate food service, retail sales, and other activities to meet visitor needs.

The site operators would also be able to adjust to local market conditions and maximize revenues. For the fifteen-year license term, it was hoped that the new site operators would invest in "program development, facilities and infrastructure."[21] Finally, the Heritage Branch hoped that "visitors will not see any decline in standards of conservation, and will be satisfied with the quality of services they receive at the sites."[22]

Request for Expressions of Interest

The RFI was issued in late May 2002, with a response date a month later. The RFI would be the first opportunity for the Branch staff to hear concerns and comments from the public about their plans to devolve the thirteen operating sites to private operators. The Branch conducted six public meetings in one week at hotels close to the historic sites to be devolved. Attendance varied but overall was good, and consisted of prospective bidders as well as groups concerned about the future of these sites.

"There was a lot of misinformation, all throughout the process, lots of concerns that the historic integrity of the site would be lost or compromised," noted Hunter. "We tried to set it right during these meetings."[23] The meetings were meant to provide information, but mostly they were used to "vent steam over the government's decision to devolve the properties" said Adams. "These meetings were really fact finding, and to identify what people thought about the devolution process," he said. "We learned a lot about what people were concerned about, and responded to those issues in the RFQ document."[24]

The six public meetings were designed to inform the marketplace that "BC Heritage proposes to develop a new model for managing provincial heritage properties in which the nonprofit and private sectors would assume responsibility as the front-line managers and operators, with government making a reduced or no financial contribution to operating, facility maintenance and curatorial costs, depending on proposals and site needs."[25] Meeting attendees heard that the Branch

would undergo a personnel reduction, thus reducing "the current curatorial, programming, and operational, facility maintenance, facility replacement, administrative and supervisory costs."[26] The Heritage
Branch staff would be reduced from fifty-five to ten people.[27]

The meetings were exploratory in that the Branch was seeking ideas
about how to shape the final model and the content of the subsequent
RFQ and RFP processes. The Branch explained that it wanted the sites
to remain open, but that the final choice of operating schedules would
be the sole responsibility of the new managers. The Branch hoped the
meetings would help proponents to "identify revenue generating opportunities and investments in new or additional facilities and services
that are in keeping with the heritage character of the site."[28] The
Branch, in return, would offer a long-term management agreement that
would allow greater operating freedoms and "more reliance on self-
monitoring of standards."[29] Third party evaluators, "secret shoppers,"
visitor satisfaction cards, and an annual onsite evaluation by Branch
staff would suffice for monitoring.

The RFI process created a list of potential bidders useful for the development of teams for later phases of the devolution process. An informal "dating service" was created, said Hunter, meaning that the Branch
staff would provide names of potential bidders with skills in particular
areas when requested by potential bidders trying to fill out their team.

However, the overall effort, driven by longtime Heritage Branch
staff member Adams, was to ensure that the historic resources were
protected. In fact, the guiding principles of the RFI stated upfront that
"protect[ing] heritage values and integrity in the areas of stewardship
and presentation" was critical to the overall success of the venture[30]

In the RFI, the Ministry acknowledged that the most recent operational
model of park use permits for its historic sites gave "considerable responsibility to nongovernment service providers (e.g., nonprofit societies, private businesses, and First Nations) under permits for the provision of visitor and public programs, retail sales, and food services." They
noted that, "Ministry staff retains overall management responsibilities for
site activities and specific responsibilities for land, buildings and historical collections, including capital maintenance, cataloguing artifacts,
conservation, security and grounds development and care" under the
park use permit system.[31] This would not be the case under devolution.

An RFI submission was voluntary and not a prerequisite for submitting a proposal under the RFQ process anticipated to follow. A survey form was included with the RFI that asked pointed questions about the devolution process, allowing the public to directly respond in writing about their concerns. Some of the questions dealt with the specifics of the RFP, such as: Do you plan to submit? Are you interested in one or more sites? Is a fifteen-year license too long or short for your needs?

Other questions dealt with what level of support from the Heritage Branch would be needed to best meet the needs of a site operator. The survey asked how the Branch should allocate any money if available (for example, to collections management, overhead, or major capital repairs at the sites). Branch staff wanted to know if there were potential revenue generating activities that would require changing existing regulations, including zoning, and would the proponent be willing to undertake those changes without assistance from the Heritage Branch? Finally, "Please provide brief comments on any other aspects of the process you want to bring to our attention."[32] Many potential bidders responded to the questions, and this helped shape elements of the next two phases of the procurement process. Seventy teams responded to the RFI phase.[33]

Request for Qualifications

The next stage, the RFQ, was designed to create a list of qualified bidders who would be invited to submit in the final stage of the process, the Request for Proposals (RFP). Prospective bidders were given six weeks to create a team to respond to the Ministry's interest in qualifications of interested parties.

The RFQ as a formal procurement opportunity set out the overarching issues for the eventual fifteen-year management agreement that would be granted to the successful team. Chief among the concerns was "protecting heritage values and integrity in the areas of stewardship, heritage conservation and presentation."[34] Also critical would be "maintaining and increasing heritage programming and heritage tourism opportunities for heritage site visitors that are self-sustaining with little or no subsidy from the provincial government."[35]

Bidders would be evaluated on three criteria: mandatory criteria (did they file the forms correctly and on time?), heritage values criteria, and

desirable criteria. Heritage values criteria included the team's understanding of "the appropriate values of conservation, respect for heritage, and sustainability of the collections."[36] Potential site operators
had to discuss their understanding of heritage conservation as it related
to ethical standards, stewardship and conservation, preservation versus
presentation, human resources, organization and management.

Desirable criteria in the RFQ were primarily the qualifications of the
individual team members, including skills in curating, facilities maintenance, programming, management, and finance.

According to the RFQ, the Ministry was seeking site managers "who
can maximize the opportunities and minimize or mitigate the constraints in order to achieve sustainable site operations that maintain or
increase heritage values."[37] In 1,000 words or less, the proponent identified how their experience and skills would allow them to achieve a
quality and sustainable heritage site operation.

Categorizing the BC Historic Sites

The sites being devolved were divided into categories (A, B, C) based
on the size of the collection, annual visitation, budget, and current staffing.
A single, stand-alone, small house museum like the Emily Carr House
was placed in the "A" category. Respondents were asked to describe their
experience and skills at small historic sites with up to 5,000 artifacts and
attendant collections management operations. Skills were sought in facilities maintenance for up to three wood frame structures on a small site, including gardens, restoration, and maintenance. Bidders would be hosting
visitors in the 10,000 range and planning special events for 200 people.
Bidders described their skills and experience with small sites that had a
maximum of three staff members, and cash flow management with potential seasonal shortfalls of $10,000 yearly and budgets to $100,000.[38]

Medium-sized sites (category B) like Point Ellice House, were those
with collections of up to 20,000 objects needing curatorial management. These sites had up to 30,000 annual visitors, hosted events with
up to 500 people, and had formal marketing plans. These sites had up
to ten wood frame structures needing cyclical maintenance, stabilization, or restoration. Bidders were asked about their experience with water lines and parking lots. Managers would need to oversee up to twelve

contractors, undertake grant writing and fundraising for up to $10,000, cope with seasonal cash flow shortages of up to $50,000, and finally, manage budgets up to $500,000.[39]

The two largest sites, Fort Steele and Barkerville Town, were the crown jewels of the historic sites owned by the Province.[40] As such, they posed much more complex issues, as these sites are sophisticated operations with many components. These two sites comprised category C.

For teams interested in the two largest sites, proponents were asked to describe their experience and skills with sites with more than 20,000 artifacts in more than sixty log or wood-frame structures needing fire protection, as well as maintenance, security, restoration, and stabilization. These sites had more than 75,000 visitors yearly, and hosted events up to 1,000 people, bus tours, and year-round interpretation to schools. They supported ancillary businesses, including heritage-themed food service, gift shops, and carriage rides, and they needed sophisticated marketing plans. Managers could expect summer staff of 100 people, including a unionized staff of fifteen, budgets of up to $1 million, and seasonal cash-flow shortages of $150,000. Ideas about managing and developing land and other resources to complement historical themes and contribute to financial sustainability were requested.[41]

The legal structure of the team did not have to be finalized prior to making a submission under the final phase, the RFP. However, the Ministry wanted to know the roles and responsibilities of each key team member in the internal structure of the team.

"Some people we felt might be good candidates decided not to submit, either because they felt that there might be too much red tape and bureaucracy or just too much work to get the property they wanted," noted Adams. "Others were still boycotting the proposal process, thinking it would go away." In the end, there were twenty-three teams that were qualified based on review of their credentials, said Adams.[42] "Because devolution was a new concept, there was a low response to the RFP initially. But one by one, capable people responded,"[43]Adams said.

Making Infrastructure Improvements

"Before the province issued the RFP, it decided that it had to put the sites in good physical condition," said Hunter. New roofs, handicapped bathrooms, and other repairs were made at the sites. "The province had limited resources to do this work, but it did the most important and expensive things first," she added. The sites developed a wish list of projects to be accomplished. "Two and a half million dollars were allocated in 2001 and 2002 to address major infrastructure needs," said Hunter.[44]

Request for Proposals Phase

The final stage in this three-phase procurement process was the (RFP). Teams that submitted during the RFQ, and were judged as being well qualified to operate a specific-size historic site (categories A, B or C), were invited to submit during this phase.

The RFP process began first with the small, or category A, sites, including Emily Carr House, Craigflower Manor, Haig-Brown House, Kilby Store and Farm, and Historic Yale. Each RFP was tailored to the unique needs of that individual site. The proposal period allowed each team to undertake its own due diligence and attend a mandatory walk-through. The walk-through was the only occasion where a potential bidder could learn who were their potential rivals for the site.

After learning that they were qualified for a category A property in the RFQ phase, the Rosses were invited to submit a proposal in the RFP phase for any category A property. They decided to bid only on the Carr House.

Recalling that period, Jan Ross said, "We circled the wagons and started a successful process to lobby for the job. We wanted to show that we had community support during the eight years we ran the Carr House under a park use permit. We included thirty letters of recommendation in our packet of materials submitted with the RFP. We got good media attention, print media mostly, talking about the devolution process and saying it was genuine and fair. We were trying to make it hard to say no to our proposal,"[45] added Ross.

For Ross and her husband, the decision to submit a proposal for a fifteen-year license to operate the Emily Carr House was not a foregone conclusion. Assuming the entire financial burden for the site, including paying for heat, light, pest control, security, gardening, and day-to-day maintenance was "a tough call," said Ross. "In the end, we decided to bid because we were fortunate. We knew the house, and knew exactly what we were getting into," said Ross. "There was a potential downside, because the Heritage Branch during our earlier two contracts had provided heat, light, gas, some exterior maintenance, and pest control, among other things. Under the devolution policy, the Ministry would provide no subsidies. Having a good business plan was critical. We spent a long time deciding whether to bid or not, but because it was a fifteen-year term, we could spread our risk out over that period of time."[46]

Ross continued, "Before the devolution process, we got lots of support. . . . There was staff at the Branch that could provide technical support. There was a full-time curator, and someone who was a specialist in visitor services, also people with good marketing and planning backgrounds, and someone who knew about security, so there was always someone you go could go to with a question," she added.[47] Under the devolution scheme, most of these positions at the Heritage Branch were eliminated by attrition, retirement, or through personnel reductions.

Ross and her husband developed a budget during this due-diligence period, and looked both at operating and capital costs for the Emily Carr House and "all the hidden costs we could think up: pest control, security, water, conservation costs for objects, and maintaining a website," she said. The RFP required that "we crunch numbers. There were several points along the way where we felt that we just could not do it. We just had to take a leap of faith with our eyes wide open, and hope that the contingencies we identified in our budget would work out," said Ross. The Carr House proposal ended up being about 100 pages, and "preparing the document had serious time and cost factors. It took a lot of time to prepare it," said Ross.

According to Hunter, "when the RFP closed, the proposals were submitted in two separate envelopes. The specific plan describing how the team would maintain, program, and administer the site was in one envelope. The second envelope contained their financial and business plan information. The second envelope was not opened unless the team could pass on the first one. The reason the province did it this way was because they wanted to be sure that the preservation mission and heritage values were driving the process, not money," said Hunter.[48]

After learning that their proposal was accepted, the Rosses entered into active negotiations on the Heritage Site Management Agreement with the Province, which ended up taking several months.[49] Hunter noted, "the negotiations with the successful proponent led to many changes in the Heritage Site Management Agreement (the fifteen-year license agreement), so no one ended up with exactly what they wanted."[50] Ross said, "It took about two or three months to finish a contract we could both agree to." The Rosses signed just before the tourist season began in April 2002.

Since then, September 11th and the SARS epidemic have cut into tourism revenues throughout Canada, according to Ross. Visitation at the Emily Carr House, which hovered at about 10,000 per year, has been down significantly. "[With SARS] 2003 was the worst year," said Ross. "We had about 7,000 visitors that year, and 2004 has not been that much better."[51]

Ross said, "The site is meeting its income expectations and there have been no big surprises. We are now considering other uses of the house to build the business. I am working with an MBA candidate at a local business school to develop a business plan to host small meetings and conferences at the Carr House and other sites in the Victoria area. The idea is develop the site for small meetings, especially on the off-season, and market the facility to book clubs, board meetings, showers, teas, and the like. Right now, we can have seventy people for a cocktail party, and thirty people for a board meeting, according to the fire code."[52]

The willingness by site managers to be open to multiple, complementary uses for the site, while maintaining public access and collections care, is exactly what the provincial government had hoped, according to Hunter. "The funding sources that the Province provided were like a meal, and it was getting smaller and smaller and dinner was a struggle to serve. What was needed was a way to build a buffet, to have multiple revenue streams for the sites," she said.

Jan Ross summarized her philosophy about being a site manager: "We realized that after the end of the fifteen-year term, the building still belongs to the people of British Columbia, and it is still owned by government. We want to be good stewards so that many people in the future would be interested in being site managers for the Emily Carr House."

POINT ELLICE HOUSE, VICTORIA, BRITISH COLUMBIA, CANADA

Point Ellice House, a verdant oasis on the waterfront on the Gorge waterway in Victoria, is in the middle of an industrial district with scrap yards and a cement factory on either side. The lush gardens and forested buffers screen out much of the surroundings. This rambling Italianate home and gardens has a superb and extensive collection of Victoriana from the O'Reilly's, one of Victoria's prominent upper-middle-class families.

For Point Ellice, the RFP process had different results. The Branch identified a qualified bidder with a history of involvement with the site during the RFQ phase, and invited that team to submit a proposal to operate the site. After several months of negotiating the terms of the Historic Site Management Agreement, the two parties could not agree and the Branch decided to reissue the RFP in November 2003. As that was unsuccessful, it was reissued again in January 2004.

After seeing a column in a local newspaper in January 2004 about the third request for submissions, the Capital Mental Health Association decided to "throw their hat into the ring."[53] This well-respected, nearly fifty-year-old mental health organization was interested in using the site to:

> Provide vocational training and a life skills center to assist persons with special needs to be more employable. The other complementary but different

Figure 12.2   Point Ellice House, Victoria, British Columbia, Canada

reason was to maintain and restore the house and grounds to enhance the enjoyment and education of visitors to the site. We believe that Point Ellice is a magical place. It needs a lot of continuing work, to build on the efforts of the many persons in the past who have worked so hard to preserve it for the people of the province. From a practical point of view, the more visitors enjoy their experience there, the more customers there will be in the future, so that our clients can have a positive learning experience and the site can produce more revenue, ensuring continuing financial sustainability.[54]

Gail Simpson of Capital Mental Health Association felt that operating the historic site would expose the organization to a new group of potential donors, and help demystify mental illness. The organization offers tours of the site and its gardens during the tourist season, operates a small gift shop, and has a tented area on the lawn where traditional cream teas are served by a mix of association clients and hired waiters. A part-time curator is on staff to manage and clean the vast collection.

Unlike the Emily Carr House, where the successful bidder had prior experience at the site, the Capital Mental Health Association did not have an ongoing relationship, and had to take the information available from the Heritage Branch about the site's financial viability at face value. Gail Simpson said, "At the walk-through, the figure was mentioned that in the past few years the gross revenue had averaged $120,000. We knew that the Branch paid much of the ongoing costs pre-devolution, and that would no longer be the case. But we thought, as we were planning to carry out the same activities (gift shop, teas, and tours) that the permitee had done, our gross hospitality income should likely be the same."[55] Simpson added, "Our gross revenue for the first year was $77,000, exclusive of subsidy. The $40,000 the Heritage Branch is allocating yearly for five years is what carried us this year."[56]

According to Simpson, being involved with Point Ellice is a "great opportunity for us to develop new partnerships and allies." The mental health association is considering complementary programming for the site to boost attendance, which last calendar year was 6,000. "Being involved with Point Ellice has been a positive thing for our organization, even though we did not make money or break even this year as hoped. Our 2005 year will be better, given that we have learned so much this first season."[57]

Reflections on the Devolution Process

For Rhonda Hunter, it was critical that the whole devolution process be "fair, diligent and transparent, could survive independent scrutiny, and that no one had the inside track. This was a very conservative process. We had to demonstrate integrity. The criteria were published and there were plenty of meetings. If there was a question, everyone got the answer. We only had one chance. It took longer than we anticipated, but we wanted to do it right. All we had to do was play it straight up."[58]

Hunter continued, "We said no to nothing, and were open to everything" that the bidders proposed. "There was never an idea that was too innovative as long as heritage values were maintained. Nothing was too bold. Rather, we found that the many of the proposals were too conservative. Key to us was artifact management, restoration and public programming,"[59] she added. Adams also noted that some of the operators are more conservative in their interpretation and exhibitions than when the sites were managed by government. Most of the interactive and hands-on displays have been removed, he said, and now most sites have static exhibits.[60]

It has only been two seasons since the bulk of the smaller sites were transferred to private management, so an overall assessment is still a bit premature. However, Adams says, some are doing well.

A wide variety of entities now manage the thirteen former provincial heritage sites. A private company operates the Grist Mill. Several nonprofit Friends groups were successful in bidding on Fort Steele, Historic Hat Creek, and Historic Yale. The province-wide Land Conservancy is operating Craigflower Manor and its adjacent schoolhouse.

The local school district is operating Cottonwood House, as a "secondary school Academy of Travel and Tourism where students receive a wide variety of training in the area of heritage interpretation, provide tours, and demonstrations of historic food preparation and farming techniques. Students also are trained in retail and restaurant service and care of artifacts."[61] The Royal British Columbia Museum operates Helmcken House. An Indian Tribal council long associated with the Xa:ytem Longhouse site is its manager.

Because of its complexity and the last-minute decision by the local government of Wells to remove its bid, the Ministry has started a new management organization to manage Barkerville Town.

Hunter feels that the greatest benefit of the devolution process has been the partnerships that were created. "Each team did not do it alone; the process had to benefit both the government and the heritage community. . . . It was important to have both someone looking out for the business side of the plan and someone looking out for the heritage side. John and I were partners in this process and it would not have been successful without both elements. We were also backed by an extremely experienced team who were outstanding in their commitment to bring this process to a successful conclusion–often at the expense of their own jobs. I am so impressed by the professionalism of people involved in this process."[62]

Patrick Frey, who took over from Rhonda Hunter at the Heritage Branch and has followed the devolved properties for the last three years, made the following observations.

Community-based management of provincial heritage properties is a positive step that places decision-making in the communities in which the historic sites are located. The Ministry continues to support initiatives that encourage greater community and private-sector investment towards the future success of the devolved properties. The Heritage Branch is working with the site managers and other parties to provide training opportunities and professional advice to building the stewardship and management capacities of the community-based site managers.

Several of the devolved sites have made significant progress in introducing new initiatives to increase revenue and visitation, but all of the sites have challenges (primarily financial) to their operational sustainability that need to be addressed in the coming years if devolution is to be effective over the long term. Worldwide, traditional historical attractions and museums have been suffering from stagnant or declining visitation even though heritage and cultural tourism has been growing and, in some cases, in spite of fairly aggressive marketing initiatives.

Two of the original site managers (Kilby and Keremeos Grist Mill) have terminated their site management agreements and the Heritage Branch is working to negotiate alternative approaches that will ensure the continuation of community-based management of these sites. In

April 2005, management of Barkerville Historic Town was successfully devolved to the Barkerville Heritage Trust, a nonprofit organization with broad–based regional participation on its Board.[63]

How to Use This Case Study

The staff of the Heritage Branch, faced with devolving all of their historic sites to the private sector, drew on successes they had pioneered over the years to make the change required by the new government in power. Realizing that they had successes with short-term relationships with outside contractors, they decided to build upon and expand these relationships. The experience of the Heritage Branch in managing the fifteen-year licenses has been good, but not an unqualified success. Most of the licensees are struggling, but others who have responded to the financial pressures of operating a seasonal historic site have developed some creative solutions.

According to Frey, "the long term success of devolution hinges not only on focused Provincial investment towards the conservation of the heritage resources and providing professional advice that helps build the stewardship capacity of site managers, but also on encouraging creativity in programming and sound business practices. All of these factors will be essential elements of management sustainability for the heritage properties."[64]

FAIRMOUNT PARK HISTORIC PRESERVATION TRUST, PHILADELPHIA, PENNSYLVANIA

Right after the War of 1812, civic-minded citizens in Philadelphia began buying up land on either side of the Schuylkill River to protect what was then the city's drinking water from industrial pollution.[65] The riverbanks contained many eighteenth- and nineteenth-century country estates with superb historic buildings that lined the cliffs overlooking the river.

Eventually, these properties were transferred to the City of Philadelphia's parks department when it was formally established in 1867. Throughout the history of the Fairmount Park, these handsome houses were used as restaurants, staff housing, and other compatible uses. However, by the 1980s, many of these sites were abandoned, deteriorated, or open to the weather.

Several Philadelphia-area foundations joined together to encourage the City of Philadelphia to consider adaptive use ideas for ten vacant but salvageable "park houses" as they were known.[66] A project was started in 1987 to identify new use ideas and solicit proposals, but the city, by law, could not offer anything longer than a four-year lease term for any real estate it owned. This undermined any reuse effort because the lease was not long enough for an investor to recoup restoration costs.

New legislation was needed to provide a longer lease term to allow potential tenants to amortize rehabilitation costs over a longer period. After much debate, and a change in administration, a thirty-year term was finally accepted. The initial premise was that a nonprofit management entity would support the properties by development and management fees. After several years, this notion was abandoned as the nonprofit had made little headway toward charging development fees.[67]

In 1992, the Fairmount Park Historic Preservation Trust (FPHPT) was established by City of Philadelphia ordinance to undertake the development and management of historic resources in the park under a thirty-year master lease.[68] The master lease required a limited amount of public access for the leased properties. In turn, the FPHPT marketed the vacant and underused historic properties to users and investors who would lease and restore them for any compatible use.

The park houses could not be rented to tenants as homes. Thirteen of the historic resources in the park are managed by nonprofit "friends" organizations and the Trust provides fee-for-service conservation consulting services to these organizations. With the change in legislation, the Trust was successful in finding users for more than twenty properties. Users range from an architectural office, Masonic lodge, art school, professional association, and health care providers.[69]

How to Use This Case

Here, the Fairmount Park Historic Preservation Trust cast a wide net to find new users for the historic properties under their management.

The master lease did not permit them to offer properties to individuals—despite that fact that many families were very willing to take on a park house if permitted. The staff went to great effort to match the organization to the house, understanding the maintenance and restoration needs of each. They matched these needs with the financial capacity of the potential lessor.

The staff also worked closely with the community, trying to find a potential tenant for a park house that would be a neighborhood benefit or anchor. In all cases, the private market played some part in the match between house and tenant. Homes in poor condition had few potential tenants. Homes in habitable condition had more prospects.

NOTES

1. I am grateful to both Rhonda Hunter and John Adams for sharing their views and experiences as leaders of the BC Heritage Devolution process. Rhonda Hunter, interview by author, typed manuscript, Victoria, BC, 8 November 2004. The agency's title changed in June 2005 to the Ministry of Tourism, Sport, and the Arts. I am grateful to Patrick Frey for reviewing this case and making suggestions. Patrick Frey, e-mail message to author, 31 August 2006.

2. "New Era Review, Three Years of Action, New Era Promises Made and Kept," updated November 2004, available at www.gov.bc.ca/bvprd/bc/content.do?brwId=@235G1%7C0YQtuW&navId=NAV_ID_province&crumb=B.C.+Home&crumburl=/home.do (accessed 12 November 2004). Rhonda Hunter, e-mail correspondence to author, 21 December 2004.

3. "New Era Review." The agency is now called the Ministry of Tourism, Sport, and the Arts.

4. John Adams, recently retired as the manager of the devolution process for the Heritage Branch, provided this capsule history of the acquisition of the Province of British Columbia's historic sites during a telephone interview with the author. John Adams, interview by author, typed manuscript of telephone interview, Victoria, BC, 14 September 2004.

5. Frey e-mail.

6. Basic information about the British Columbia historic sites can be found on the British Columbia Heritage Branch website www.tsa.gov.bc.ca/heritage_branch/index.htm (accessed 21 December 2004).

7. John Adams, e-mail correspondence to author, 3 January 2005.

8. Adams e-mail, 3 January 2005.

9. Adams interview, 14 September 2004.

10. Adams interview, 14 September 2004.

11. I am grateful to Jan Ross for sharing information about her experiences as a Park Use Permitee and now a site manager for the Emily Carr House. Jan Ross, interview by author, typed manuscript, Victoria, BC, 8 November 2004.

12. Canada, Official Report of the Debates of the British Columbia Legislative Assembly, 2002 Legislative Session, 3rd Session, 37 Parliament, Hansard, Wednesday 27 March 2002, Afternoon Sitting, volume 5, number 1, page 2191, as found at www.legis.gov.bc.ca/hansard/37th3rd/h20327p.html (accessed 21 December 2004).

13. Debates, 2192.

14. Debates, 2189.

15. Debates, 2191.

16. Hunter, e-mail correspondence, 21 December 2004.

17. Ministry of Community, Aboriginal and Women's Services, Request for Expressions of Interest, dated 24 May 2002, 2. The Ministry is now called the Ministry of Tourism, Sport, and the Arts.

18. The other seventeen sites that the Branch managed had no programming, minimal interpretation or signage, and were held by government primarily to protect the resource. These non-operating sites would be devolved in a separate process.

19. Minutes of City of Victoria Heritage Advisory Committee, 23 September 2003, 5, available at www.city.victoria.bc.ca/cityhall/minutes_boards/min030923_heritage;pdf#xml=http. Frey e-mail.

20. RFI, 6.

21. RFI, 5.

22. RFI, 6.

23. Hunter interview, 8 November 2004.

24. Adams interview, 9 November 2004.

25. RFI, 2.

26. RFI, 2.

27. Hunter, e-mail correspondence, 21 December 2004.

28. RFI, 3.

29. RFI, 4.

30. RFI, 4.

31. RFI, 4.

32. RFI, 10.

33. Adams interview, 9 November 2004.

34. RFI, 10.

35. Ministry of Community, Aboriginal and Women's Services, Managing and Operating Provincial Heritage Sites in British Columbia, Request for Qualifications, no.133023, issued by BC Purchasing Commission, 30 July 2002.

36. RFQ, 14.

37. RFQ, 15.

38. RFQ, 15–16.

39. RFQ, 16–18.

40. Frey e-mail.

41. RFQ, 19–20.

42. Adams interview, 9 November 2004; Hunter e-mail correspondence, 21 December 2004.

43. Adams interview, 14 September 2004.

44. Hunter interview, 8 November 2004; Hunter e-mail correspondence, 21 December 2004

45. Ross interview, 9 November 2004.

46. Ross interview.

47. Ross interview.

48. Hunter interview, 8 November 2004; Hunter e-mail correspondence, 21 December 2004.

49. Ministry of Community, Aboriginal and Women's Services, draft Heritage Site Management Agreement, Emily Carr House, no date. Also see Ministry of Community, Aboriginal and Women's Services, Guidelines and Principles for Preparing Heritage Site Management Agreements, no date.

50. Management Agreement, Emily Carr House.

51. Ross interview.

52. Ross interview.

53. I am grateful to Gail Simpson, former Executive Director of the Capital Mental Health Association for sharing her experiences. Ms. Simpson is now retired and serving as the volunteer site manager at Point Ellice. Tina Lowery, the part time curator, also provided useful insight about the operations of Point Ellice. Gail Simpson, e-mail correspondence to author, 3 January 2005. Gail Simpson, e-mail correspondence to author, 18 October 2006.

54. Capital Mental Health Association, "Request for Proposals, Managing and Operating Point Ellice House," 13 February 2004; Simpson e-mail correspondence, 3 January 2005.

55. Simpson e-mail, 3 January 2005.

56. Gail Simpson, interview by author, typed manuscript, Victoria, BC, 8 November 2004; Simpson, e-mail correspondence, 3 January 2005. Point Ellice will receive a grant of $40,000 a year for five years from the Heritage Branch

as part of its transition to a new site manager. Three other sites are also receiving annual appropriations: Barkerville Town, Fort Steele, and the Grist Mill.

57. Simpson interview, 8 November 2004; Simpson e-mail correspondence, 3 January 2005.

58. Hunter interview, 8 November 2004.

59. Hunter e-mail correspondence, 21 December 2004.

60. Adams interview, 14 September 2004.

61. Secondary Tourism Educator's Group, "Cottonwood House Historic Site," available at www.steg.ca/ (accessed 20 November 2004).

62. Hunter, e-mail correspondence, 21 December 2004.

63. Patrick Frey, e-mail correspondence with author, 31 August 2006 and 11 September 2006.

64. Patrick Frey, e-mail message to author, 11 September 2006.

65. Hosmer, *Presence of the Past,* 77.

66. John Carr, interview with author, 26 June 2003.

67. The author was personally involved in the startup of the Park House Project while working as Vice President for Program Development at the Philadelphia Historic Preservation Corporation. Also see "Philly Park Group to Restore Neglected Manors." *Associated Press* 25 November 2005 as found at www.abclocal.com/wpvi/story?section=local&id=3667047.html.

68. Fairmount Park Historic Preservation Trust website, www.fairmount-parktrust.org/ (accessed 20 June 2003). Carr interview. Also see Master Lease Agreement By and Between The City of Philadel-phia (Acting through the Fairmount Park Commission) and Philadelphia Industrial Development Authority, Execution Copy 10 August 1993.

69. Carr interview.

CHAPTER 13

Case Studies:
Sale to a Private Owner with Easements

ELFRETH'S ALLEY ASSOCIATION, PHILADELPHIA, PENNSYLVANIA

As the fourth professional director of the Elfreth's Alley Association (EAA), Robert Vosburgh started his new job in December 2004 by looking backwards. Vosburgh, an attorney by training and a museum professional by vocation, started his tenure at the historic house museum organization by reading the minutes of the meetings of the Elfreth's Alley Association board of directors since the organization's inception.

Vosburgh was fortunate that the EAA has kept good records throughout much of its seventy-one-year history and that a recent grant from the Pennsylvania Historical and Museum Commission allowed the EAA to organize and house its papers in a proper archive.[1] Vosburgh learned through his tour of almost three generations of preservation activity that "the Elfreth's Alley Association has been at various times a lessee, lessor, purchaser and seller of several properties" along the Alley.[2]

Vosburgh came to Elfreth's Alley after working as a planned giving officer at a much larger art museum and school in Philadelphia, and was seeking an opportunity to manage a cultural organization that was poised for greater things. Elfreth's Alley Association was in the midst of a real estate transaction where the organization would receive, through donation, two parcels of land on the alley: 128 Elfreth's Alley, the only noncontributing property in the National Historic Landmark district but dating from 1868, and the so-called Flagpole Lot, a 4,455 square-foot parcel at the west end of the alley adjacent to Second Street that has long been privately owned but used as open space.[3] This donation brought to the fore issues raised countless times during the history of the EAA about the substance of the mission of the organization and its property stewardship responsibilities.

Alley History

Elfreth's Alley, located in Old City Philadelphia, is a rare eighteenth-century survivor, a tiny street of just thirty-one homes amidst what was once a largely industrial neighborhood. Throughout its history, the EAA has been a driving force in its neighborhood for the preservation of the buildings along the alley. One of the earliest National Historic Landmarks—designated in 1960—the site is marketed today by the EAA as "our nation's oldest residential street."[4]

The Alley was originally a cartway through one of William Penn's great blocks in his "Greene Countrie Towne." The thirty-one surviving homes on Elfreth's Alley date from circa 1724–1836. "The Alley's history begins in 1702 when it was a cartway for bringing goods from the docks along the Delaware River. By the mid-eighteenth century, Jeremiah Elfreth, the Alley's namesake and a blacksmith along Second Street, was one of the Alley's largest property owners. As such, he rented many of the homes to sea captains, shipwrights, and colonial artisans, including pewter smiths and furniture makers."[5] The houses are all modest, two- and three-story working-class rowhouses made of brick with wooden shutters and cellar doors in front of the house to access the basement. Bladen's Court, a small alleyway at the east end, contains three homes from the early nineteenth century and is part of the National Historic Landmark district.

Most of the street's small houses were built by speculators and rented out or used as boarding houses, according to records collected by EAA historians. As the Philadelphia port declined in the early nineteenth century, skilled artisans moved in. These craftspeople lived upstairs, worked in their backyards and sold their wares out the front door. A recent history of the Alley noted that "in the nineteenth century, the Alley also had numerous cottage industries, with a commercial bake shop, grocery store and tavern operating out of the homes. Alley houses had a tenement quality in the late nineteenth and early twentieth century, as immigrants from all over the world moved to Philadelphia and lived with extended family and boarders."[6]

According to census records collected over the years about alley residents, "In 1910, a Russian Jewish widow, Annie Bick, lived in No. 116 with her seven children, two stepchildren and a boarder, and supported her family as a dressmaker. The 1930 census has revealed that Robert Morton, an African-American factory worker, lived in No. 135 with his wife and daughter."[7]

The Old City neighborhood of Philadelphia, where Elfreth's Alley is located, had "evolved into a manufacturing center in the nineteenth and early twentieth centuries and as a result Elfreth's Alley was an island of residential properties surrounded by warehouses, showrooms, and factories.[8] By the early twentieth century, the alley was described by contemporary newspapers as a 'slum.'" [9] The industrial neighborhood that surrounded the Alley suffered economic decline as the manufacturing base that made Philadelphia once the "workshop of the world" began to erode significantly. Many of the homes on Elfreth's Alley were unoccupied and had fallen into disrepair by the 1930s.

The Founding of the EAA

Early Elfreth's Alley Association publications credit Mrs. Dolly W. Ottey as the EAA's founder.[10] Mrs. Ottey operated a small restaurant, the Hearthstone, at No. 115. It was there "on a cold and rainy evening of March 28, 1934, that she gathered the residents of the street" to form the EAA.[11] For several years, the EAA sponsored an "At Home" event with tours of the homes with an admission fee of ten cents. Advertising posters show that by 1937 this event had evolved into the "Pageant of Elfreth's Alley," a two-day event, which included a full-scale theatrical production of the "Windows of Old Philadelphia."[12] These early efforts were aimed at increasing public recognition of Elfreth's Alley as a historic treasure of Philadelphia, worthy of preservation.

According to the EAA archives, "Although spearheaded by residents, records indicate that concerned individuals from throughout the city were assisting in the preservation efforts of the Association. A 1942 membership list, the earliest found in the Archives, records 143 members, of which 108 were nonresidents."[13]

Figure 13.1   Nos. 124 and 126 Elfreth's Alley, the Museum Houses operated by the Elfreth's Alley Association, Philadelphia, Pennsylvania

In 1943, the Elfreth's Alley Association was officially established as a corporation in Pennsylvania. The original purpose statement for the EAA read:

The purpose for which said corporation to be founded are to enshrine Elfreth's Alley in the annals of historic Old Philadelphia; to preserve, improve and restore Elfreth's Alley; to invite Philadelphia and others interested to visit Elfreth's Alley; to examine and preserve the history of Elfreth's Alley permanently; to encourage owners and tenants of property located on the Alley to preserve the identity and original character of this historic street; or encourage and develop interest therein by the public and such other persons who many become members of the corporation.[14]

In the early years, "the Association operated with a fifteen-member board of directors and numerous volunteer committees. Funds were raised primarily through June Open House (now known as Fete Day) but also through card parties, raffles, teas, and other social events. Groups of costumed guides were trained to conduct tours and act as "hostesses" on Fete Day."[15]

Property Acquisition and Stewardship

The EAA sought to acquire by gift, lease, or purchase threatened properties to ensure that the character of the street as a whole was protected. Throughout the 1930s and 1940s they were concerned with responding to condemnation orders filed for various properties on the alley.

The first properties acquired by EAA were Nos. 1 and 2 Bladen's Court. "One day in 1948 Mrs. Florence Nyce, an active member of the EAA, saw two men walking down Bladen's Court. She followed them and found that they had come to tear down the two little houses on the east side of the court, Nos. 1 and 2. Mrs. Nyce asked if there were any way to save the houses and the owner told her that $500 by noon that day and $1500 the next morning would purchase the houses and spare them from wrecking. Public spirited citizens helped the Association meet these demands."[16] The EAA owned Nos. 1 and 2 Bladen's by 1949.[17] In addition, the EAA owned and maintained a small garden courtyard opposite these houses.[18]

The EAA continued to respond to opportunities to save buildings on the street. In 1943, the EAA signed a lease agreement for Nos. 114 and 124 with the George D. Wetherill and Co., a paint manufacturer and owner of the properties. The EAA made needed repairs to the properties and opened No. 114 as the EAA headquarters.[19] In 1949, the EAA was raising funds to make No. 114, the "Hostess" house, or headquarters, "more livable."[20]

In 1955, the EAA decided to move their headquarters to No. 124 and renovate No. 114 as a rental property. By 1956 the EAA owned Nos. 1

and 2 Bladen's Court without a mortgage, and continued to lease from Wetherill and Co. Nos. 114 and 124, which they maintained and improved despite their lack of ownership.[21] The EAA subleased No. 114.[22]

In 1957, No. 126 Elfreth's Alley was condemned by the city. It was acquired by the Philadelphia Society for the Preservation of Landmarks (Landmarks).[23] Landmarks was begun by "upper-class and upper-middle-class women. . .such as Miss Frances Anne Wister, who in the 1930s had saved her ancestral home, Grumblethorpe, and also the notable Powel House in Society Hill."[24] The effort to rescue old houses in Elfreth's Alley was one of many such efforts being undertaken in Philadelphia starting in the late nineteenth century.[25]

After renting it for five years, in 1962 the EAA purchased house No. 126 from Landmarks.[26] By 1958, the EAA shop was moved out of No. 124 and temporarily installed in the cellar of the Coach House.[27] The shop was located in the back of No. 126 in 1964, and the EAA met resident opposition when it attempted to resume shop operations in No. 124 during the summer of 1965. In 1958 the following properties were insured by the EAA: No. 1 Bladen's for $6,000, No. 2 Bladen's for $5,000, No. 114 for $5,000, and No. 124 for $2,500.[28] Although No. 126 was being leased by the EAA at this time, it doesn't seem to have been insured by the EAA.[29]

In 1964, after twenty years of repairing and managing these properties, the EAA finally purchased Nos. 114 and 124 from the paint company, and used both as rental properties.[30]

Vosburgh noted that, throughout the years "money has been raised through special events such as Fete Days and Deck the Alley, dinners, and the old Hearthstone Restaurant in the 1930s and 1940s. There was a thrift shop in the 1940s and perhaps into the 1950s. Later development efforts were more professionalized, including government and foundation grants. The shop has been around for a long time, at various [places] starting in the 1960s, not always in No. 124."[31]

By 1964 the EAA owned a total of five properties, the most it would ever own. In addition to the properties it owned, EAA "performed or facilitated exterior work on a number of other houses including Nos. 120, 122, 118, and 139."[32]

Stewardship Responsibilities

Preserving threatened properties along the alley had been the main goal of the organization since its beginnings. However, other than renting the properties to tenants, the EAA did not have a long-term plan for how these properties would be maintained, restored, or endowed. It seemed that it was enough to save the houses from destruction. The EAA's standard operating procedure during this period was the most common paradigm for the preservation movement at the time.

Charles Hosmer, the first historian of the America historic preservation movement, wrote in his 1964 book *Presence of the Past: A History of the Preservation Movement in the United States before Williamsburg* that it was rare for a local preservation organization in the early years of the movement to take a longer view of its stewardship responsibilities.

> whenever a historic building was to be saved. . .funds would have to be raised for the purchase of each property. . . .Payment of the purchase price only changed the ownership; it did not insure that the stability of the structure for years to come. Few preservationists could see beyond the glorious days when the old house was purchased, nor could they trouble themselves with the sordid, day to day maintenance problems.[33]

The EAA remained content that renting the properties would provide enough income to make basic repairs. Funds for restoration efforts were problematic, as the EAA began to consider whether it would mortgage their properties to pay for these costs. It is clear from the minutes that the Elfreth's Alley Association never began raising funds for an endowment. Hosmer described the fundamental problem with starting an endowment fundraising effort during the early years of the preservation movement.

> Within a few years of the purchase of a historic house, a preservation group usually realizes that it was necessary to campaign for some form of endowment to close the gap that existed between admission fees and running expenses . . . but campaigns for endowment funds ended in failure almost every time. First, announcing the need for an endowment to cover running expenses seemed to be an admission that a preservation organization was a failure because people were not visiting a historic building in large enough numbers to maintain it. Second the goal of an endowment

is simply a sizable sum of money, which really did not have much appeal to potential donors. In most cases, an endowment had to exceed the purchase price of a house in order to be of any use.[34]

Becoming a Historic House Museum

In the earliest days of the EAA, the Alley was promoted to visitors through special events a few times a year to bring attention to its unique collection of colonial dwellings. Having a "museum" inside one of the houses, in conjunction with the shop, would add to the visitor's experience of this authentic place.

The first discussion about a museum is in the Board Minutes of May 21, 1957. "Number 126 has been condemned...It was suggested that we lease it from the Society for the Preservation of Old Landmarks [Landmarks] for $1.00 per year with the purpose of restoring it and perhaps having a permanent museum. . . .With No. 126 as a museum, the headquarters could be rented as a dwelling."[35] The term of the lease for No. 126 was a period of twenty years commencing September 1, 1957, with the stipulation [from Landmarks] that the lessee agree that it would be converted into a museum within five years. However, EAA was free to sublease the property until such time as it became a museum.[36]

Through the assistance of George Batchelor, an architect, and Penny Hartshorne Batchelor, an architect and preservationist with the National Park Service, No. 126 was restored to an eighteenth-century appearance, and opened to the public with a collection of furniture and decorative items on loan from the Philadelphia Museum of Art.[37]

The organization had a curator on staff on a voluntary basis since 1965.[38] The first professional part-time staff member was Susan Winslow Hodge, who served as the Museum's curator and designed its first special exhibit, "Hearths and Crafts," which opened in 1984.[39] Full-time directors have been in place since 1986.[40]

The Future of the EAA Properties

"By 1963 the EAA's fervor to acquire as many properties as possible began to wane."[41] The Board minutes from its September 9, 1963, meeting gives inkling that the Association's preservation mission needed review.

Regarding the methods of achieving purposes. . .restoration and preservation of houses on the Alley is more expensive and will become increasing[ly] more expensive as time goes on. Agreed that the Association should encourage individuals to preserve and restore the houses on the Alley whenever possible. In addition agreed that Association could not and should not own all or most of the houses on the Alley, felt that it should own no more than a maximum 20 or 30 percent of these houses. Further agreed that Association should purchase houses, within this limit, whenever they become available, provided, of course, that sensible, adequate financing can be arranged. Once houses are owned, restoration and preservation plans should be prepared. Houses would then be restored and preserved by the Association and resold or the houses should be sold to individuals who would agree to restore accordance with Association's plans. Whenever the Association sells a house, agreement of sale should include clause to the effect that new owners would offer it to Association before selling it to others. Noted that Association may have to partially subsidize restoration and preservation of houses purchased but in the long run this would be more economical than doing complete job ourselves.[42]

Vosburgh noted that "this statement shows a major shift in the board's thinking *vis a vis* the methods of achieving" the EAA purposes.[43] Many of the preservation techniques outlined in the September meeting minutes were very forward thinking for the times and not in widespread use in Philadelphia. But this sentiment about EAA's stewardship responsibilities was not to last.

Two years later the board was still grappling with its overall mission regarding the houses. The minutes of the June 1965 meeting note "What is the goal of the Association with respect to houses and capital investment, should there be a revolving ownership, should the Association buy to rent, buy to sell, buy to sell to restore? Buy to restore and sell?"[44] Throughout the 1960s, the minutes contain numerous references to typical landlord issues: tenants breaking leases and emergency repairs on houses that needed more than just patching.

Seven years later, in 1972, the disposition of the houses again came up, and the membership was invited to a meeting to discuss the issue.

The board was clearly conflicted about their stewardship responsibilities, but the meeting with the membership did little to clarify their choices. The day-to-day management of multiple tenant-occupied houses was wearing and causing discord. No one would entertain the option of selling the houses outright without some reassurance that they would be restored and preserved. By the end of 1976, all of the EAA's rental properties were subject to mortgage. According to Vosburgh, it is unclear from his review of the minutes when these properties were mortgaged and why. During the intervening eight years, the organization was still responding to preservation crises on the street, but time was also spent planning for the development of No. 124 as a house museum.

It was not until September 9, 1980, during the property committee meeting that the organization first identified how the properties could be sold with legal agreements to guarantee they would be maintained over time. "It was noted that. . .one option would be to sell the properties with restrictive covenants and preservation easements attached, thus ensuring the preservation of the properties."[45]

A façade easement (in some states called a restrictive covenant) is a voluntary legal agreement in the form of a deed to ensure that a historic building is permanently protected, affirmatively maintained, and remains unchanged in perpetuity. Nonprofit easement-holding organizations like the Philadelphia Historic Preservation Corporation (PHPC) were being organized to accept the donation of façade easements. PHPC's pilot program began in the Old City neighborhood in 1979 and several EAA board members were familiar with the program and its goals.[46]

Easement agreements could satisfy the EAA's need to ensure that its properties were permanently protected, and shift the burden of maintenance and restoration from the EAA to the new private-sector owners who had the financial means to restore the houses. However, another eight years would pass before the organization would make a final decision to sell the properties with these restrictions.

In 1988, the board began to take serious action on the sale of the buildings. "It was agreed to form a subcommittee to discuss the sale of the properties on Elfreth's Alley and Bladen's Court currently owned by EAA." It was noted that the subcommittee would investigate the possibility of keeping No. 124 in order to expand the museum shop.[47]

Deciding to Sell

Unlike many nonprofit organizations that have difficult decisions to make, there does not seem to have been a specific triggering event that pushed the board to finally take action. Rather, a series of small or incremental changes to the organization as a whole created a climate ripe for change.

First, the organization had received grant funds in 1987 to participate in a Comprehensive Historic Assistance Program for historic house museums sponsored by the National Trust for Historic Preservation to "address issues ranging from what we need to do to maintain the physical structure of the Museum house to building a program that benefits the membership and the public."[48] This assessment, according to former director Beth Richards, concluded that the "organization [should] get out of the property management business and become a historic house museum."[49]

Second, Richards felt that the presence of a curatorial staff person with training in museum administration might have swayed the board toward developing a better interpretive program at its museum house. A trained curator, who provided organizational continuity, would be most interested in advancing museological issues, not dealing with tenant issues. Third, the longstanding frustration with being a landlord had not abated. It is clear that by hiring a curator, undertaking studies, and professionalizing their operations, the organization was moving away from its historic preservation roots toward managing a historic house museum. These incremental changes seem to have pushed the board to finally ask for a membership vote about disposing the properties.

To prepare for the membership vote, the board during its June 1988 meeting discussed the major points to be included in their letter to the membership:

> The letter must explain that Board feels that the houses are not a financially sound investment as they stand. We have not been making the kind of money we should. It is possible that the houses will need major work (i.e. new roof) that will cost money the Association just doesn't have. The money received from the sale of the houses will go into a *very restrictive account*. It is possible that the Association can "live" very comfortably on the interest of the money from the sale; therefore the money

should be placed in a high interest bearing account, where only the interest will be used. The principal will be used only in emergencies that may arise in the future. Some of the principal will be set aside for capital improvements and the refurnishing of the museum house. The letter must also emphasize that covenants will be put on each property so they will be in no danger of having the façade altered in any way.[50]

Vosburgh noted that "even though they do not say it exactly, what they are talking about is [starting] an endowment" for the museum houses.[51] The board's letter to the membership, dated July 31 1998, said:

> By unanimous vote, the Board is recommending to the Association membership that we sell three of the four rental properties owned by the Association and establish, with the proceeds from the sale, a trust fund to finance museum improvements and fund the education and preservation operations of the Association. . . .The Association's properties have been restored. . .and if the sales were permitted, the Board could turn its energies from being a landlord to broader preservation and educational efforts. . . .Proceeds from the sales would be placed in an endowment . . . providing investment income to support ongoing museum operations and capital improvements. The principal would remain untouched. . . . Under the bylaws of the EAA your consent is necessary before the Board can sell the properties.[52]

Members were asked to vote in favor of the "Board's resolution to sell the properties at No. 114 Elfreth's Alley, No. 1 Bladen's Court, and No. 2 Bladen's Court and to establish, with the proceeds, a trust fund to provide investment income for the maintenance and capital improvement of the museum and support of Association operations."[53]

The Board's letter unleashed many concerns from the neighbors. A group of thirty-eight residents signed a petition asking the EAA to "to avoid too hasty a decision to sell the Association's properties." The concerns centered on the fate of the tenants in the properties, the potential that many properties put up for sale at once might depress the value of their homes, the covenants, and long-term preservation goals.[54] A full membership meeting was held on September 24, 1988, to address questions and solicit the vote of the members. A resolution passed permitting the sale of the three rental properties by a vote of 29 to 4.[55]

The first property sold was No. 114, because it was already vacant. By 1991 the EAA had sold Nos. 1 and 2 Bladen's Court. All three properties were sold subject to façade, interior, and open-space easements to protect interior and exterior features and the open space of the backyards.[56] The easements, which would run with the land and be difficult to extinguish, would ensure that the building would never be demolished and be affirmatively maintained. They would bind the current and any future owner, obligating them to obtain the easement-holding organization's prior approval for any additions or repairs to the features itemized in the easement document. The EAA decided to become the easement-monitoring organization for these properties and now has the obligation to inspect them periodically and to enforce the terms of the agreements.[57]

The EAA's easements put the organization in the position of monitoring both the inside and outside of houses they once owned. This has proven to be an uncomfortable arrangement, as some of the neighbors on the street are still close-knit, and negotiations about violations can degenerate into neighbor-versus-neighbor disagreements. On the whole, however, the sale of the properties to private owners has been successful. One easement violation was noted and a settlement negotiated between the parties without litigation.

With the sale of the properties completed, No. 124 was retained for an expansion of the museum, already open next door at No. 126. The uppermost floors are used as the EAA offices. The expansion of the museum took place between 1997 and 1999. In retrospect, the decision to expand the museum had a serious financial impact on the organization.

The $700 monthly rental from No. 124 had not only supported the carrying costs for the building, but part of the organization's overhead. The loss of this rental income, coupled with the loss of the rental income from the three houses sold off, was only partially offset by the income from the endowment.[58] Beth Richards noted that several program officers of area foundations thought the EAA's move to sell the income-producing properties was unwise because the endowment income would not replace all of the rental income.[59] Indeed, the organization entered into a period of consistent annual deficits between $47,000 and $22,500 during the years 1997 and

2001, despite museum attendance that averaged about 15,000 people each year.[60]

In an effort to shore up the organization's finances and long-term prospects, Richards, along with the board, worked hard from 2001 to 2004 to bring the annual deficit down to a net operating deficit of $19,440 for the year ending December 2004.[61] Vosburgh has built on the strict fiscal discipline of recent years and, with the Board, has a plan to raise revenues in the shop, from guided tours, and through a more comprehensive annual fund campaign.

The legacy of deferred maintenance continues to haunt the organization. According to Vosburgh, "Some of these past deficits resulted from unexpected capital expenditures—such as a new furnace at the end of [fiscal year] 2004. Beginning in [fiscal year] 2007, the EAA will separate the capital budget from the operating budget, thereby giving us a better picture of the relationship between the expenses of providing services distinct from the expenses of addressing long-neglected maintenance issues on particular physical assets."[62]

"The EAA ran a surplus in 2005 but only because of several one-time corporate gifts. This is not a sustainable strategy for balancing future budgets. The surplus will be credited towards several capital repairs (and a percentage of those gifts were credited toward the operating budget), but even with the capital budget segregated from operating, we have yet to identify a long-term strategy for increasing operating dollars relative to expenses."[63]

Vosburgh continued, "Can the EAA continue its mission of preserving the historic structures of Elfreth's Alley and interpreting the 300-year continuum of life here without the burden of maintaining two mid-eighteenth century homes? Should it? These are critical questions and as the EAA prepares its Interpretive Plan in [fiscal year] 2007, we'll have a better understanding of what physical assets we need to accomplish our mission. House museums are a strategy; they are not EAA's raise d'etre. The EAA has installed its first new exhibit in some time. It's not about a colonial era theme, and it's not inside the house museum. (The exhibit, about immigration to the alley, is displayed on panels attached to a temporary construction fence at the head of the alley.) There are other strategies for achieving our mission besides maintaining a house museum, and the organization is critically considering some of these alternatives."[64]

Conclusion

Elfreth's Alley Association is a microcosm of the historic preservation movement itself. The EAA was born as an aggressive historic preservation organization, saving properties from demolition on this important street, a tangible and authentic reminder of our colonial past. As the organization matured, it evolved into a historic house museum organization whose primary mission focused on the care and interpretation of its collection and the museum properties. Even though the EAA still discussed property acquisitions well into the 1990s, no new properties were purchased by the organization after 1964.

In making this gradual but fundamental shift from a preservation organization to a house museum operation, the EAA's longstanding historic preservation mission became muddled, especially for the neighbors who had come to rely on the EAA as their "eyes and ears" for insensitive development projects that might affect the setting or individual buildings on the street. While the EAA is highly supportive of the neighborhood association when development projects affect the district, the organization now focuses on the interpretation of the museum houses to the public.

The process the EAA used to finally sell its properties is instructive for other house museum organizations. For more than forty years, the EAA maintained the houses, but only managed to fully restore one of them, which was converted into a house museum. Landlord responsibilities took up huge amounts of the board's energy. While moderately profitable, being a landlord was ultimately unsatisfying because the requisite funds could not be raised to fully restore all the properties. Caught in an unsatisfactory arrangement and without a mechanism to ensure that the properties would be protected long-term, the properties remained in the organization's inventory from the 1940s through the 1980s.

Having finally identified façade easements as a flexible legal tool to permanently protect their properties, the organization could finally consider selling them. The façade easement agreement would guarantee that the EAA's work would not be undone, and the EAA could assign to the new private owners the responsibility to adequately restore these small homes as they were unable to raise sufficient funds to do the work themselves.

For the Elfreth's Alley Association, the sale of the houses to new owners, who were more likely to have the financial means to take care of them properly, was a successful resolution to a longstanding problem. The property sales partially endow the EAA, giving it a small cushion to weather uncertain times. As a result, the endowment provides stability for a small nonprofit organization now responsible for monitoring and enforcing the easement agreements on the homes once owned and so long identified with the Elfreth's Alley Association.

How to Use This Case Study

This option, the sale of the historic house museum to a private owner with easements, seems to be the most preferred option based on interviews conducted with a wide variety of house museum organizations during the last two years. Whether your board would consent to returning your historic house museum to the private sector will depend on local traditions and community sentiment. While this is the most often-used option by house museum peers across the country, a sale with easement may not be the right solution for your specific organization. You are urged to consider the entire range of options presented here before making a decision about the future stewardship of your historic site.

ROBERT E. LEE BOYHOOD HOME, ALEXANDRIA, VIRGINIA

Located in Alexandria, Virginia, the Robert E. Lee Boyhood home, a notable 1795 Federal-style brick home, had been owned by the Lee-Jackson Foundation since 1967.[65] The foundation was organized to own and preserve properties associated with General Robert E. Lee and General "Stonewall" Jackson. In addition, the foundation provided scholarships to Virginia students to strengthen awareness of these two Civil War generals as exemplary role models for future generations.[66] The Foundation purchased General Jackson's Lexington, Virginia, home and the Lee Boyhood Home in Alexandria, Virginia, and operated both as house museums.[67]

In the 1990s the Foundation's interests shifted and it decided to sell the Jackson home.[68] A nonprofit organization came forward to buy the house and the property is open daily, has more than 30,000 visitors a year and an active educational program.[69] For the Lee Boyhood Home, restoration needs were mounting, and the Foundation decided that it should be sold and proceeds added to its scholarship program.[70]

Without putting the property on the market, the Foundation accepted an unsolicited offer of $2.5 million in March 2000 from a local family who was willing to invest considerable sums for its restoration and turn it into their private home.[71] The sale, said to be "shrouded in secrecy," stunned the community and unleashed a fierce backlash.[72] Neighbors contacted the Virginia attorney general's office. He tried to intervene to persuade the Foundation to void the sale and return the money to the family, but the Foundation declined to change course.[73]

Realizing the sensitive nature of the matter, the family decided to craft a process whereby the house would be offered for sale to a qualified nonprofit organization with the financial ability to purchase and restore the building as a museum open to the public.[74] An invitation for proposals was issued, and two organizations submitted offers.[75] After review by a distinguished panel, the panel recommended that both proposals be rejected as both lacked realistic plans for raising funds or sustaining the property as a public museum.[76] The family has completed the restoration work and now lives in the home.[77]

In response to the surprise sale of the Lee Home, a state law was passed the following year that requires that nonprofit owners of historic sites give notice of intent to sell to the city, state, and attorney general's office ninety days prior to sale.[78]

How to Use This Case Study

This case illustrates situations to avoid. While the Lee-Jackson Foundation had every right to sell the property and concentrate its efforts on its scholarship mission, the Foundation could have circumvented the local controversy by selling the property on the open market rather than accepting a private offer. As fiduciaries, we can only speculate that the Foundation board may have felt that the adverse publicity they received was the "price to pay" in order to secure the sale and add substantially to the organization's scholarship fund.

In this case, the sale was allowed to proceed because the Foundation board was acting within its stated mission. The attorney general's office intervened but was unable to persuade the Foundation to void the sale.

House museum stewards concerned about negative press should more every effort to involve stakeholders as part of the decision-making team, make members aware of the range of uses being discussed, and actively manage how information is distributed to the media.

NOTES

1. I am indebted to Robert Vosburgh, formerly Executive Director of the Elfreth's Alley Association, for providing two memos to me that detail the specific meetings when the Board discussed property transactions for Elfreth's Alley. My thanks also to Beth Richards, another Executive Director of Elfreth's Alley, who provided useful background information for this case study. The archives at the Elfreth's Alley Association are organized with a finding aid. Elfreth's Alley Association, *Guide to the Archives*, October 2004.

2. Robert Vosburgh, Memo to Property and Preservation Committee, "EAA History as a Property Owner," 21 February 2005, 1.

3. Vosburgh Memo. Robert Vosburgh, e-mail message to author, 31 March 2005.

4. Elfreth's Alley Association. *Inside These Doors: A Historic Guidebook of the Homes of Elfreth's Alley, a National Historic Landmark,* 2004. 3.

5. *Inside These Doors,* 3.

6. *Guide to the Archives,* 2.

7. *Guide,* 2.

8. *Guide,* 2.

9. *Inside These Doors,* 15.

10. *Guide,* 2. *Inside These Doors,* 15.

11. "By serving chipped beef on toast (15¢) to local businessmen she and the Association were able to raise funds and awareness for the preservation of Elfreth's Alley." *Guide,* 2.

12. *Guide,* 3.

13. *Guide,* 3.

14. *Guide,* 3.

15. *Guide,* 3.

16. "EAA History as Property Owner," Vosburgh quotes from Eliza Newkirk Rogers, *Elfreth's Alley Guidebook,* The Elfreth's Alley Association, 1964, found in Elfreth's Alley Archives, Box 15, Series VIII: Sales and Promotion.

17. Vosburgh Memo, "EAA History as Property Owner," 2.

18. *Guide*, 3.

19. *Guide*, 3.

20. EAA Archives, Box 1, Series 1: Administration, Board of Directors, 1949, Member newsletter, 21 July 1949.

21. EAA Archives, Box 1 Series 1: Administration, Board of Directors, 1955. Minutes of the Board of Directors, 19 April 1955.

22. EAA Archives, Box 1, Series 1: Administration, Board of Directors, 1955. Minutes of the Board of Directors, 19 May 1955.

23. Vosburgh Memo, "EAA History as Property Owner," 3.

24. John M. Groff, "To Thine Own Self Be True: The Small Historic House Museum in the 21st Century." A paper delivered at American House Museums in the 21st Century: An Athenaeum of Philadelphia Symposium, 4–6 December 1998, available at http://www.philaathenaeum.org/hmuseum/groff.htm (accessed 20 April 2003).

25. Groff. Charles Hosmer, *Presence of the Past: a History of the Preservation Movement in the United States before Williamsburg.* New York: G. P. Putnam's Sons, 1964, especially Hosmer's index for information about the earliest efforts to preserve historic houses in Philadelphia.

26. EAA Archives, Box 1, Series 1: Administration, Board of Directors, 1962. Minutes of the Board of Directors, 5 April 1962. Matthew Schultz, telephone conversation with author, Philadelphia, PA, 17 March 2005.

27. EAA Archives, Box 1, Series I: Administration; Board of Directors, 1958. Minutes of the Board of Directors, 5 May 1958. "A manager is needed to run the shop of the Association, now moved out of No. 124 and temporarily installed in the cellar of the Coach House. There are six volunteer girls who will work on the weekends." The EAA never owned the Coach House, according to Richards. Beth Richards, interview with author, 4 April 2005.

28. EAA Archives, Box 1, Series I: Administration; Board of Directors, 1958. Minutes of the Board of Directors, 5 May 1958.

29. Minutes, Board of Directors, 5 May 1958.

30. *Guide,* 3.

31. Robert Vosburgh, e-mail message to author, Philadelphia, PA, 19 March 2005.

32. "EAA History as Property Owner," 3.

33. Hosmer, 288.

34. Hosmer, 295.

35. EAA Archives, Box 1, Series 1: Administration, Board of Directors 1957, Minutes, 21 May 1957.

36. EAA Archives, Box 1, Series 1: Administration, Board of Directors, 1958, Minutes, 6 October 1958. The Association purchased No. 126 from Landmarks in 1962.

37. *Guide*, 3.

38. EAA Archives, Box 1, Series 1: Administration, Board of Directors, 1965. Minutes 7 January 1965. "Mr. Schall announced the following appointments: Mr. Dorman as Curator of the Museum. He will oversee the entire Museum complex operation and committees working on any aspect of Nos. 124–126 will clear their programs with him." EAA Archives, Box 1, Series 1: Administration, Board of Directors, Minutes, 26 April 1968 note that an assistant curator had been hired to "work out a plan of operation for the museum."

39. *Guide,* 4.

40. *Guide*, 4.

41. Vosburgh Memo, "EAA History as Property Owner," 4.

42. EAA Archives, Box 1, Series 1: Administration, Board of Directors, 1963. Minutes, 9 September 1963.

43. Vosburgh Memo, "EAA History as Property Owner," 4.

44. EAA Archives, Box 1, Series 1: Administration, Board of Directors, 1965. Report to the Membership, 9 September 1965.

45. EAA Archives, Box 1, Series 1: Administration, Property Committee, 1980. Property Committee Report, 9 September 1980.

46. The author managed the Philadelphia Historic Preservation Corporation's façade easement program from 1986–1992. The easement program is now managed by the Preservation Alliance for Greater Philadelphia.

47. EAA Archives, Box 1, Series 1: Administration, Board of Directors, 1988, Minutes, 18 February 1988.

48. EAA Archives, Box 1, Series 1: Administration. Board of Directors, 1988. Elfreth's Alley Association, Letter to the membership, 31 July 1988. Janet Klein to Toni Collins, 4 November 1988.

49. Beth Richards, interview with author, typed manuscript of telephone conversation, Philadelphia, PA, 26 June 2003.

50. EAA Archives, Box 1, Series 1: Administration, Board of Directors, 1988. Minutes, 30 June 1988.

51. Robert Vosburgh, e-mail message to author, Philadelphia, PA, 19 March 2005. According to Beth Richards the "endowment" is really a Board designated or restricted fund, and not formally constituted as a legal endowment. Richards interview, 26 June 2003.

52. EAA Archives, Box 1, Series 1: Administration, Board of Directors, 1988. Letter from the Board of Directors of the Elfreth's Alley Association to Members, 31 July 1988.

53. Letter to the Board of Directors, 31 July 1988.

54. EAA Archives, Box 1, Series 1: Administration, Board of Directors, 1988. Signed petition from 31 Alley residents to EAA Board of Directors, 12 August 1988.

55. EAA Archives, Box 1, Series 1: Administration, Board of Directors, 1988. Minutes of the Meeting of the Membership, 21 September 1988. Sometime after the three properties were sold, the organization changed its bylaws to become a nonprofit organization without a membership, thus investing in the Board of Directors all responsibility for the use of the assets of the organization. *Guide*, 3.

56. Deed of Façade, Interior and Open Space Easement, 1 Bladen's Court, 5 August, 1991. The easement deeds are part of the EAA Archives.

57. According to Beth Richards, the EAA discussed with Philadelphia Historic Preservation Corporation if they would accept the easements for the three properties to be sold. PHPC declined. The Association decided to monitor the easements themselves, thus creating a perpetual obligation to enforce the restrictions and inspect the buildings. The Association has not inspected the easement properties in several years. Robert Vosburgh and Beth Richards, interview with author, typed manuscript of telephone conversation, Philadelphia, PA, 10 February 2005.

58. Richards interview, 26 June 2003.

59. Richards interview, 26 June 2003.

60. In 1996 the Board restricted fund amounted to $347,330 from the sale of the three properties. By 2000 $272,600 remained. According to the Strategic Plan, "For at least the past four years (1997 through 2000), the Elfreth's Alley Association has been operating at a loss . . . That loss (averaging $47,000 annually) has been subsidized in two ways: 1) by interest and dividends from endowment investments at an average of $22,500 annually. . .and 2) by sale of shares of the Alley's endowment. . . .Fortunately, the net sale of equity shares to subsidize operations has slowed dramatically in recent years." Elfreth's Alley Association, *Strategic Plan 2002–2005*, 6, 9. According to Richards, the endowment's current value in 2004 is about $170,000. These funds are divided into two accounts, the "Endowment Fund" with about $100,000 and the "Preservation Fund" with about $70,000. Interest from the "Endowment Fund" supports the operation of the Association. The "Preservation Fund" was created to purchase additional properties, pay for easement inspections, and give short-term loans for restoration and small grants to residents for studies needed for restoration. According to Richards, the organization no longer gives grants and all loans have been repaid. Richards, interview, 26 June 2003. Strategic Plan, 6. According to Richards,

museum attendance has grown to about 50,000 annually. Beth Richards, e-mail message to author, 8 April 2005.

61. Robert Vosburgh, e-mail message to author, 8 April 2005. Richards, e-mail, 8 April 2005. Robert Vosburgh, e-mail message to author, 22 August 2006.

62. Vosburgh e-mail, 22 August 2006.

63. Vosburgh interview, 3 March 2005.

64. Vosburgh e-mail, 22 August 2006.

65. Thompson Mayes, interview with author, typescript of telephone conversation, 13 May 2003.

66. The Lee-Jackson Foundation of Charlottesville, www.lee-jackson.org/ (accessed 14 December 2004).

67. Mayes interview.

68. Ann O'Hanlon, "Sold Sign on Lee House Jarring," *Washington Post*, 7 March 2000, Metro 1.

69. See www.stonewalljackson.org for further information about this site.

70. Ester M. Aaron, "$2.5 M for History," *Alexandria Gazette Packet*, 9 March 2000, 1.

71. Ann O'Hanlon.

72. Ester M. Aaron.

73. Commonwealth of Virginia. Office of the Attorney General, "Statement by David Johnson, Counsel to Attorney General Mark Earley, Re: Sale of Robert E. Lee Boyhood Home," Press Release, 28 July 2000. Office of the General Counsel, National Trust for Historic Preservation, Washington, DC. See also Ann O'Hanlon, "Sale of Historic Lee Home in Alexandria Is Put on Hold; Va. Attorney General to Review Purchase that Stunned Officials, Residents," *Washington Post*, 11 March 2000, B1.

74. "Invitation for Proposals Robert E. Lee Boyhood Home, Alexandria Virginia," no date, Office of the General Counsel, National Trust for Historic Preservation, Washington, DC. Also see Kington Management Corporation and National Trust for Historic Preservation, "Kington Family Seeks Nonprofit Organization to Purchase Robert E. Lee's Boyhood Home, Invites Proposals from Nonprofits for Restoration, Operation of Museum," Press Release 11 May 2000, Office of the General Counsel, National Trust for Historic Preservation, Washington, DC.

75. Vaughn interview.

76. Kington Management, National Trust for Historic Preservation, Virginia Historical Society, and the Civil War Preservation Trust, "Kington Family and Historic Preservation Groups Agree on Alternative Plan to Save Lee's

Boyhood Home," joint Press Release issued 14 September 2000, Office of the General Counsel, National Trust for Historic Preservation, Washington, DC.

77. Ann O'Hanlon, "Panel Backs Couple's Plan to Renovate Lee's Alexandria Home," *Washington Post*, 15 September 2000, B8. Daniel Drummond, "Lee's Boyhood Home Won't Reopen as Museum," *Washington Times*, 15 September 2000, C3.

78. Commonwealth of Virginia, House of Delegates, House Bill 2165, "Certain historic properties: Notification prior to sale legislation," 2001 session; available at legl.state.va.us/cgi-bin/legp504.exe?011+sum+HB2165 (accessed 17 December 2004). See also "Lee Boyhood Home Bill Passes," Boyhood Home Bulletin Board at www.leeboyhoodhome.org/ (accessed 14 December 2004).

CHAPTER 14

Case Studies:
Sale to a Nonprofit Stewardship Organization

CASA AMESTI FOUNDATION, MONTEREY, CALIFORNIA

The National Trust for Historic Preservation was less than ten years old when Casa Amesti, an 1834 California Adobe in Monterey, California, became one of the first historic properties donated to the fledgling organization.[1]

Chartered by Congress in 1949 to "facilitate public participation in the preservation of sites, buildings and objects," the National Trust was organized by individuals, historical groups, and others that shared an interest in the nation's past as evidenced by its architecture and historic places.[2] The organization's Congressional Charter states its purposes as: "to receive donations of sites, buildings and objects significant in American history and culture, to preserve and administer them for the public benefit."

Envisioned as a national historic property steward like its counterpart in England, the British National Trust, it was not until the early 1950s that stewardship and public outreach became twin goals.[3] Today the National Trust for Historic Preservation owns twenty-five historic properties around the country that are open to the public. Most are managed through cooperative agreements with local property councils that oversee fundraising and day-to-day management of these sites.

Historic Casa Amesti

In 1953, a telegram arrived at the Trust headquarters in Washington saying that Frances Adler Elkins (1888–1953), a California-based interior designer and sister of the noted Chicago architect David Adler (1884–1949) had willed her California Adobe to the Trust. The house at 516 Polk Street and its contents came to the Trust without an endowment for maintenance or restoration. Elkins, who had started an interior design business in the mid-1920s, had lavished attention on the historic California Adobe and engaged her brother to update the structure shortly after she and her husband purchased the property in 1919. The house that the Trust received was the signature creation of Frances Elkins' interior design talent, its noteworthy early 1920s interior remarkably unaltered.

Casa Amesti began as a four-room, one-story adobe dwelling, constructed for Don Jose Gallo Amesti and his wife Prudenciana in 1834.[4] Today, the house is located in the midst of downtown Monterey.

After building Casa Amesti and living there for less than fifteen years, the Amesti family left Monterey for San Francisco with the California Gold Rush in 1849. They gave their house to their newly married daughter, Carmen. Casa Amesti was "Americanized" in the 1850s when the second story was added, a central hall created, and glass windows and fireplaces introduced. The historic home was cherished by generations

Figure 14.1   Casa Amesti, Monterey, California

of the Amesti family until World War I when it was rented out as a boarding house. The family would have preferred to donate the house to serve as a retirement home for Roman Catholic women, but the complications of the estate forced the home's sale in 1918 to the Elkins.[5]

Across the street from Casa Amesti is another restored home, the Cooper-Molera Adobe, which was donated to the National Trust in 1972. The Cooper-Molera Adobe is a three-acre compound, but unlike Casa Amesti, where the adobe had been subsumed by "modernizations" in the 1850s, the Cooper-Molera Adobe remains intact as it was built in 1823. The Cooper-Molera Adobe is managed by the State of California as a historic site under a cooperative agreement with the Trust, as the property is still owned by the National Trust.[6]

Interior Design at Casa Amesti

Newlyweds Felton and Frances Elkins bought Casa Amesti for $5,000, and Frances set about retaining the character of the old, but installing all the modern conveniences. She called upon her brother, David Adler, an architect of substantial suburban estates for the wealthy in Chicago, to bring her vision for the classic adobe to reality.[7]

In installing pipe chases, wiring, and other infrastructure, Adler removed, but replaced in kind, adobe and wooden features. He then added elaborate classical moldings and mantels, while retaining the old wide wood-plank floors, the 1854 stairs, beamed wooden ceilings, and the wraparound second-floor porch. The simple, whitewashed walls were framed by the dark wood-plank ceilings above and polished wood floors below.

When the house was completed, Adler turned his attention to the walled garden, creating a formal setting reminiscent of the Spanish courtyard gardens of Seville with "clipped hedges, a fountain, and lines of whitewashed flower pots" which he and his sister had seen during their grand tour of Europe. Adler's interior and garden work was completed in 1920, and Frances then turned to furnishing the home.

"Santos from Spain, silk cushions, painted French and Italian armchairs, a candle-burning chandelier, rich mahogany tables, antique prints, and handsome old volumes bound in leather were some of her purchases."[8] Fortunately for historians, Elkins documented her interior decor in stereopticon views. These photos show the house much as it remained when the Trust received the property in 1953. Considering that interior decoration is often ephemeral, changing at the whim of new owners or through efforts to keep up-to-date with changing "taste," this was a remarkable legacy.[9]

Three historic rooms on the second floor retain their 1920s furnishings and decor, in much the same condition as they were designed by Elkins. They include the Sala, the large living room or parlor that was once lined with chairs and used for entertaining by the Amesti clan. Here, Frances Elkins created conversation groupings in the corners with a large desk in the center. The deep, wood-paneled reveals of the windows and paneled passageways between the rooms, painted cream, were added by Adler. The classically inspired door and window surrounds, molded with round corner blocks, were introduced during Adler's renovation. A classical mantel and over-mantel, and deep cornice moldings frame the original wide planked ceiling. Banquettes and antique daybeds mix with upholstered wing chairs and lyre-backed dining chairs. The room looks startlingly familiar today, even timeless, a refined interior created seventy-five years ago.[10]

David Adler's bedroom, the second of the three historic rooms designed by his sister, has a blue toile-de-Jouy "Les Monuments of Paris" wallpaper and yellow bed hangings with a crenulated valance.[11] Finally, the dining room also retains the décor and significant pieces from the Elkins' tenure.

Frances Elkins and her daughter Katie lived in the house for thirty-five years. Elkins' interior design business, called Casa Blanca, was run from an adobe in town once owned by Robert Louis Stevenson. Casa Blanca was supported by an uncle who also gave her brother his first large architectural commission.[12] Mrs. Elkins made yearly buying visits to France to scour the markets for choice pieces for her clients, and met some of the avant-garde during those years. She was taken with Jean-Michael Frank's furniture and Alberto Giacommeti's lamps, as well as the modern painters of the day. She encouraged her clients to purchase works by these contemporary artists.[13]

Elkins transformed Casa Amesti into a signature interior with an eclectic combination of American and European case goods, Chinese rugs, modern tables and lamps, and porcelains against whitewashed walls. An article in *House Beautiful* magazine in 1942 described

Elkins' home as "the finest of the restored old adobes...in its original character and in its completeness yet fitting simplicity with which it has been rehabilitated....There is no attempt at period consistency, no attempt. . . to reproduce the valueness crudities of the so-called mission style or. . . the Spanish Colonial."[14]

The Trust and Casa Amesti's Stewardship Needs

Frances Elkins willed her property to the nascent National Trust. The Trust would hold the property "in trust by it and maintained in perpetuity as a historic California Adobe."[15] There were provisions in the will that, should the National Trust decide not to accept the donation, the property would revert to one of Mrs. Elkins' grandsons.

By 1955, the property had been legally transferred to the National Trust. The organization, based in Washington, D.C., only managed one other property at the time, Woodlawn Plantation in suburban Virginia. According to Thompson M. Mayes, Deputy General Counsel of the National Trust, the organization was relatively new, and not set up to administer a historic property "far away" in California.[16]

The property came to the Trust without an endowment to pay for needed maintenance or repairs. In order to maintain the property in perpetuity as specified in Frances Elkins' will, the Trust would need to find an entity that would be willing to maintain Casa Amesti and allow public access to the historic site. In seeking a viable organization to maintain the property, and open it occasionally, the Trust could avoid the expense of managing a site some 3,000 miles away. Renting the property to another party may have been a radical notion in 1955 for a new national stewardship organization, but this solution solved many problems.[17]

The Old Capital Club, a nonprofit private social and dining club, stepped forward. The Club took over the building, entering into a twenty year occupancy agreement with the Trust in 1957, which was renewed again in 1977.[18]

Maintenance and Preservation of the Site

In establishing the occupancy agreement, the Trust sought to ensure "the operation, maintenance and preservation of the Premises for public benefit as a historic California Adobe."[19] The Club would be responsible for "operating, maintaining and preserving the Premises on behalf of the National Trust in exchange for making the property available to the Club for continuing of the Club's cultural and educational activities."[20] The Club would assume all expenses incurred in "maintaining, administering, protecting and operating the Premises," including real and personal property taxes, utilities, insurance premiums, repairs, improvements, construction, or alterations, except those paid directly by the Trust in the event of a casualty loss.[21]

The Club would protect the historic integrity of the features, materials, appearance, workmanship, and environment of the old adobe. The Club would seek the advice and counsel of the Trust on any proposed changes to the physical fabric of the structure or grounds and landscaping, and submit proposals for written approval prior to commencement of work.[22]

The furnishings and décor of the historic structure were to be maintained in a manner consistent with its historic character. The historic furniture, paintings, and other objects were itemized for insurance purposes and the Club was responsible for a systematic inspection of their condition and for obtaining any necessary conservation. The Club provided an annual accounting of all costs associated with capital improvements, structural repairs, and expenses for conservation and restoration of the historic objects.[23]

Public Access and the Decision to Transfer Ownership

The Trust sought limited public access for the house. The Trust saw visitation at Casa Amesti as crucial to the organization's statutory mandate to facilitate public participation in historic preservation.[24] The garden and the three historic rooms on the second floor were cited in the occupancy agreement, and were to be made available for public visitation at mutually agreeable times, after 3:00 p.m. on weekdays except by special arrangement, after 10:00 a.m. on weekends, and upon request. It was intended that the Club make the site available for public visitation more frequently, but not less than, twelve days a year. This minimum stipulation was a requirement that the Trust was obligated to carry out under the Historic Preservation Grants-in-Aid Policies and Procedures then in effect by the U.S. Department of the Interior.[25]

In the early 1980s, the Trust began internal discussions about a new stewardship arrangement for Casa Amesti. The Club had been exemplary managers of the site throughout the years, and considered the house "its beloved adobe."[26] But as a private club, the Trust, according to Mayes, was feeling increasingly uncomfortable about whether the public perceived that there was sufficient public access available.[27] Both the Trust and the National Park Service had introduced new antidiscrimination policies for entities that received federal grant funds. At the time, the Trust received federal funds for its operations, and was therefore bound by these regulations.

The Trust consulted with the State of California Department of Parks about the future of Casa Amesti. This agency has a successful cooperative agreement with the Trust to operate the Cooper-Molera Adobe across the street from Casa Amesti.[28] The Trust began discussions with the Old Capital Club in the mid-1980s to establish if they would be interested in entering into a new stewardship arrangement. It would be fifteen more years before the final agreements would be signed in 2001.

Transferring Casa Amesti

The initial conversations between the two organizations were cordial, and for close to ten years, the Trust and the Club discussed a new stewardship arrangement that would ensure that the property be restored and maintained. According to Mayes, "all of the stakeholders, including the family, local preservation organizations, and the leaseholder, all had to agree on the direction, which took years." David Boyd, Mrs. Elkins' grandson who retained a reversionary interest in the property from his grandmother's will, and his mother, Katie Elkins Boyd, were also parties to the discussions. "Everyone had to be comfortable that this change made sense," said Mayes.[29] "Significant funds had to be raised to support an endowment because one had never existed before."[30]

A letter dated September 26, 1995, set out the terms of the transfer. The Club would raise $500,000 toward an endowment, to be held by the Community Foundation of Monterey County. The Club would complete improvements to Casa Amesti as recommended in a historic structures report. These included archeological monitoring of all work requiring ground disturbance, creation of a disaster plan, inventory and condition assessment of the contents of Casa Amesti, repair of objects in the three historic rooms according to the condition assessment, the creation of an interpretive plan, and a small exhibit on the history of the property.[31] A final condition was to place a permanent preservation restriction attached to the title of the property as a preservation easement to ensure that the property was preserved in perpetuity.

The Trust and the Club agreed to create a new organization called the Casa Amesti Foundation as a 501 (c) (4) nonprofit organization. The Club would comprise less than half of the Board membership. The Casa Amesti Foundation was organized during the fundraising period, 1998–1999, according to Sidney M. Morris, a member and secretary of the Old Capital Club Board of Directors during this time.[32] The primary purpose of the Foundation was to be the title holder of Casa Amesti.

Among the Trust's concerns was establishing the long-needed endowment for the property. Recent object conservation costs in the historic rooms provided a basis for a suggesting that a $500,000 minimum endowment was needed to maintain the historic objects in the house.[33]

Katie Elkins Boyd became involved with the Foundation, eventually becoming president. She provided critical insight about her mother's design intent and served in an unofficial capacity as a consulting curator for the conservation of objects in the historic rooms.[34]

According to Morris, Club members took the lead to raise the money necessary for the endowment and restoration. During the five-year period between 1995 and the final transfer of the property in 2000, Club members were successful in gathering more than $1.5 million.[35] Morris said, "the Club had a limited membership at the time of perhaps no more than 300 people. Our board president sent a letter to our Club members saying that we needed to raise money for the retrofit and restoration and that a fund had been sent up at the local community foundation to receive gifts. His letter suggested that each member contribute $5,000, which would not be quite enough for the project, but would be a start. Some of our senior members have limited means or are retired. Other members had corporate connections and matching gifts were received. A few members provided larger gifts. But all were glad to do it."[36]

The Trust's initial estimates to restore the building were about $325,000, said Morris, but the Club members decided that they wished to seismically retrofit the property during the restoration work, which added additional costs. "In the end, we spent just under $525,000 on the property restoration, raised half a million for the endowment, and spent just over $525,000 on the garden restoration. About 20 percent of this cost is for consulting."[37]

The target date for the transfer was October 1997, when the current cooperative agreement would lapse. Because the property was held in trust, any transfer of ownership would have to be approved by the California Probate Court, which had jurisdiction over Frances Elkins' will and by the National Trust's board of trustees. The National Trust acted first by voting on a resolution authorizing the president to enter into an appropriate agreement for "transfer of Casa Amesti and the long-term preservation of that property on terms and conditions satisfactory to the President and subject to compliance with applicable legal requirements" on May 22, 1995.[38] Still, six more years would pass before the transfer was completed and the easement recorded.

Perpetual Preservation

Another primary consideration of the Trust was to ensure that the property would be preserved and well-maintained after it left the organization's ownership. As a condition of transfer, the Trust required that the new foundation enter into a perpetual preservation restriction on the property. An easement is a voluntary legal agreement in the form of a deed between a qualified organization, such as the Trust, and a historic property owner. In the easement agreement, the historic building owner agrees not to demolish or subdivide, and to affirmatively maintain, the property forever.

Easements are an effective tool to ensure maintenance of a historic property over time, as the agreement runs with the land and is difficult to extinguish. Easements bind the current and all future owners of the land. The building is inspected by the qualified organization yearly, and the terms of the easement are enforced by the easement holding organization if there are violations.

Most easements are donated for the exterior of buildings, and only occasionally to protect historic interior features. Easements are used to ensure the preservation of open space and can be utilized to ensure that the grounds, if they are significant to the setting of a historic building, are maintained. In the case of Casa Amesti, the house, gardens, and historic rooms are included as protected features and were documented in the easement at the time of the closing on the easement. In this case, the agreement was between two nonprofit organizations, so there were no federal tax incentives involved.[39]

The easement negotiated between the National Trust and the Casa Amesti Foundation notes that the property is a significant example of Monterey Colonial architecture, and that Frances Adler Elkins "imparted her uniquely American style of decoration to the Property's interior which remains substantially intact throughout the Historic Rooms."[40] The agreement is specific that the property and its buildings and historic rooms must be kept in good repair, structurally sound and substantially in the form and condition of the effective date of the closing. The Foundation cannot make additions, remove or alter the existing landscaping, build temporary structures, or add signs, awnings, and satellite dishes without the express prior written approval of the Trust.

Public access to the historic rooms was addressed in the easement. The rooms are to be "made generally accessible on Saturdays if the demand exists, through a reservation system. Interpretive staff need only be available when reservations are scheduled. The Foundation shall also make the historic rooms accessible on those days featuring the historic adobes of Monterey. Students and historical societies shall be admitted to the rooms at reasonable times."[41] Morris noted that individuals and groups wishing to see the property contact the Club for an appointment and a docent is provided. "Mrs. Elkins' work is well known here and most of our visitors are interested in history, architecture, and Mrs. Elkins' historic style of decorating. Hundreds of people visit during the Monterey Adobe events."[42]

Maintaining Harmonious Relations

Throughout the many years of negotiations, the Trust was mindful that the organization had to maintain good and harmonious relationships with the Club, its officers, and then with the newly created Casa Amesti Foundation Board of Directors, because the easement would establish a perpetual relationship between the organizations, according to Mayes, of the Trust. The "go slow" nature of the negotiations, over so many years, is partially due to the physical distance between the parties. However, the enormity of change being proposed and the financial implications made the transfer process seem unending.

"The Casa Amesti Foundation decided to continue the lease with the Old Capital Club because they had been good stewards of the building for over 50 years," said Mayes. With this transfer, the Trust achieved a satisfactory way to ensure that Casa Amesti was permanently protected through the easement agreement.

In November 3, 2000, the transfer was completed through an Order on Petition for Approval of Transfer.[43] The easement was subsequently signed on January 25, 2001.[44] The Casa Amesti Foundation continues the traditions established by the Old Capital Club by opening the house for tours by appointment and during the annual events when the adobes of Old Monterey are available for public viewing.

Lessons Learned

Despite the fifteen-year period between the decision to find a new steward for Casa Amesti and the signing of the paperwork allowing its transfer, the process used by the National Trust can be replicated and is instructive for other historic property stewards.

By encouraging local stakeholders to create a local nonprofit organization to hold title to the property, and to raise funds for its preservation and perpetual maintenance, the Trust has furthered its organizational mission by increasing public participation in the historic preservation movement. The perpetual easement the Trust holds and annually inspects allows the organization to continue its relationship with local people who now own Casa Amesti and regard the venerable adobe with great affection.

How to Use This Case Study

Creating another stewardship organization may be a worthy option to consider if the current board is unable or unwilling to recruit new board members. This type of change, however, requires great foresight on the part of the current board that recognizes the short-term limit of its tenure. Identifying a new cadre of people to take over the steward-ship responsibilities as a new organization might be worth considering when the board membership has significantly dwindled due to resigna-tions or "retirements," and retaining a house museum use is imperative. This solution may not work if there are significant time pressures. In the case of Casa Amesti, the transition took seventeen years to negoti-ate and implement.

HEURICH HOUSE FOUNDATION, WASHINGTON, D.C.

The Heurich House, located in the Dupont Circle neighborhood of Washington, D.C., is a grand and substantially intact thirty-one-room, 13,000 square-foot 1897 Victorian mansion located on a prominent cor-ner. The house retains all of its furnishings and decorations, including an elaborate curved staircase said to be made of brass, marble and onyx; carved wooden fireplaces in almost every room; and gold leaf in abundance.[45] This spectacular home and large garden, known locally as the Brewmaster's Castle, was left to the precursor organization of the Historical Society of Washington, D.C. through the will of Mrs. Heurich, who died in 1955. The will specified that the property was to be known and used as the "Christian Heurich Memorial Mansion."[46]

"Until the Society acquired the building, it had no home," said Mark G. Griffin, the former historical society president and current chairman of the Heurich House Foundation. The Historical Society, founded in 1896 as the Columbia Historical Society, organized lectures and pre-sentations of papers by academics about the history of the District of Columbia and published proceedings of their meetings.[47]

The Historical Society, in accepting the house as a bequest from Mrs. Heurich, "had to demonstrate for twenty years that they could maintain the property, or else it would revert to a German orphanage," said Grif-fin.[48] As someone who has long been involved with the Historical Soci-ety, Griffin served as a volunteer curator in the 1970s. He then became general counsel and, finally, president in 1981, stepping down in 1985.

During his tenure, the Society was able to raise about $1.3 million as part of a National Endowment for the Arts challenge grant to upgrade and restore the building. At that time, investments were made in new wiring, heating system, roof, and an elevator linking all four floors and the basement, all to bring the building up to code "as close as historically possible."[49] For nearly fifty years the Historical Society used the house, which was the first poured concrete (and therefore fireproof) structure in the city, as its offices, research library, and house museum.

The Historical Society had access to two sizable funds to maintain the house, according to Griffin. In the mid-1970s, a developer approached the Historical Society to join with him in an application for a zoning change to allow the developer to build a larger building than would normally be permitted on the site of a surface parking lot located behind the Heurich House. This planned unit development application would permit the developer to transfer the zoning's floor area ratio of the commercially zoned Heurich House to the parking lot, thus enabling the developer to build a much larger structure there. The Heurich House agreed to this because it would reduce the floor-area ratio on the historic house, thus eliminating any future development threat. In addition, the developer agreed to pay the organization $500,000, which was placed in a board-designated fund for the maintenance of the historic building.

Around the same time, one of the Heurich children created a $1 million trust to be used for the maintenance of the structure.[50] The income from these two funds paid for annual upkeep and maintenance over the years, but the needs of the house were always growing, according to Griffin, to the point where the house became the "tail that wagged the dog."[51]

Planning for the City Museum of Washington

"In the late 1980s, a group of citizens began initial planning for a museum of the city of Washington, but this effort stalled," said Griffin. Several years later, the City of Washington declared the old Carnegie Library on Mount Vernon Square as surplus property. The Historical Society entered into an agreement with the City of Washington to lease the Carnegie Library for $1.00 a year on a ninety-nine year lease to rehabilitate and use the library as the City Museum of Washington.[52] A well-coordinated capital campaign ensued with prominent and well-regarded area people participating as co-chairs of the campaign.[53] The City Museum of Washington, a 60,000 square-foot facility at the old library, was developed to "tell stories of Washington's fascinating past and encourage DC visitors to explore off-the-Mall historic sites."[54]

Sale of the Heurich House

During the planning for their new facility, the Historical Society Board decided, according to a press release announcing the sale, that "the Board of Trustees realized that it would not be economically feasible to operate both the Heurich House and the City Museum in the restored Carnegie Library at Mount Vernon Square. After lengthy consideration, the Board approved a resolution to sell the Heurich House to an appropriate buyer at an appropriate price."[55]

It was reported in local newspapers that the Historical Society briefly considered selling the property to "a restaurateur that planned to disperse the site's original furnishings and collections and convert it to a private club."[56] Learning about the possible sale, a number of prominent citizens interested in the house, including two grandchildren of the original owner, stepped forward to assist a newly formed foundation with the purchase the house from the Historical Society, and to maintain it as a house museum open to the public.

The purchase, at the fair market value of $5.5 million, was concluded in March 2003. The buyers formed a new nonprofit stewardship organization, the Heurich House Foundation, to open the site for tours and special events. They gathered together a high-quality board populated with people prominent in the arts and preservation in the District.

Opening of the City Museum

In the meantime, the Historical Society opened the City Museum in May 2003 after a careful restoration of the library. The new facility was planned to have "exhibit galleries, a multi-media introductory show, an educational center with meeting space, an archeology lab, and a public research library and reading room, a café and museum store."[57] Appropriations from Congress, area foundations, and corporations were raised during the $20 million capital campaign.

However, after a year, the board of trustees decided to close its exhibit galleries in April 2005 because of low visitation. Even with a city appropriation, the facility never lived up to the anticipated visitation of more than 100,000 yearly. Reflecting on the closure, the co-chair of the Board, Leslie Shapiro, noted in a *Washington Post* article about the closing, said "the initial mistake was opening without enough money to sustain the museum's ambitions and advertise its content."

Today, the Historical Society retains its library and research facility at the library, and continues to rent the space for special events, which have been especially lucrative, according to the *Post* article. "When the anticipated crowds didn't materialize, the museum dismissed 12 of its 28 employees and began to rely heavily on renting out its space for parties and dinners. Those special events raised $415,000 in 16 months, compared with $78,000 from admissions."[58]

The Heurich House Foundation Today

The years after the sale of the Heurich House to the Foundation have not been easy. To purchase the property, the Foundation took out a five-year, $5,450,000 adjustable rate mortgage from an area bank, guaranteed by the Heurich grandchildren. Interest rates crept up from 4.25 percent to 7.25 percent during this period. The two maintenance funds for the building were passed along as part of the sale, but after two years the $500,000 fund was depleted. The unexpected death of a prominent board member, together with operational and economic difficulties, led to the resignation of several other board members.

By February 2006 the organization needed to raise funds to continue its operations. The organization mounted an urgent appeal to raise $250,000 from neighbors and interested parties to continue its operations. The appeal was successful.

Griffin, the current chairman, and another community member were asked to serve on the board, and have worked hard in the intervening months to find tenants for the upper floors of the building, to seek special event bookings, and to collect donations from tourists. Griffin worked closely with the bank and with friends of the Foundation to restructure the loan. A friend of the Foundation has stepped forward to purchase the loan as a private investor, and the debt service is now based on the cash flow of the property. Tenants are being sought for the third and fourth floors, while the rest of the building and garden is open for tours and events.

To ensure that the property remains open to the public, the Heurich House Foundation says it "must raise $1,750,000 to reduce the debt and be self-supporting" before December 2006. Most recently, the Washington D.C. Council member representing the Heurich House neighborhood, Jack Evans, sought an appropriation of $500,000 in the fiscal year 2007 city budget to apply toward the challenge.

These funds, if they are approved, would represent about 30 percent of the funds needed toward the fundraising goal this year of $1,750,000. The organization is trying to dispel the myth that the Heurich House has been "saved," which began circulating at the time of the urgent $250,000 fundraising appeal in March 2006.

"Had this property been just a historic building without all its original features and furnishings, then a respectful sale to a law firm or a trade association would have been an acceptable alternative," said Mr. Griffin. "If there was no debt, we probably would be ok."[59]

How to Use this Case

New stewardship organizations are formed out of necessity or invention. The Heurich House, a special property because it is almost wholly intact, was threatened by its potential sale to a user who did not appreciate the totality of the historic structure. Friends and family members banded together to assure that this unique property could remain open to the public. The purchase price at fair market value has created severe financial stresses on the new Heurich House Foundation and they have done an admirable job finding tenants, booking events, and developing a viable friends group to support the structure. They are most fortunate to have found a private investor who is willing to tie repayment of the purchase price to the cash flow generated by the house. This arrangement will allow the organization to develop the property's tourism potential and financial support over time unrelated to monthly loan payments.

NOTES

1. William Seale, *Of Houses and Time: Personal Histories of America's National Trust Properties*. New York: Harry N. Abrams, 1992, 109.

2. Congressional Charter, National Trust for Historic Preservation, 1949, www.nthp.org/charter (accessed 8 February 2005). I am grateful to Thompson Mayes, Deputy General Counsel of the National Trust for Historic Preservation for suggesting this case study, and for his willingness to supply documents to me. Seale, 18.

3. Seale, 19.

4. Seale, 109. Amesti married Prudenciana, the daughter of Encarnacion Cooper. They built Casa Amesti across the street from her parents' home.

5. Seale, 109.

6. Seale, 108.

7. Seale, 108.

8. Seale, 191.

9. Pauline Metcalf makes this point in her essay in a book about Frances Elkins' collaboration with her brother on Casa Amesti and other projects. See Martha Thorne, ed. *David Adler Architect: The Elements of Style.* New Haven: Yale University Press, 2002, 36–37.

10. Thorne, 36–37.

11. Thorne, 36–37.

12. Thorne, 36–37.

13. Thorne, 45.

14. As quoted in Metcalf article, in Phyllis Ackerman, "An Old Adobe Comes Into its Own," *House Beautiful* 56, no. 6, December 1942, 566–67.

15. Superior Court of the State of California, in and for the County of Monterey. In re: the Estate of Frances Adler Elkins, Deceased, 1, Office of the General Counsel of the National Trust for Historic Preservation, Washington, DC.

16. Thompson M. Mayes, interview by author, typed manuscript of telephone conversation, Washington, DC, 13 May 2003.

17. Thompson M. Mayes, interview by author, typed manuscript of telephone conversation, Washington, DC, 6 December, 2004.

18. Cooperative Agreement between the National Trust for Historic Preservation and The Old Capital Club, Monterey, CA, 4 November, 1977, Office of the General Counsel of the National Trust for Historic Preservation, Washington, DC, 1.

19. Cooperative Agreement, 1.

20. Cooperative Agreement, 1.

21. Cooperative Agreement, 2.

22. Cooperative Agreement, 2.

23. Cooperative Agreement, 3–4.

24. Cooperative Agreement, 2.

25. Cooperative Agreement, 3.

26. Lewis L. Fenton to Richard Moe, 13 March 1997. Office of the General Counsel, National Trust for Historic Preservation, Washington, D.C.

27. Mayes interview, 6 December 2004.

28. Mayes interview, 13 May 2003.

29. Mayes interview, 13 May 2003.

30. Mayes interview, 13 May 2003.

31. Richard Moe to Lewis L. Fenton, 26 September 1995, Office of General Counsel, National Trust for Historic Preservation, Washington, DC.

32. Sidney M. Morris, telephone interview by author, Monterey, CA, 4 May 2005. Thanks are extended to Mr. Morris for his willingness to provide needed background information for this case.

33. Mayes interview, 13 May 2003.

34. Fenton letter to Moe.

35. Morris interview.

36. Morris interview.

37. Sidney M. Morris, e-mail message to author, Monterey, CA, 11 May 2005.

38. Resolution of the Board of Trustees of the National Trust for Historic Preservation 22 May 1995.

39. Easements can offer substantial tax benefits if donated by a private individual to a qualified organization. See the National Trust for Historic Preservation's website, explaining their easement program and the tax benefits available to individuals and corporations, available at www.nationaltrust.org/law/easements.html (accessed 23 April 2004).

40. Deed of Preservation and Conservation Easement Casa Amesti, 25 January 2001. Office of the General Counsel, National Trust for Historic Preservation, Washington, DC, 1.

41. Easement, 5.

42. Morris interview, 4 May 2005.

43. Superior Court of the State of California in and for the County of Monterey. In re: the Estate of Frances Adler Elkins, Deceased. Order on Petition for Approval of Transfer, 3 November 2000. Office of the General Counsel, National Trust for Historic Preservation, Washington, DC.

44. Deed of Preservation and Conservation Easement Casa Amesti, 25 January 2001, Office of the General Counsel, National Trust for Historic Preservation, Washington, DC.

45. www.cr.nps.gov.nr/travel/wash/dc56.html (accessed 5 July 2006).

46. www.brewmasterscastle.org (accessed 29 August 2006).

47. Mark Griffin, telephone interview with author, 18 September 2006. I am grateful to Mr. Griffin for sharing information about the Heurich House with me.

48. Griffin interview.

49. Griffin interview.

50. Griffin interview.

51. Griffin interview.

52. "Historical Society Signs Contract to Sell Heurich House," available at www.citymuseumdc.org/media/releases/News Release 031103.asp (accessed 13 June 2006).

53. www.BrewmastersCastle.org. Griffin interview.

54. "Historical Society Signs Contract to Sell Heurich House."

55. "Historical Society Signs Contract to Sell Heurich House."

56. www.brewmasterscastle.org.

57. "Historical Society Signs Contract to Sell Heurich House."

58. Jacqueline Trescott, "City Museum to Close its Galleries," *Washington Post*, 9 October 2004, page A01, available at www.washingtonpost.com/wp~dyn.articles.A18694-2004Oct8.html (accessed 30 August 2006).

59. Griffin interview.

CHAPTER 15

Case Study:
Donation to a Governmental Entity

ADEL HISTORICAL SOCIETY, ADEL, IOWA

The Adel Historical Society bought the local old school house in 1973 to house its collection of Adel and Dallas County, Iowa, artifacts and archives. The Society intended to open the building as a museum for this small rural central Iowa community. Built in 1857, this two-story brick building was one of the earliest houses in the community, and for twenty years served as the local schoolhouse. The property was cared for by the board of the historical society. They used the building as a "card party house" for a senior group, who set up card tables inside the building a few times a year.

By 1998, the Adel Historical Society board of directors determined it could no longer manage the building due to lack of funds and diminishing membership. The Society approached the city with an offer to donate the property to them. The building had various maintenance problems, including a nonworking furnace, no air conditioning and termite damage throughout. The Society did not require or place an easement on the property prior to its donation to the city.

The city agreed to accept the donation and perform ongoing maintenance, if the local Main Street organization, Adel Partners, would move its offices to the site and staff the museum during regular public hours. Adel Partners formed and chaired a Museum Steering Committee. The committee included representatives of the former owners, Adel Historical Society and the local Historical Commission. Adel Partners managed the restoration project on behalf of the city, the new owner, with advice from its design committee. All construction work was completed by local firms or volunteers to meet the *Secretary of Interior's Standards*, a standard preservation benchmark.

A community-wide fundraising campaign began in 1999 and raised just over $60,000 to pay for restoration and repairs, a significant accomplishment in this city of 3,400. The City Manager was successful in obtaining a $14,271 grant from the Revitalization Assistance for Community Improvement program of the Prairie Meadows Racetrack and Casino. An additional $7,000 was obtained from the Historic Resources Development Program of the State Historical Society of Iowa. The city's initial $7,500 contribution increased to almost $18,000 when sponsor sources appeared to be exhausted. Families and institutions were encouraged to give larger gifts to sponsor rooms in the structure. Individual donations ranged from $10 to $500.

Opened with fanfare in 2002, the Adel Historical Museum building still hosts changing exhibits about local history and accepts donations to its small collection for display. The local Main Street manager provides tours of the museum during its open season from April 15 to October 15 and during the holidays. The building is open for visitors from 10 a.m. to 3 p.m., Tuesday to Saturday.[1] Members of the local historical society still manage the objects on display and the archives.

How to Use This Case Study

The Adel Historical Society was lucky to find a willing partner in the city, which was interested in accepting the donation of the property, despite its poor condition. The Society did not require that an easement be placed on the property prior to the donation, which would have ensured the property's protection in perpetuity.

Perhaps because they were donating the property to the city, the Historical Society felt this was unnecessary. Or, they may have feared that the city would have rejected the donation if they required an easement. City government administrations change over time, as well as city fortunes. Boards considering this option should discuss the need for an easement with the potential donor and act to place on easement on the property if at all possible.

The condition of your building will govern whether many reuse options are viable. The table located at the end of chapter 8 will help you determine which options are the most likely, based on the current condition of your building.

SUMMARY OF PART II AND PREVIEW

Part II of this book, comprised of case studies of a dozen historic house museums that successfully transitioned their historic site to a new owner or new user, is meant as inspiration for house museum boards that are struggling with insufficient funds or people power to sustain their site to the level that their historic building needs and deserves.

The range of case studies profiled, from Boston to California, from South Dakota to Atlanta, and in the United States and in British Columbia, Canada, all show the breadth of innovation being undertaken by your house museum peers. Well-known and distinguished organizations are confronting the future of their house museums, alongside, small and rural house museum organizations. Every one of these organizations faced the same concerns you are finding and took action.

In the final chapter of this book, I will discuss the initial motivations of the case study organizations to seek a use or user change. My hope is that, by discussing the reason and methods these organizations used to initiate reuse discussions, your board will be inspired to take steps to ensure the future of your historic house museum.

NOTES

1. Information for this case study comes from Main Street Iowa, "Experience the Magic! Fifteen Year Report, 1986–2001," 32, 42. Jo Berry, interview with author, Adel IA, 7 and 14 June, 2005. Adel Partners, Main Street Iowa Downtown Revitalization Awards 2002 Nomination Form Design, Adel Historical Museum project, 2002. I am grateful to Jo Berry for supplying information about Adel Partners to me for this case.

CHAPTER 16

Conclusion

At the outset of this book, I described the intended audience: board, staff, and volunteer members of historic house museums owned by nonprofit organizations that are struggling with insufficient funds or people power to sustain their site to the level that it needs and deserves. To conclude this book, I would like to review the initial motivations of the boards of the twelve organizations profiled in chapters 8–16.

All of these historic house museum stewards made the successful transition to a new use or owner after wrestling, in some cases for almost forty years, to ensure that their historic site will be maintained for future generations. While each organization had unique circumstances, its motivation can provide general lessons that may be applicable to your organization. I hope that these cases might give you and your organization the courage and perseverance to take positive action to transition your house museum to a new owner or user to ensure its long-term preservation.

The case study organizations I profiled seemed to be driven by one of three motivating factors to make their use change: operational issues, preservation concerns, or financial pressure.[1] Each of these motivators will be discussed in turn.

OPERATIONAL MOTIVATIONS

Several case study sites chose to find a new use or owner as part of an overall review of their organization's operations, most often through a long-range strategic-planning process. In these cases, the institution managed the use or ownership change as part of a formal or informal organizational planning process that looked at how the historic building fit within the organization's overall mission. They took action when the historic building's needs did not mesh with the overall vision for the future of the organization.

Organizations that routinely use a strategic-planning process are already looking toward the future and how their organization fits within changing realities. Groups that wish to envision the future and make a clear statement of what the future holds for the historic site can then take incremental steps each year toward achieving their overall vision and future.

Historic sites that plan for their future and set clear goals can manage the house use/user transition well, because they think deliberately about the whole of the organization and all its component parts. While no transition process is easy, museum organizations that use a well-managed strategic-planning process to sort out the future of their historic site can make transitions that are easy to understand and successful.

For the Nantucket Historical Association, their first-ever interpretive plan drove their effort for change. In this case, the interpretive plan grew out of a strategic-planning process as new leadership took hold of the organization to guide its future. The interpretive plan, designed to broaden the stories told by the organization for its visitors, led to an assessment of all of their twenty-five properties to identify which ones could most clearly be used to tell the stories in the identified themes.

Finding three sites in their inventory that did not fit into the new scheme, the Board of Trustees ultimately decided to reprogram two sites that were considered "non-essential to the interpretive plan" for educational purposes. The reuse of the 1800 House for Nantucket-area decorative arts and crafts seems to have struck a nerve, based on the outpouring of enthusiasm and financial support.

Faced with a new political regime as a result of an election, staff members at the Heritage Branch of the British Columbia Ministry of Community, Aboriginal and Women's Services responded to the grim news that all of their historic sites were to be "devolved" or privatized to new private-sector operators.[2] Using their annual operational planning process, the staff developed a plan that concluded in a two-year-long procurement process to find financially capable stewards for the

Ministry's thirty historic sites. Under license for fifteen years, these organizations, mostly nonprofits and private individuals, must maintain the site, open it for tourists, and retain public access.

The National Trust for Historic Preservation also faced operational issues. Specifically, they were concerned about unwittingly violating new federal antidiscrimination laws. This concern led them to seek a new stewardship arrangement for one Trust site, Casa Amesti, an 1834 California Adobe, in Monterey, California. In this case, the user, a private social and dining club, had been a superb steward of the property under two, twenty-year occupancy agreements. The Trust, over a seventeen-year period, worked with the family of the donor, the Club, and other stakeholders to fashion a new stewardship organization. The Casa Amesti Foundation raised significant endowment and restoration funds. Here, the National Trust responded to changing federal government rules and took action toward creating a new future for this historic site.

Rather than develop expertise in a new area, the University of Chicago, owner of the Robie House, Frank Lloyd Wright's masterpiece of Prairie School architecture, turned to the already-successful Frank Lloyd Wright Home and Studio to manage restoration and public visitation at the Robie House. The lease between the University and the Preservation Trust allows the University to focus on its educational mission while permitting a skilled and well-regarded nonprofit to provide the necessary interpretation and restoration skills.

In this case, the Home and Studio board made a strategic choice to initiate discussions with the University to manage and restore the Robie House. They made a compelling case to the University that the preservation organization would make a better steward for the site, leading to the long-term lease and a new name, the Frank Lloyd Wright Preservation Trust.

In the case of the Historic Adams House in Deadwood, South Dakota, the unusual management arrangement pioneered in the 1930s at the Adams Museum became a template for a co-stewardship agreement. This agreement ensures that the two components of the historic site—the building and its completely intact collections—are preserved by the City of Deadwood (owner of the building) and the Historic Adams House board (owner of the collections).

The owners of the Margaret Mitchell House and Museum sought out the much larger Atlanta History Center to discuss a possible merger. Already a successful organization that had restored Mitchell's home, opened a visitor center, and rehabilitated another building as a museum dedicated to the *Gone With the Wind* film, a merger would allow the programming at the organization to continue to grow and thrive. The asset transfer and eventual merger was a strategic move for both organizations, allowing each to expand its mission and create more opportunities as a merged entity.

PRESERVATION MOTIVATIONS

Focusing on the care of the structure and its long-term needs, these case study organizations chose new solutions for their buildings to ensure that their buildings would have users who could afford to maintain them long-term.

Boards that resolve to act on a transition to a new user or user because of the growing preservation needs of the building are acting responsibly to their stewardship obligations. Many boards fail to act before the building has seriously deteriorated or needs substantial investment to remain a viable site for visitation. Boards that are motivated to change because of the preservation concerns of their site, and make the decision to act before a crisis ensues, are making the transition deliberately, as part of a thoughtful and reflective process.

These transitions are not easy, because the organization must admit that it no longer has the means to care for the site properly. By placing the site with other organizations or individuals with the necessary funds, the board is acting responsibly on its stewardship mission.

During a thorough review of the organization's operations in the late 1970s, the Society for the Preservation of New England Antiquities (SPNEA) identified certain historic sites within their inventory with only limited appeal to visitors because of their location or other factors. This overall review was not a short-term fix. Rather, it was part of an extended period of conflict in the 1970s, forced on the organization because reversals in the economy required SPNEA to alter its operating style. Maintenance of the houses had been so long deferred that it became imperative and, unfortunately, more costly than if it had been performed earlier.

The organization sold some sites with easements to private individuals who restored them, and retained ownership of others. SPNEA formulated a new management approach for several of their houses, designating them as "study houses," which are fully furnished and restored homes open by appointment only. These homes are retained in the organization's inventory.

The Heurich House Foundation was formed when the Historical Society of Washington, D.C., chose to sell their former home when they expanded their efforts to a new site. Grandchildren of the original owners and other friends of the superb and largely intact site stepped forward to purchase the property from the Historical Society to make sure that the property and its contents would not be dispersed and the house could remain on public view.

Motivated to save several houses from demolition or insensitive alteration, the Elfreth's Alley Association purchased five properties along this tiny street of Colonial- and Federal-era homes in Philadelphia and rented them to residential tenants. As the preservation movement matured in the city and region, the board decided to open one home as a museum house. Never able to raise sufficient funds to restore all five properties as they had hoped, the board, after nearly forty years of ownership, decided to sell three of the houses to private owners with easements to ensure they would be restored and maintained. The organization continues to monitor the easement agreements.

Public agencies, especially park systems, are loathe to sell real estate assets acquired with public monies. Yet, few agencies seem to have the financial resources to preserve and maintain historic sites that happen to sit on land that was acquired for its open space values rather than for the historic building.

The Maryland-National Capital Park and Planning Commission in suburban Washington, D.C., developed a public-private partnership with a private individual. In return for a forty-year lease, the resident curator will invest hundreds of thousands of dollars in Hazelwood an important, but deteriorating, historic house. The resident curator is responsible for investing in the historic house, rather than the park agency.

The Fairmount Park Historic Preservation Trust was founded in the 1980s to find new users for ten deteriorating historic properties within Fairmount Park in Philadelphia, owned by the city and managed by the park agency. These sites, many superb early and mid-nineteenth-century examples of summer homes along the Schuylkill River, had deteriorated since the 1970s. At that time, the last of the park employees who had lived in them nearly rent-free, were removed after newspaper articles described the practice.[3]

The nonprofit organization was formed to find new uses for these sites to ensure their long-term preservation. The Fairmount Park Historic Preservation Trust's mandate has since grown to include close to fifty historic properties on park land throughout the city that need new users with the financial ability to maintain and restore them under long-term leases.

Wishing to ensure that the historic house museum Upsala, located strategically across the street from Cliveden, the site of the 1777 Battle of Germantown in Philadelphia, would be retained for public access, the boards of the Historic Upsala Foundation and Cliveden, a National Trust property, merged their operations. The new entity uses Upsala for meetings and office space. Cliveden continues to be used for interpretive purposes as a museum. This arrangement ensures that Upsala will be well-maintained and preserved.

FINANCIAL PRESSURE

It can take years for boards face up to the "perfect storm" for house museums—mounting maintenance and restoration needs and dwindling finances. How the organization chooses to communicate the changes to their stakeholders can have broad implications for the institution.

Organizations that are unable to plan for or even grasp the implication of their poor stewardship of their properties will eventually face a crisis of some kind that compels them to act. Crisis situations are fraught with problems because the board is unprepared to deal with the outcome, be it financial or from a public relations standpoint. Typically, house museum organizations that initiate transition discussions during a crisis will be unable to make an adequate search for viable solutions.

Or they will precipitously latch onto the first viable solution that comes along. Either way, the historic property is not well-served, because the board has neglected its stewardship role.

The Board of Directors of the Robert E. Lee Boyhood Home in Alexandria, Virginia, had, since its inception, a dual mission of maintaining the historic site and also providing scholarships to Virginia students. Wishing to concentrate on its scholarship program, which it had every right to do, the Foundation shut the house after accepting an unsolicited offer to sell their site to a private owner. Here, the organization did not undertake a strategic planning process, or methodically reach the conclusion that they had to find a better steward for their site.

Rather, they acted on a tempting offer that unleashed a firestorm of protest by area residents. The sale concluded after a protracted effort by the new owner failed to find a credible nonprofit steward with the financial wherewithal to restore and maintain the site. As a result of this "surprise" sale, the State of Virginia enacted legislation that requires public notice prior to the sale of a cultural site open to the public.

Board members at the Adel Iowa Historical Society appealed to their municipality to take responsibility for their property for a nominal sum because their dwindling membership could not restore or maintain it. Again, the Historical Society had made no attempt to plan for the future of their site or find another steward to ensure its preservation. They approached the only source that might take on their deteriorated property, the City of Adel.

The municipality accepted the donated property with several conditions. A community-wide fundraising campaign was launched to raise $60,000 needed to bring the building up to code and restore the interior and exterior. In return for maintaining the site, the city also required that the local Main Street organization locate their office there so that the site could be open daily, thus providing the public access that the Historical Society board had been unable to accomplish.

A CALL TO ACTION

It is not uncommon for the ultimate objective of the house museum organization—the preservation of the historic house—to become confused if the institution is unstable or unsustainable despite the board's efforts. This confusion occurs because organizations often take on a life of their own as they are human creations, made up of well-intentioned people.

It is critical for struggling house museum boards to clearly understand their fiduciary duty to the historic building and act in its best interests; even if that means that the building must be sold to a new owner or leased to a new user. The building has no champion other than its board. Your board must do right by the historic resource and think about its future.

If you see parallels to your organization in any of the case studies—no matter how slight—consider whether your historic house museum is sustainable. Should you believe that your site is unsustainable due to lack of an endowment or regular, predictable income that exceeds 50 percent of your yearly operations, start the discussion with your peers on the board about the variety of solutions available for struggling house museums contained in this book.

Start by reviewing your mission statement to see if you are fully living up to your organization's responsibilities of being a good steward to your historic site. As noted in the case studies throughout this book, several well-known and well-regarded historical organizations have assessed their stewardship responsibilities and taken action to ensure the future of their sites. If you feel your house museum could do better, then begin working today to chart a new future for your precious resource.

NOTES

1. I am extremely grateful to William Higgins for his insights about the case study organizations in his early review of this manuscript. He provided the concept around which this final chapter is based.

2. This agency is now called the Ministry of Tourism, Sport, and the Arts.

3. Carr interview.

Bibliography

GENERAL HISTORIC PRESERVATION AND MANAGEMENT LITERATURE

American Association for State and Local History Standing Committee on Standards and Ethics. "When a History Museum Closes." Ethics Position Paper #2. Final Draft. Presented at American Association for State and Local History Annual Meeting, 12–15 September 2006.

Bamberger, Richard. "Establishing a Plaque Program: Bringing Local History to the Community." Technical Leaflet No. 168. American Association for State and Local History, 1989.

Baum, Willa K. *Oral History for the Local Historical Society,* 3rd ed. AltaMira Press, 1995.

Brackett, Carolyn. "Why Is Historic Site Visitation Down?" *Forum Journal* 19, No. 3 (2005), forum.nationaltrust.org/default.asp.

Butcher-Younghans, Sherry. *Historic House Museums: A Practical Book for Their Care, Preservation, and Management.* New York: Oxford University Press, 1993.

Campbell, Robert. "Making Properties Pay Their Way." *Historic Preservation* 34, no. 1 (1982): 24–28.

Campbell, Colin. "Sustainability: The Ongoing Challenge for Historic Sites." *Forum Journal* 20. no. 3 (2006), 18–20.

Carlson, Mim, and Margaret Donohoe. *The Executive Director's Survival Guide: Thriving as a Leader.* San Francisco: Jossey-Bass Publishers, 2003.

Coleman, Laurence Vail. *Historic House Museums.* Washington, DC: American Association of Museums, 1933.

Connors, Tracey Daniel. *The Non-Profit Book: Management,* 2nd ed. New York: John Wiley and Sons, 1999.

———. *The Non-Profit Book: Management*, 3rd ed. New York: John Wiley and Sons, 2001.

Davis, Terry L., and Kenneth M. Wolfe, "Planned Giving." Technical Leaflet 222. Nashville: American Association for State and Local History, 2003.

Esler, Jennifer. "Historic House Museums: Struggling for Survival." *Forum Journal* 10, no. 4 (1996). forum.nationaltrust.org/default.asp.

Feldman, Allyn, Beth Hansen, and Gloria Chun Hoo. "When Volunteers 'Own' the House." *History News* 60, no. 1, (2005): 17–20.

Feeney, Suzanne. "Governance Framework for Collaborations and Mergers," in Tracey Daniel Connors. *The Non-Profit Book: Management*, 3rd ed. New York: John Wiley and Sons, 2001.

Garg, Naren. "Study of Philadelphia Area Non-profit Owned Historic House Museums Through Their IRS 990 Tax Returns for the Heritage Philadelphia Program," July 2006.

George, Gerald. "Historic Property Museums: What Are They Preserving?" *Forum Journal* 3, no. 1 (1989). forum.nationaltrust.org/default.asp.

———. "Historic House Museum Malaise: A Conference Considers What's Wrong." *History News* 57, no. 4 (2002): 4.

———. *Starting Right: A Basic Guide to Museum Planning,* 2nd ed. Walnut Creek, CA: AltaMira Press, 2004.

Groff, John M. "To Thine Own Self Be True: Making a Success of the Smaller Historic House Museum in the 21st Century." A paper presented at American House Museums, an Athenaeum of Philadelphia Symposium, 4–5 December, 1999. philaathenaeum.org/groff.html.

Harris, Donna Ann. "Field Research for Heritage Philadelphia Program, Internal Revenue Service Form 990 Reports for 27 Historic Sites." Heritage Philadelphia Program, December 2005.

———. "Materials Needed for Attorney Review, Living Legacy Project." Heritage Philadelphia Program, May 2005.

———. "Survey of Landmark Transfer of Development Rights Programs, Interim Report for the City of Miami." Unpublished report for the National Trust for Historic Preservation, April 2006.

———. "Telephone Interviews with 24 Historic Site Administrators." Heritage Philadelphia Program, May 2003.

Harris, Donna Ann, and Barbara Silberman. "Exploring Alternative Stewardship Arrangements for Historic Houses." Joint grant proposal to the William Penn Foundation and The Pew Charitable Trusts, November 2004.

Harris, Samuel Y. "Alternate Use as a Preservation Strategy: The Eastern State Penitentiary Case Study." *Forum Journal* 7, no. 5 (1993): forum.nationaltrust.org/default.asp.

Heritage Philadelphia Program website. heritagephila.org.html/.

Herrington, Bruce. *Financial and Strategic Management for Non-profit Organizations.* San Francisco: Jossey-Bass Publishers, 2002.

Hosmer, Charles. *Presence of the Past: A History of the Preservation Movement in the United States Before Williamsburg.* New York: G. P. Putnam's Sons, 1965.

Kammen, Carol. "The Future Survival of Historical Societies." *History News* 59, no. 3 (2004): 3–4.

La Piana, David. *The Non-Profit Mergers Workbook: The Leader's Guide to Considering, Negotiating, and Executing a Merger.* St. Paul, MN: Amherst H. Wilder Foundation, 2000.

Light, Paul C. *Sustaining Nonprofit Performance: The Case for Capacity Building and the Evidence to Support It.* Washington, DC: Brookings Institution Press, 2004.

Lincoln Nebraska Community Foundation Inc. "Agreement Designated Fund, March 2004." Lincoln Community Foundation Inc. website. www.lincoln communityfoundation.org.html/.

Malaro, Marie C. *A Legal Primer on Managing Museum Collections*, 2nd ed. Washington, DC: Smithsonian Institution Press, 1998.

McDonald, Travis C. "Restoration, Re-Restoration, and Real History: Trends and Issues in Historic House Museums." *Forum Journal* 7, no. 6 (1993). forum.nationaltrust.org/default.asp.

McKay, Tom. "Standing in the Local Societies' Shoes." *History News* 51, Vol. 1, 22.

Merryman, John Henry, and Albert E. Eisen. *Law, Ethics, and the Visual Arts*, 2nd ed. Vol. 2. Philadelphia: University of Pennsylvania Press, 1987.

O'Connell, James. "Research on Historic House Museum Mergers and Sales" for the Heritage Philadelphia Program, July 2006.

Moe, Richard. "Are There Too Many House Museums?" *Forum Journal* 16, no. 3 (2002). forum.nationaltrust.org/default.asp.

Moss, Roger W. *Historic Houses of Philadelphia: A Tour of the Region's Museum Houses.* Philadelphia: University of Pennsylvania Press, 1998.

Pearce, Peter H. "Preservation for Pleasure: A New Life for Old Buildings through the Work of the Landmark Trust." A paper presented at American House Museums, an Athenaeum of Philadelphia Symposium, 4–5 December, 1999. philaathenaeum.org/pearce.html.

Rees, James C. "Forever the Same, Forever Changing: The Dilemma Facing House Museums." A paper presented at American House Museums, an Athenaeum of Philadelphia Symposium, 4–5 December, 1999. philaathenaeum.org/rees.html.

Rutgers University, Camden New Jersey, Professor Howard Gillette's Public History Class, "Research Project on Historic House Museum Sales, Mergers, and Closures In the Last Five Years." Fall 2006 for the Heritage Philadelphia Program, 2006.

Sanchis, III, Frank E. "Looking Back or Looking Forward? House Museums in the 21st Century." A paper presented at American House Museums, an Athenaeum of Philadelphia Symposium, 4–5 December, 1999. philaathenaeum.org/sachis.htm.

Secretary of the Interior's Standards for Treatment of Historic Properties, 1995. www.cr.nps.gov/hp/tps/secstand1.htm.

Silberman, Barbara Warnick. "Get Historic Houses in Order." *Philadelphia Inquirer*, 8 February 2005.

———. "Stumbling Towards Excellence: The Heritage Philadelphia Program" *History News* 60, no. 2 (2005): 12–16.

Smiley, Marc. "Board Development for Nonprofit Preservation Organizations." Washington, DC: Preservation Press, 2000.

Sommer, Barbara W., and Mary Kay Quinlin. "A Guide to Oral History Interviews." Technical Leaflet No. 210. Nashville, TN: American Association for State and Local History, 2000.

Stapp, Carol B., and Kenneth C. Turino. "Does America Need Another House Museum?" *History News* 59, no. 3 (2004): 7–12.

Thompson, Richard L. "Contingency and Emergency Public Affairs," in Tracey Daniel Connors, *The Non-Profit Book: Management*, 3rd ed. New York: John Wiley and Sons, 2001.

Tolles, Bryant F, editor. *Leadership for the Future: Changing Directorial Roles in American Museums and Historical Societies*. Nashville: American Association for State and Local History, 1991.

Walker, Patricia Chambers, and Thomas Graham, compilers. *Directory of Historic House Museums in the United States.* Walnut Creek, CA: AltaMira Press, 1999.

Williams, Donna. "Great Expectations: Historic House Museums in State History Programs in the 21st Century." A paper presented at American House Museums, an Athenaeum of Philadelphia Symposium, 4–5 December, 1999. philaathenaeum.org/williams.htm.

Wolf, Thomas. *Managing a Non-profit Organization in the Twenty-first Century*. New York: Simon and Schuster Inc., 1999.

Wood, Anthony C. "Celebrating Preservation's Story: It's Your Memory. It's Your History. It's Worth Saving." *Forum Journal* 18, no. 2 (2006): 7–10.

CASE STUDIES

Adams House and Museum (chapter 9)

Co-stewardship Agreement Between the Adams Memorial Museum, The City of Deadwood and The City of Deadwood Historic Preservation Commission for the Restoration and the Operation of the Adams House Museum in Deadwood, South Dakota, 13 July 1998.

Co-stewardship agreement for 150 Sherman Avenue, Deadwood, South Dakota. www.northernblackhillsweeklygroup.com/articles/2005/11/26/lawrence_county/publicnotices/notices868.txt.

Homestake-Adams Research Center Overview www.adamsmuseumandhouse.org/harc.html.

"Historic Adams House Restoration," News Article 30 November 2003, www.adamsmuseumandhouse.org /house/article.php?readit=2.html.

Transfer by Gift of Adams House Contents and Related Materials. City of Deadwood and Adams Memorial Museum, 13 July 1998.

Adel Historical Association (chapter 15)

Adel Partners. Application for Main Street Iowa Downtown Revitalization Awards 2002 Nomination Form, Design, Adel Historical Museum, June 2002.

Main Street Iowa. "Experience the Magic! Fifteen Year Report 1986–2001." Des Moines, Iowa: Main Street Iowa, 2002.

British Columbia Heritage Branch (chapter 12)

Barkerville Coalition. "Barkerville and the Devolution Process," Help Save Barkerville (British Columbia, Canada) website. www.barkervillecolaition.com/backgrounder.

Canada, Ministry of Community, Aboriginal and Women's Services. Annual Service Plan Report 2003–2004.

———. Barkerville Task Force Report Presentation. www.mcaws.gov.bc.ca/heritage_branch/barkerville.html.

———. "The B.C. Heritage Legacy Fund." Backgrounder, 24 March 2003. www2.news.gov.bc.ca/nrm_news_releases/2003MCAWS0036-000286-Attachment.

———. Draft Heritage Site Management Agreement, Emily Carr House, no date.

———. Draft Managing and Operating Provincial Heritage Sites in British Columbia, Request for Qualifications, no date.

———. "Emily Carr House." Heritage Branch website. www.heritage.gov.ca/emily/emily.html.

———. "Endowment Fund to Boost Heritage Conservation," News Release, 24 March 2003. Available at www2.newsw.gov.bc.ca/nrm_news_releases/2003MCAW0036-000286.html.

———. Guidelines and Principles for Preparing Heritage Site Management Agreements, no date.

———. Managing and Operating Provincial Heritage Sites in British Columbia, Request for Qualifications, no.133023, issued by BC Purchasing Commission, 30 July 2002.

———. Minster for State Deregulation. "Quarterly Progress Report, April 2003." www.gov.bc.ca/deregulation.

———. "Point Ellice House and Garden." Heritage Branch website. www.tsa.gov.bc.ca/heritage_branch/heritage_sites/point_ellice_house.html.

———. Request for Expressions of Interest, RFI HB 2002-1, 24 May 2002.

———. Request for Expressions of Interest, 24 May 2002.

———. Service Plan 2004/05-2005/06.

———. "Welcome to BC Heritage, BC Heritage...It's Worth a Closer Look." Heritage Branch website. www.tsa.gov.bc.ca/heritage_branch/index.html.

Canada, Official Report of the Debates of the British Columbia Legislative Assembly. 2002 Legislative Session, 3rd Session, 37 Parliament, Hansard, Wednesday 27 March 2002, Afternoon Sitting, Volume 5, no. 1, 2191. www.legis.gov.bc.ca/ hansard/37th3rd/h20327p.html.

Capital Mental Health Association, Victoria, BC, Canada. "Request for Proposals, Managing and Operating Point Ellice House," 13 February 2004.

———. Annual Report 1 April 2003–31 March 2004. Victoria, BC: Capital Mental Health Association, 2004.

Grant Thornton LLP. "Heritage Site Management Issues Report for the Ministry of Small Business, Tourism and Culture." Victoria, British Columbia, Canada, March 2000.

"New Era Review, Three Years of Action, New Era Promises Made and Kept." Updated November 2004. www.gov.bc.ca.

Orr, Sheila. Management of Point Ellice House. www.shielaorrma.bc.ca/667/3336/.

Casa Amesti Foundation (chapter 14)

"Christmas in the Adobes Offers Unique View of Monterey's History." www.parks/ca.gov/events/event_detail.asp?is=1016.

City of Monterey, Historic Preservation Commission Minutes. Special Meeting, 21 February 2002. www.monterey.org/boards/hpc/m.

——. Cooperative Agreement between the National Trust for Historic Preservation and the Old Capital Club, Monterey, CA, 4 November 1997.

——. Resolution of the Board of Trustees regarding transfer of Casa Amesti to non-profit charitable organization in Monterey, CA, 22 May 1995.

Elfreth's Alley Association (chapter 13)

Board of Directors Minutes. Archives, Elfreth's Alley Association, Philadelphia.

Elfreth's Alley Association. *Guide to the Archives*. Philadelphia: Elfreth's Alley Association, October 2004.

——. *Inside These Doors: A Historic Guidebook of the Homes of Elfreth's Alley, a National Historic Landmark*. Philadelphia: Elfreth's Alley Association, 2004.

——. Strategic Plan 2002–2005.

Minutes of the Meeting of the Membership. Archives Elfreth's Alley Association, Philadelphia.

Property Committee Reports. Archives Elfreth's Alley Association, Philadelphia.

Report to the Membership. Archives Elfreth's Alley Association, Philadelphia.

Rogers, Eliza Newkirk. *Elfreth's Alley Guidebook*, The Elfreth's Alley Association, 1964.

Fairmount Park Historic Preservation Trust (chapter 12)

"Philly Park Group to Restore Neglected Manors." Associated Press 25 November 2005 as found at www.abclocal.com/wpvi/story?section=local&id=3667047.html.

Master Lease Agreement By and Between The City of Philadelphia (acting through the Fairmount Park Commission) and the Philadelphia Authority for Industrial Development, execution copy 8/10/93.

Lee Boyhood Home (chapter 13)

Commonwealth of Virginia. Office of the Attorney General. "Statement by David Johnson, Counsel to Attorney General Mark Earley, Re: Sale of Robert E. Lee Boyhood Home," Press Release, 28 July 2000.

Commonwealth of Virginia, House of Delegates, House Bill 2165, "Certain historic properties: Notification prior to sale legislation," 2001 session; available from legl.state.va.us/cgi-bin/legp504.exe?011+sum+HB2165.

"Lee Boyhood Home Bill Passes," Boyhood Home Bulletin Board at www.leeboyhoodhome.org.html/.

Maryland-National Capital Park and Planning Commission (chapter 11)

Cox, Rachel, S. "Resident Curators: Private Stewards of Publicly Owned Historic Houses." *Forum News* 6, No. 1 (1999). forum.nationaltrust.org/default.asp.

Maryland-National Capital Park and Planning Commission. Department of Parks and Recreation. "Announcement Historic Curatorship Lease Availability," News release, 30 July 1999.

———. "Report to the Prince George's County Council on the Historic Sites of the Maryland-National Capital Park and Planning Commission in Prince George's County," 1997.

———. "The Marketing and Management of the Historic Sites of the Maryland-National Capital Park and Planning Commission." January 1998, Vol. 1 of 3.

———. "Planning Board and County Council Approve Residential Curatorship for Historic Hazelwood." *Views*, newsletter of Maryland-National Capital Park and Planning Commission, Department of Parks and Recreation, Prince George's County, MD, Winter 2005.

———. Request for Proposals (RFP), P 24-137. "Historic Curatorship Lease of Hazelwood Scope of Services," 4 November 2003.

Nantucket Historical Association (chapter 8)

Nantucket Historical Association. "The Campaign for the Nantucket Historical Society, Starting with History, Starting Now," 2001.

———. "Interpretive Plan, Approved by the Board of Trustees with Question and Answer Supplement," 25 May 2001.

———. "Community Preservation Committee Application for Funding FY 2005," 11 September 2003.

———. "Making Nantucket History: NHA Breaks Ground for the New Museums." *The Gam*, the Newsletter of the Nantucket Historical Association 5, Winter 2003, 1.

Newell, Aimee." 'That pride in our Island's history': The Nantucket Historical Association." *Nantucket History* 49, Winter 2000: 9–12.

Skramstand, Harold, and Susan Skramstand. "Nantucket Historical Society Goals and Strategies 2001–2003," Spring 2001.

Stover, Dorothy. "Letter from the President." *Nantucket History* 49, Winter 2000:5.

Webster, Chip. "1800 House Rehabilitation Study for the Nantucket Historical Association," November 2002.

———. "Greater Light Rehabilitation Study for the Nantucket Historical Association," November 2002.

Index

About the Author

Donna Ann Harris has served in executive and project manager capacities in the historic preservation field for more than twenty years. In 1990, Ms. Harris began preliminary research that led in 1991 to the funding of the Historic House Museum Challenge Grant Program, the first program supported by The Pew Charitable Trusts to begin to organize the historic house museum community in the Philadelphia region. This program provided $2 million for restoration and planning grants on a competitive basis to begin to address restoration, deferred maintenance, and professional development for the more than 300 historic sites in the six-county region served by the foundation. Since then, the program has been renamed and continues to provide restoration and planning grants to a much more organized and vocal house museum constituency.

In the intervening time, Ms. Harris has prepared request for proposals for alternate ownership arrangements for historic sites, spearheaded an organizational merger of two conservation organizations, negotiated façade easements on historic sites being sold, and assisted preservation organizations to identify new uses for historic buildings in downtown settings. She has lectured on historic preservation topics and is author of academic and lay articles about preservation issues.

Most recently, Ms. Harris worked for six years with the Illinois Main Street program as a manager and was named State Coordinator in 2001, where she led the largest staffed downtown revitalization program in the country. Ms. Harris provided organizational development assistance for fifty-six community-based preservation organizations. She retired from state government in 2004 to set up a Chicago-based, nationwide consulting firm Heritage Consulting Inc., which provides training and consulting services in historic preservation, commercial district revitalization, and nonprofit organizational development.

Ms. Harris holds a Master of Science in Historic Preservation from the nation's oldest historic preservation program at Columbia University's School of Architecture, Planning, and Preservation. She also earned a Master of Governmental Administration from the Fels Center of Government at the University of Pennsylvania in Philadelphia.

This project is an outgrowth of a Mid Career Fellowship awarded to Ms. Harris by the James Marston Fitch Charitable Foundation, a New York-based foundation that gives a highly competitive grant annually to leaders in the historic preservation, landscape architecture, and architecture fields to undertake research and publications vital to the field.